The Secret Life of
FOOTBALL

The Secret Life of
FOOTBALL

Alex Fynn and **Lynton Guest**

with Peter Law

Macdonald
Queen Anne Press

A *Queen Anne Press* BOOK

© Alex Fynn, Lynton Guest and Peter Law 1989

First published in Great Britain in 1989 by
Queen Anne Press, a division of
Macdonald & Co (Publishers) Ltd
66–73 Shoe Lane
London
EC4P 4AB

A member of Maxwell Pergamon Publishing Corporation plc

British Library Cataloguing in Publication Data
Fynn, Alex
The secret life of football.
1. Great Britain. Association football
I. Title II. Guest, Lynton III. Law, Peter
796.334'0941

Typeset by Selectmove Ltd, London
Printed and bound in Great Britain by BPCC Hazell Books,
Aylesbury

ACKNOWLEDGEMENTS

In addition to the people directly featured in this book, we would also like to thank
the following:

Hugh Adam, Hans Akkerman, Lidy Aldershoff-Gaemars, Francis Alonso,
David Barber, Pierre-Laurent Baudey, Bernie Coleman, Liz Casani, Guy
Chauvel, Jim Farry, Bruno Govers, Mel Goldberg, Roberto Gaspari, Giancarlo
Gallivotti, John Grundy, Rob Hughes, Marcus Horwick, Gerd Jessel, Stuart Jones,
Roger Kennedy, H. G. Van Leeuwen, Robert Lasagna, Vera MacPherson, Nick
Schon, Ger Storck, Guido Togioni, Tadele Tassema, Philip Wells.

Special thanks are due to Cliff Francis of Saatchi & Saatchi Advertising, John
Barr, Dennis Roach and David Shapland of PRO, Tom Clarke and Keith Smith of
The Times, and Caroline North, Alan Samson and Peter Champion of Macdonald
Queen Anne Press.

Picture credits

All pictures courtesy of *The Times* except:
Jacket, back cover: David Dein (*Daily Mail*) and Michel Platini (*The Sun*).
Plates: David Dein (*Daily Mail*), Jesús Gil & Ron Atkinson and Michel Platini (*The
Sun*), Franz Beckenbauer (*Bongarts*), Kevin Keegan (*Press Association*), and Peter
Mead (*David Steen*).

CONTENTS

For Tim Dicken, Mike Greenslade and Roger Morris

40 YEARS ON

In England, we have come to rely upon a comfortable time lag of 50 years or a century intervening between the perception that something ought to be done, and a serious attempt to do it

H.G. WELLS

In the beginning was the game. It was the game of the people, who invented and played it until it was banned by those in authority. Such was its appeal, however, and so great its attraction, that it eventually conquered even the elite, by whom it had previously been shunned. It was a game which the British codified and exported to virtually every country on earth until it became the most popular game ever devised.

On 27 May 1947 the England football team went to Lisbon for a match against Portugal. Stanley Mortensen and Tommy Lawton scored four goals each as the England side, which also included Stanley Matthews and Tom Finney, won 10–0. In the 1947–48 season 40 million paying spectators watched English football. Manchester United, playing at Manchester City's ground, Maine Road, because of war damage to Old Trafford, averaged nearly 55,000 supporters a game. It was the golden age of English football and the nation considered itself almost invincible at the sport it had given to the world.

At the end of the 1987–88 season, despite the fact that 100 more games were played than had been 40 years earlier, attendances had slumped to 18 million. England lost three successive matches to crash out of the European Championships and English clubs remained banned from European competitions for the fourth successive season. The intervening years had seen huge upheavals in English society but the game seemed incapable of adapting to the changing environment in which it found itself. Meanwhile, other countries made great strides and created systems of play and administration that left England far behind.

This book charts the story of that decline, particularly the story of its recent years. It is a drama played out by powerful individuals in a large number of countries; industrialists, politicians, financiers, media owners, bureaucrats and property developers, who are making decisions about the game in the context of its international and commercial future. In some countries, though sadly not in England, it is also the story of footballers and ex-footballers and how some of the greatest talent the world has ever seen is harnessed and utilised for future generations. For while England has gone inexorably backwards since those halcyon days, others have taken the initiative and the point has finally been reached when English football is becoming less and less important, not only in the world and in Europe but in Britain itself, where Scotland now leads the way in both the quality of play and administration of the game. How and why this has happened, who is responsible for it and what can now be done to recover the game, as the final minute of the 11th hour approaches, are the questions this book attempts to answer. It is a story about football, but it is also a story about our past and our future and how we relate to the rest of a world undergoing tumultuous change.

On 19 April 1989 AC Milan produced one of the greatest displays of football yet witnessed in European club contests when the Italian team defeated the mighty Real Madrid, six times winners of the Champions' Cup and approaching their fourth successive Spanish League title under Dutch coach Leo Beenhaaker, by 5–0 in the second leg of the semi-final of Europe's premier tournament. Amid the celebrations that followed in the San Siro stadium, Milan president Silvio Berlusconi basked in the reflected glory that events on the field had brought, unusually finding the time to give interviews to any reporters that asked. These included Jimmy Greaves, who had gone to Milan in his role as television presenter to report on crowd control in Italy following the disaster at Hillsborough four days previously. An effusive Berlusconi declared that the final in Barcelona would be 'a big show' and Greaves described the entertainment provided by Milan, a club for which he played briefly in 1961, as 'one of the greatest performances ever seen in the competition'.

For most clubs and their presidents, winning the European Champions' Cup would be the pinnacle of achievement. Getting to the final or even into the competition at all would be enough to fulfil even the loftiest of footballing ambitions. However, for Silvio Berlusconi, one of Europe's most successful businessmen, winning the Cup against Steaua Bucharest in Barcelona on 25 May was a means to an end. It did not stop there; in fact it would be just the beginning of Silvio Berlusconi's 'big show'.

In London, meanwhile, developments had been taking place in the ownership and management of two of the country's top football clubs as a younger generation began to assert itself. In their turn, these newcomers were to fuel a movement for change throughout the English game. Try as they might, however, the Football League, under the weight of its own tradition, reduced any debate over constructive change to a series of bitter squabbles as self-interest took over. At the beginning, it had all seemed so different: anything was possible.

1
SUGAR DADDIES

Football hooligans? Well, there's 92 club chairmen for a start
BRIAN CLOUGH

The wood panelled office in Pall Mall, as far removed from the north bank at Highbury as you could get, seemed to produce a more confident, purposeful David Dein. Here, in his exclusive domain in one of London's most expensive streets, Dein was more forthcoming than he had been when we had spoken to him on footballing occasions. In the arcane world of the commodity market David Dein reigned supreme, ever alert to the minutest fluctuation that might interrupt the 6,000-mile chain from the humid fields of Caribbean islands to the breakfast tables of the nation. But when Dein had pushed for change in football, he found it more difficult to achieve. At first the game was a passionate hobby, one which Dein's wife referred to as his mistress as even then he seemed to spend more time on it than on domestic matters. However, once he began to inhabit the jungle that football's leaders had created in the highest echelons of the sport, Dein realised that as the English game faced the biggest crisis in its 100-year history, to continue as a part-time enthusiast would no longer be enough. Early in 1989 Dein organised a management buy-out of his London office, in order, he said, 'to devote more time to Arsenal and football in general, which gives me far more job satisfaction than my own business'.

David Dein's rise to prominence in English football had been meteoric. His London and Overseas Sugar Company had been built up following long years of trading that he began as an importer of exotic food among the small businesses of Shepherd's Bush in west London. Elected following the television debacle of 1985,

Dein was the only member of the Football League Management Committee who was not chairman of his club, yet as vice-chairman he was becoming more and more responsible for both the image and the substance of a resurgent Arsenal. If chairman Peter Hill-Wood, an old Etonian merchant banker whose family connections with Arsenal went back to the 1920s and spanned three generations, represented the old footballing establishment, Dein was a man who epitomised the new commercial thinking within the Football League. He became closely identified with the League administration which, under the presidency of Philip Carter, was to be the breath of fresh air which would provide the organisation with the means to take advantage of new marketing opportunities. In the words of president Carter, the Football League, under his leadership, had become a 'proactive, rather than a reactive' organisation, which had learned the lessons of 1985 and was intent on taking the game into the 21st century.

There can be no question that David Dein is a committed supporter of Arsenal. He spoke with genuine feeling of the days when, as a youngster, he was taken to Highbury by an uncle. 'One of my earliest memories,' he said, 'and one which has lasted ever since, was seeing Tommy Lawton soar above everyone on the edge of the penalty area and power a header into the net.' He could not understand those who could be directors of one club then switch their interest to another, a conservative view shared, among others, by Irving Scholar, chairman at Tottenham. Dein had reputedly paid £300,000 to join the Arsenal Board in August 1983, later becoming the majority shareholder, and was not the kind of person who would be content to remain in the background. Peter Hill-Wood was happy to let Dein have his head. Hill-Wood described the injection of cash Dein provided as 'dead money' and said that if a person wished to give the club that amount, he was pleased to take it.

Within two months Dein was one of the group of directors that engineered the removal of manager Terry Neill following a poor start to the season. Matters came to a head when, on 29 November 1983, Third Division Walsall went to Highbury for a League Cup fourth round tie and beat the mighty First Division side 2-1. The result was all the more galling to Arsenal supporters as it echoed another famous defeat by Walsall in the third round of the FA Cup in 1933. The next day Neill bought the England Under-21 international defender Tommy Caton from Manchester City for £500,000 but the following Saturday, amid 'Neill out' chants from a section of the crowd, Arsenal lost at home again, this time 1–0 to West Bromwich Albion, and dropped to 15th in the table. Supporter dissatisfaction with Neill, expressed in demonstrations outside the stadium, and speculation in the press brought pressure on the Board to act. Hill-Wood was quoted as saying, 'No one has a divine right to be employed by this club'. For two more weeks Neill's future hung in the balance. Some members of the Board supported the manager for his integrity and hard work and because the loyalty inherent in Arsenal's tradition made it difficult for them to get rid of such a longstanding servant of the club.

To David Dein, Neill was not doing his job and had lost the support and respect of both players and fans. 'He was not the right person to lead us into the next decade', was the way Dein saw it. He recommended to the Board that Neill be fired and on 16 December the axe fell. Neill accused Dein of interfering in player-manager relations and it was certainly true that Dein had been a friend of Tony Woodcock and Graham Rix long before he became a director of Arsenal. Rix became uneasy with the relationship once Dein had joined the Board and clearly Dein found the transition from being a devoted fan and friend of the players to a director of the club difficult. Nonetheless, it did not prevent him from carrying out what he saw as a necessary change. 'Where surgery was needed, I was prepared to recommend it,' he said. Don Howe, who had been coach under Neill and previous incumbent Bertie Mee, was appointed caretaker manager. Results began to improve and he was given the job until the end of the season. Howe must have given some credence to the stories of Dein's special relationship with certain members of the side as one of his first actions as caretaker manager was to invite Tony Woodcock into his office to solicit the player's views on the state of the team. Howe himself also left Arsenal in controversial circumstances in 1986 when the club made an approach to Barcelona manager Terry Venables, who had taken the Catalan team to the European Champions' Cup final. Venables turned down the offer because of the way he alleged Howe was being treated. Dein said of the incident: 'It was no secret that Venables wanted to leave Barcelona and he had actually delivered the goods. He had tremendous success in Spain. We were having second thoughts about the long-term viability of Don Howe. He found himself in an invidious position and resigned'. After a short spell under caretaker manager Steve Burtenshaw, George Graham, an ex-Arsenal player and manager of Millwall, was appointed to the job.

Arsenal had been prone to acrimonious partings with managers long before the Neill-Howe problems. Bertie Mee, who had produced the double-winning team of 1970-71 with Don Howe, could not be accommodated at the club and had taken his talents and experience to Watford. Earlier, Billy Wright had suffered a similar fate to that of Neill and Howe when the crowd had begun to bay for his dismissal following a dismal run of results in the mid-1960s. Given this aspect of the club's history it would be wrong to lay the entire responsibility for the Terry Neill situation at David Dein's door, although he was seen in some quarters as the hatchet man because of his involvement in the incident. He said: 'I didn't regard myself as a hatchet man, rather an action man'. It obviously did him no harm – months later he was vice-chairman of Arsenal and two years after that was sitting on the Management Committee of the Football League.

While David Dein was making his impact at Highbury, events a few miles across north London at Tottenham were also gathering pace. The Gunners' traditional rivals were undergoing a process of profound change following the turmoil of revolution which had marked the arrival of a new Board of Directors in 1982. The new owners were led by property developer and tax exile Irving Scholar, who at the time was living in Monaco. A forceful and articulate personality, he was one of the few people within football who had given any thought to the relationship between the game and television, although his expertise was spurned by his fellow chairmen when he was rejected in his bid to become a member of the Management Committee in 1984. Irving Scholar had built up a sizeable property business, the Holborn Property company, after small beginnings as an estate agent. Scholar, like Dein, was taken to his first games as a small boy by an uncle and is as devoted to

Spurs as Dein is to Arsenal. The similarities do not end there: both were grammar school boys from Hendon in north-west London, both played schoolboy football in the same north London league and both had been extremely successful in business; yet they did not meet until both were in powerful positions within the game.

Critics of the Dein-Scholar style of football administration tend to concentrate on simplistic themes: 'They're ruining the game by commercialism and marketing' or the 'They think more about making money than football' school of analysis. The real problem lies in the differing perceptions of football among the game's supporters. Dein and Scholar, both highly successful operators in what are essentially financial empires, love the game as much as anybody and their clubs more than most, but their perspective of management is a world away from football's traditions. Yet British football clubs, like most businesses, are limited companies and as such are likely to be run by one person of wealth and power. These owners then make decisions. Others might make different decisions. For every football supporter there are as many theories on how the game should be run. Whoever is in charge invites criticism. The problem does not lie with individuals but with the system of ownership itself. Under the British system there is no requirement for the Board of Directors to have any community links whatever and no impetus exists to propel them towards finding a consensus of supporters' views when important decisions are being made. England's other national sport, cricket, does not operate in this way. Cricket clubs are exactly that – clubs, in the true sense of the word, where members vote on important issues, as events in Yorkshire and Somerset in recent years have shown.

A similar system operates in Spanish football although it is under threat from a 'limited liability' lobby led by Jesús Gil, president of Atletico Madrid. In English football it is just a matter of good fortune if the man in charge turns out to be an Elton John, who is prepared to undergo arduous tours in order to raise money for Watford Football Club. This unbridled power is not something the chairmen are willing to impart to those charged with running their own organisation, the Football League. The contrast could not be more telling. While decision-making, unfettered by inconvenient notions such as supporter participation, is promoted at club level, the League itself is saddled with the most unwieldy structure that makes the implementation of even the simplest of decisions seem like one of the 12 labours of Hercules.

Irving Scholar's chance to mount a take-over bid for Tottenham Hotspur in 1982 arose out of the financial fiasco surrounding the rebuilding of the whole of the west side of the club's White Hart Lane stadium. By the autumn of 1982 Spurs' finances were in a mess. The construction work had cost over £5 million and while FA Cup wins in 1981 and 1982, which had brought in double the expected receipts as both finals went to replays, had masked the true nature of the shortfall, it was becoming increasingly obvious that something was seriously amiss at the famous old club. In fact it was teetering on the brink of disaster. The new stand had already claimed one victim when longstanding chairman Sidney Wale resigned amid mounting criticism of the costs of the project. Local businessman Arthur Richardson, who had himself been a member of the Spurs Board since the 1960s and was also closely identified with the decision to rebuild, took over the reins.

The contrast between Richardson, retired waste paper merchant and old-style patrician, and Scholar, streetwise young property tycoon, could not have been more marked. Richardson had proudly brushed aside Scholar's offer of assistance after a meeting to discuss the financing of the new stand in 1980 and continued to rebuff him for the next two years, although his services as a property consultant were being offered free of charge. Richardson had claimed that the building work would cost £3 million, to be raised by selling 72 executive boxes in advance at £30,000 each, by income from an impending sponsorship deal worth, according to Richardson, £1 million, and by forming a Centenary Club which would recruit 200 members at £1,000 each. In the event, the building work cost £5.25 million, the executive box sales were slow and the sponsorship deal never materialised under his regime. Although Spurs made a profit of £200,000 in 1981–82, this was achieved after the club's most successful season ever in terms of gate receipts and appeared less than convincing when looked at in terms of a turnover of £3 million plus. And the really disastrous news was that loan repayments totalling £850,000 were due to be paid in the succeeding 12 months.

The take-over of Spurs proved to be far easier than the participants had envisaged, although it must be said that the plan was meticulous and precise in its conception and execution. At the time, the notion of a completely new consortium successfully bidding for a football club was about as likely as Watford reaching the FA Cup final. While a struggling small town club might welcome the advances of entrepreneurs like Scholar, this was Tottenham Hotspur, one of the biggest clubs in England and, along with Arsenal, the standard-bearer of London's football pride. Scholar himself was initially sceptical of his chances of success: 'Tottenham was always known as a club that was, in a sense, impregnable to outsiders and at that time there were not many take-overs of football clubs. What normally happened was that father passed on to son who passed on to grandson and so forth. It was very hereditary'. He might well have been talking about the Hill-Woods at Arsenal! With his expertise as a property developer, it was apparent to Scholar that more often than not costs get out of hand when substantial building projects are carried out by people who are not professionals in that business. And Spurs simply did not have the finances, nor were they generating the income, to cover the £5 million plus the new stand would eventually cost.

Having been rejected in his offers of professional assistance it took an article in the London *Evening Standard* in 1981 to begin the process of a more direct involvement for Scholar. The story was accompanied by an artist's impression of the new stand. Scholar received a phone call from fellow property developer and Spurs fan Paul Bobroff. Expressing his concern, Bobroff was keen to see if Scholar saw the development in a similar light. 'You know they are going to get themselves into the most terrible trouble, don't you?' 'Yes, I've seen the plans and I've seen the building costs and in my view the building costs are way out', was Scholar's response. The two men agreed to monitor developments and to see whether their misgivings were shared by shareholders, directors and other influential Spurs supporters. By the end of 1981 their worst fears had been realised. Spurs were now facing a potentially crippling debt and concerned supporters in the know could see the club facing bankruptcy and even possible liquidation if nothing was done. It was beginning to look as if Spurs, once one of the biggest clubs in Europe, would go the way of west London rivals Chelsea, who had almost gone out of existence when the costs of building the new east stand spiralled as attendances fell.

Irving Scholar, Paul Bobroff and a group of friends discussed the club's problems on the way north for a match against Leeds United in December 1981. The car reverberated to the sounds of discontent. 'The club's not right, it's not being run in the right way', was the general thrust of the conversation. Like millions of football fans all over the world they were sure they knew a better way. The difference was that this particular group had the financial muscle, the determination and the knowledge of business to make their discussions more than just idle complaints. Scholar said: 'I knew that there would be problems with the repayment of this loan because all you had to do was really look at the state of the club financially and you knew that it was a very expensive project. I thought to myself, this is ridiculous, we keep on moaning about this, but unless someone actually tries to do something about it then the club could get itself into the most serious difficulties'. The game, which ended 0–0 and has probably been long since forgotten by all but the most diehard of Spurs fans, was in fact a watershed in the club's history. Scholar came away from the match determined to become directly involved and by Christmas had decided to make approaches to Spurs shareholders in order to secure for himself a significant stake in the club and establish a presence on the Board.

There was nothing haphazard about the next moves of Irving Scholar. In fact they bear all the hallmarks of a precise and systematic manoeuvre to gain control of at least a substantial minority of shares. Scholar first made a written offer to all the female shareholders in the belief that most of them had probably inherited their shares and were not particularly interested in either football or the club. By January 1982 a number of them had agreed to sell and while Scholar thought it was probably impossible actually to take over the club, subsequent events proved that these purchases represented the first shots in an all-out war with the old guard in the persons of the Richardson family.

Paul Bobroff bought a substantial slice of the club from the Bearman estate, which held a sizeable block of shares inherited from F.J. Bearman, who had been a director of the club for many years until the mid-1960s.

Richardson's response to what was happening, symptomatic of the football establishment's self-assured attitude, was relaxed to say the least and the strategy the family adopted eventually proved to be no match for the shrewd tactics of the rebel group. Arthur Richardson's complacency rested on the outcome of events that had happened more than 50 years earlier, in the 1930s. A test case established the right of directors to refuse to sanction the buying of shares in their company by people of whom they disapproved. The case was Berry versus Tottenham Hotspur Football and Athletic Club and had arisen when a Mr Berry, who had been a thorn in the side of the Board for some time, bought shares in the club. The directors refused to recognise the transfer and hence Mr Berry was unable to exercise his rights as a shareholder. The club won the case in the courts having redrafted its Articles of Association following a similar case in the 1920s, which the club had lost. As far as Arthur Richardson was concerned this rule, Article 14, still had the force of law. No matter how many shares Irving Scholar and Paul Bobroff managed to acquire, they could be kept out as long as the Board held firm and refused to recognise the share transfers. Relying on this, the Richardsons felt they didn't have to counter Scholar by buying shares themselves, thus avoiding a direct financial confrontation. This decision was to be their greatest mistake.

Unknown to the Richardsons, Irving Scholar was also aware of Article 14 and its implications for his ambitions. The scheme devised for surmounting this apparently impregnable legal restriction was simple and devastating. When purchasing the shares Scholar did not seek to transfer them to his own name but instead obtained the proxy voting rights of the existing named shareholders. This meant that when the group controlled more than 50 per cent of the shareholders' votes it could call an extraordinary general meeting and vote the existing Board of Directors out of office. It also meant that the purchase of shares remained secret. News of the Scholar group's strategy did not surface in the press until 18 November 1982, by which time the rebels had been joined by two disaffected members of the Richardson Board, Frank Sinclair and Douglas Alexiou, the son-in-law of former chairman Sidney Wale. They were now in control of the required 51 per cent of shareholders' votes and were within a month of completing one of the more remarkable coups in English football history. Arthur Richardson, in the last phase of the Scholar onslaught, took refuge in the fact that his old friend Sidney Wale, who owned 14 per cent of the club, would stay loyal. After all, Wale's father Frederick had been chairman and Sidney had been on the Board since 1957 and held the chair himself from 1969 until his resignation over the cost of the new stand in 1980. In fact, on 4 December 1982, 16 days after news of the impending take-over broke, Wale approached Scholar and within 24 hours the two had concluded a deal whereby Scholar bought Wale's holding. Irving Scholar, combining the *modus operandi* of the City of London with the hard-nosed determination of the construction industry, had completely outmanoeuvred the naïve dinosaurs of the traditional football establishment and had acquired one of the most marketable sports organisations in Britain. Moreover, the number of issued shares in Tottenham Hotspur had remained low, less than 5,000, since the original share offer had not been completely taken up in 1905. This meant that the purchase of 'impregnable' Spurs had cost the rebel group no more than £600,000.

Surprisingly, Scholar did not join the administration immediately despite being the largest shareholder, preferring to watch from the sidelines in Monaco as Douglas Alexiou was installed as chairman and a new Board of Directors, including Paul Bobroff, was appointed. Their first act was to remove Article 14 from the club's constitution. Alexiou, in his public statements after the take-over, claimed that the new Board's priority would be success on the field. 'Spurs must win the League. We are looking to emulate Liverpool', he said. Alexiou's ambition remains unfulfilled, however, as the club is as far away from lasting success now as it was then. On the commercial side, Alexiou was even more optimistic – 'Sponsorship of Spurs is worth £1 million' – but again, finding a suitable sponsor would take longer than had been anticipated.

The new owners had inherited the largest debt in English football history: almost £5 million. They found the Spurs organisation hopelessly old-fashioned and inefficient. There were strange rumours circulating about a missing £50,000 in gate receipts and stories of a mountain of cash piling up in the ticket office which had been swept up by cleaners. On 22 December 1982 the club faced charges at Tottenham magistrates court in connection with non-payment of VAT. Despite the problems, Scholar had realised that if the debt could be overcome, Spurs were actually in a position to increase profits dramatically by taking over lucrative marketing and merchandising operations which at the time were earning little for the club. Scholar and Bobroff developed a three-point plan to wipe out the debt. A rights issue would bring in over £1 million from existing shareholders and consolidate Scholar's position through a further acquisition of stock. The club's training ground at Cheshunt, Hertfordshire, a prime development area on the northern fringes of London, was to be sold after being revalued at £1.5 million. But, most remarkably, Scholar and Bobroff were to attempt something never previously envisaged by football club directors. They were going to offer shares in Tottenham Hotspur to the public on the London Stock Exchange. Moreover, the football club would be split from other operations and administered as a separate company. Other companies would handle commercial activity and any future diversification. Each would be a wholly-owned subsidiary of a new holding company, to be called Tottenham Hotspur plc. Spurs was about to become a very public company.

Take-over fever and unsavoury stories of financial irregularities gripped the Football League in the wake of events at Tottenham. Suddenly chairmen were making more news than the teams they owned in a disturbing development fuelled by the media. Until Herbert Chapman in the 1920s and '30s no one bothered too much about managers. The press, eager for explanations of Arsenal's phenomenal success in the latter decade, created the cult of the manager, who gained in importance with every passing year. Now, in 1982 and '83, the newspapers were full of boardroom coups and possible bankruptcies. On 23 November, the day that Irving Scholar publicly confirmed speculation concerning the imminent take-over at Tottenham, rumours surfaced that control of the biggest club in the English midlands, Aston Villa, was about to be relinquished by the Bendall family amid a tax fraud investigation and allegations that meetings of the Board of Directors had been bugged following the discovery of surveillance equipment on the club's premises. The story was confirmed when Doug Ellis bought control. One of his earliest actions was to make himself the club's first paid director. 'Only women and horses work for nothing', he said!

Within the next 12 months Robert Maxwell had taken over at Oxford United, bought a significant stake in a neighbouring club, Reading, and was proposing their merger into the Thames Valley Royals; television pundit and former manager Jimmy Hill sold out of Coventry City after sustaining a huge loss for the club in an investment in Detroit Express of the North American Soccer League; and Viscount Chelsea and David Mears were removed from the Chelsea Board at an extraordinary general meeting following allegations by new chairman Ken Bates that the two had sold their shares, not to the club, himself or the public, but to yet another property company, SB Properties, which was later taken over by the acquisitive Marler Estates. Bates had identified what would become a major area of concern to London football supporters in the coming years when he accused Mears and the Viscount of 'displaying an amazing lack of loyalty which could threaten the long-term future of Chelsea at Stamford Bridge'.

These were some of the more lurid events of the period. At the same time most League clubs were carrying serious debts and were technically insolvent. Notable among them were Bristol City and Derby County, which were in danger of going out of business altogether. Underlying these developments was the growing realisation that the world of football was once again changing. Football has never been static, which is why it has survived so long. In the 19th century the universities wrested control of the game from the urban mobs who had popularised it to the horror of the ruling elite. In their turn the universities could do nothing as the working class reclaimed football as its own. Amateurs gave way to professionals. The British game was forced to come to terms with the spread of football round the world. The maximum wage was removed in 1961. Television arrived to change everything. The emphasis had switched from players to managers to directors. The difference now was a harsh financial climate where 83 of the 92 Football League clubs were in serious debt. Moreover, there was a worrying trend of declining crowds eroding the financial base. Hyper-inflationary transfer fees in the late 1970s had disillusioned the public, most football grounds were old and decaying and many clubs that had attempted rebuilding, including Tottenham, Chelsea, Fulham and Wolverhampton Wanderers, were facing financial ruin. Worse still, all this came at a time when many thought that standards of play in England had reached an all-time low. English club sides, now containing an influx of overseas players alongside the traditional Irish, Scots and Welsh, were still doing well in European competitions but the performance of the national team in the 1982 World Cup and its inglorious failure in the qualifying rounds of the 1984 European Championships further sapped confidence in the national game. More chillingly, football-related violence was on the increase, or at least was gaining yet more press coverage. Whatever the case it was clear to everyone but those charged with running football that not enough was being done.

In contrast to the public upheavals elsewhere, David Dein's arrival at Arsenal had been a relatively quiet affair, notwithstanding the Terry Neill episode, which could be attributed to the normal vicissitudes of the world of football. Although the majority shareholder, he was not about to bring about the revolutionary changes that were occurring at Tottenham, although change there would certainly be. Highbury stadium needed upgrading but the lessons of grandiose building projects had been learned. Dein, while on a family holiday, went to see the magnificent Joe Robbie stadium in Florida, home of the Miami Dolphins, which had been financed from day one by advance income from executive boxes (skyboxes as they are called in America) and the rich pickings of corporate hospitality. The rebuilding of Highbury's open south terrace, known as the Clock End, would follow exactly this concept.

By securing a sound power base at Arsenal, albeit in a more conservative fashion than that employed by some of his counterparts elsewhere, Dein began to look beyond mere parochial concerns to the wider world of the administration of the Football

League. Some years later, in May 1988, when his stock on the Football League Management Committee and within the game was at its highest, he made clear exactly what he was working towards. Dein's vision of English football might well be viewed with alarm by a large number of supporters, although this does not necessarily mean that he is wrong. However, it was clear that the interests of the big clubs were uppermost in his mind. He was keen to promote a number of changes although he doubted if some of them could be achieved. 'In an ideal world I would like to see 12 or 14 of the top English clubs and the top four Scottish clubs in one (British) league. I believe ultimately and within our lifetime we will see changes in structure . . . the lower divisions will have to go part-time.' The voting structure of the League was wrong. It was a case of the 'tail wagging the dog'. These attitudes are founded on the premise that the big clubs generate the income which subsidises smaller clubs and keeps them in business, while at the same time these small outfits control enough votes in general meetings to resist much needed reform.

In the light of subsequent events, it is worth quoting in full what the Arsenal vice-chairman said in support of his claims. 'I can see, if the big clubs got together and said "we think we should get a bigger slice of television income" . . .' – the incomplete phrase was left hanging in the air as Dein moved on – 'Now there's an amendment coming to the AGM [the annual general meeting of the Football League] to dismiss compensation [the system in which clubs whose matches are screened live on television receive compensation for reduced attendances]. So big clubs lose money at the gates because of live television. It is felt that perimeter advertising and sponsorship make up the money. It's a nonsense. We should get that in any event.'

On a more practical level, but one which still follows the logic of the 'big city' argument, Dein was pushing for the removal of the League's head office, hidden away in sleepy Lytham St Annes in Lancashire, to London. Even this proposal was opposed and eventually a compromise was worked out whereby the League's new promotion and marketing division, under ex-Beecham executive Trevor Phillips, was established at the Wembley stadium complex while the main administration stayed 250 miles away in the north-west. Such episodes made serving on the Management Committee, according to Dein, 'purgatory'.

The Tottenham Hotspur share issue of 1983 was over-subscribed fourfold and Irving Scholar joined the Board, though not yet as chairman. Restructuring left Paul Bobroff in charge of the public holding company, Tottenham Hotspur plc, while Douglas Alexiou remained chairman of the wholly-owned subsidiary, Tottenham Hotspur Football Club. The next day, the second half of a home game against West Bromwich Albion was delayed by floodlight failure, one of a series of bizarre episodes that have plagued Spurs in recent years. At the beginning of the 1983–84 season in August, Tottenham had employed the advertising agency Saatchi and Saatchi, which had run a series of much-publicised television commercials to attract extra support. At the first home game of the season, against Coventry City, the club was totally unprepared to cope with the resultant increased crowd and large numbers of the Spurs faithful were unable to get into the ground until the game had been in progress for some time. On 22 October 1983 the club was fined £10,000 by the Football League for having made irregular payments to the two Argentinian players, Ricardo Villa and Osvaldo Ardiles, under the previous administration.

Despite the set-backs, as 1984 arrived there was good reason for optimism on the part of both Irving Scholar and David Dein. The boyhood fantasy had actually come true for Scholar. Although he occupied no executive position, the power at Tottenham Hotspur was his. He now owned one of the greatest names in British football: double-winners in 1961; the first British winners of a European trophy in 1963; the club of Arthur Rowe, of Danny Blanchflower, of Dave Mackay, of Bill Nicholson, of Jimmy Greaves. Not only that, the debt which had led to the resignation of two chairmen had been removed at a stroke with the success of the Stock Exchange flotation. Results on the pitch were good – there had been seven Wembley appearances in 18 months. The removal of Terry Neill at Arsenal meant that David Dein was making his presence felt. He was able to turn his thoughts to the future. An upturn in results under new manager Don Howe would soon see the crowds flocking back. Further ahead was the crucial building scheme that would prove the worth of Dein's involvement. When

David Dein arrived on the Board at Arsenal, no development had taken place at Highbury for 50 years. 'It serves two purposes', Dein said. 'It was a natural development to put a roof on the Clock End and the new building now satisfies the demand for executive entertaining, yet it also provides improved facilities for standing fans.'

So the commodity trader and the property millionaire had become the sugar daddies of the Football League: unwelcome intruders lavishing vast sums when necessary on their obsession. As David Dein said: 'It's a great challenge to be involved. It's my personal goal to help make Arsenal the number one football club in the world'. This is certainly a laudable ambition, and Arsenal have made an impact since George Graham took over, winning the Littlewoods Cup and challenging for the League title with a number of young players (in fact seven of the 13 players used in the final match of the 1988–89 season were products of the youth development programme). In addition, crowds of 50,000 have been seen again at Highbury, the team won an international tournament at Wembley, beating Bayern Munich and Spurs in the process and the new side have finally dispelled the 'boring Arsenal' image of years gone by.

And they did finally manage to bring the League Championship back to London in 1988–89, the first time the title had returned to the capital since the double year of 1971. The way in which the League was captured also augured well for the club's future. Needing to win by two clear goals in the last match of the season at Anfield, of all places, Arsenal stopped Liverpool's seemingly inevitable march to a record 19th title and second double with one minute of the season to go. The crucial second goal came at the end of a match in which Arsenal had attacked and pressurised the Liverpool team in a way that has rarely been seen in the 1980s. The drama of the night's events prompted David Dein to say: 'I was ecstatic. It's one of the great moments of football history because the game is based on passion. It's sensational. It's Roy of the Rovers stuff. It doesn't really happen but it did'. More enigmatically Dein agreed that winning the title now put him into a 'position of strength'. After the euphoria of the Championship victory, though, manager George Graham brought a note of reality to the proceedings. On being elected manager of the year he said: 'We have all suffered by not being able to learn from top-class European opposition at first hand'. The League Championship was certainly a prerequisite in Arsenal's quest for the position of the world's top club. By the mid-1980s, however, such a dream was impossible to realise for any English club.

Spurs had also made progress, particularly in the club's finances, diversifying into leisurewear, publishing, computing and a Hummel sportswear franchise. The Cheshunt training ground was eventually sold in 1987 for over £4.5 million. Irving Scholar had always believed that Spurs was a big club on the field but a small one off it. After his boardroom coup Spurs won the UEFA Cup in 1984, and came close to a League title under two managers, Peter Shreeve and David Pleat. However, the UEFA Cup victory saw the resignation of manager Keith Burkinshaw after Scholar had made it clear that he could not have full control of the club. Burkinshaw's successor, Peter Shreeve, left after stories of indiscipline and drinking among the playing staff appeared in the press. The appointment of Terry Venables came after another bizarre incident in which David Pleat, who had succeeded Shreeve, was alleged by the *Sun* newspaper to have been caught kerb-crawling by police. Nevertheless, Scholar's regime has continued to provide healthy profits, although sometimes at the cost of alienating the club's traditional support. Scholar's ideas for redevelopment at White Hart Lane, with the emphasis on executive boxes and facilities for wealthier fans, have continually run into criticism as the club has begun to be viewed as a money-making project. To be fair, Scholar agreed to accommodate what he called 'the best standing view in London' (the Shelf), in his redevelopment programme for the east stand. The football club turned in a profit of £931,000 in 1986–87, though results on the pitch under Venables have so far been generally disappointing, and for a time during the 1988–89 season they were struggling against relegation.

Despite the successes of Arsenal and Spurs, the dream of David Dein to make his the number one club in the world can only be examined in the context of world football. No matter how well they think they are doing, neither Spurs nor Arsenal can come anywhere near the giants of other countries. Barcelona, for instance, is the richest club in the world with a turnover of £18 million in 1987–88. Real Madrid is the biggest club in the world in terms of reputation, having won 5,700 multi-sports trophies since its inception. But it is not just these mega-clubs that outstrip the biggest in England. Even a second-ranking club in Spain makes the operations at Spurs and Arsenal seem small-time by comparison.

2
SURREAL MADRID

Anyone who invests in sports has an ego problem to start with

HERMAN SARKOWSKY
Owner of Portland Trail Blazers (basketball)

On 17 April 1988 an unexpectedly large crowd of 50,000 people made their way along the banks of the river Manzanares in Madrid towards the Vicente Calderon stadium. In a strangely subdued mood, the assembled masses supplied nothing more than polite applause as the object of their devotions, Atletico Madrid Football Club, defeated a modest Las Palmas team, variously described in the Spanish press as 'lazy' and 'feeble', by the only goal of an undistinguished match. The victory all but secured a place for Atletico in the UEFA Cup competition but this was not the reason for the size of the attendance. Nor was it due to the pleasant warmth of the Madrid spring. Delightful though both of these must have been for the massed Madrileños, the real reason became apparent only when the game was over. In an astonishing display of spontaneous emotion the entire crowd rose to its feet and began a lengthy standing ovation, aimed not at the team or the coach, but at the unlikely figure occupying the president's seat. With the fans' chant, roughly translated, 'You're the only decent one', ringing in his ears, Jesús Gil y Gil raised his right arm and with a regal gesture appealed to the crowd for calm.

If the recipient of this spontaneous vote of confidence had been at the head of a successful and unified club the rapture would have been understandable. But despite the unison of the crowd's chants, Jesús Gil's football empire was riven by discontent and deep divisions, most of them fuelled by the president himself. Only days before, a number of Atletico players had issued an unprecedented public rebuke to their leader for his disparaging remarks about their ability and lifestyle. After an indifferent run of results in mid-season Gil informed the media that the Atletico players spent most of their time at discotheques and night clubs, did not conduct themselves in a professional manner on or off the pitch, and worst of all, some of them weren't married! Such is the style of Jesús Gil, who has taken confrontation and verbal intimidation beyond the limits of accepted norms and fashioned them into the very cornerstone of his management ethos. If arguments and disputes were settled by those who shout the loudest, Jesús Gil would be king of the world.

Ten months earlier, in June 1987, control of Atletico Madrid was subject to a bitter internal power struggle. Unlike executive changes in so many other countries this battle was not fought behind an impenetrable barrier of secrecy such as that which surrounded Irving Scholar's coup at Spurs. This was a contest conducted with the mixture of open public debate and behind the scenes wheeler-dealing more reminiscent of American politics than the running of a football club. Moreover, the outcome of the battle was decided, not by furtive share deals and the vagaries of company law, but by the members of the club itself, in an election which was the epitome of the democratic process. Spanish football clubs are clubs in the true sense of the word, not limited liability companies or subsidiaries of holding companies or larger conglomerates. As such, executive positions are decided by membership election and confer authority only for a short fixed term, in the case of the presidency of Atletico Madrid, three years.

The election campaign of 1987 became necessary following the death in the previous March of long-serving president Vicente Calderon, after whom the Atletico stadium was named. There were only two candidates: vice-president Salvador Santos Campano and Jesús Gil, an outspoken 55-year-old property developer. Campano, a mild-mannered man who had lived in the shadow of Calderon for many years, was no match for the outrageous Gil who, by accusing the former administration of embezzlement, tarred Campano with the allegations without accusing him directly. It was an obvious issue for Gil as Atletico's finances were indeed in a mess – their debts were estimated at £7.5 million – and it was a theme Gil had taken up before, when he resigned from a club committee in 1978 alleging financial impropriety on the part of the ruling junta. In response to these attacks Campano had promised the members that if elected he would bring former Manchester United manager Ron Atkinson and English international midfielder Ricky Hill to the club. Atkinson went so far as to visit Madrid for a press conference and a meeting of supporters' clubs. Perhaps sensing that raising financial allegations would not be sufficient, Gil rose to this new challenge by going to Milan in late June, on the face of it to watch the *Mundialito,* a club competition organised by Italian entrepreneur and Milan president Silvio Berlusconi. But Gil had other, more important business on his mind. Appearing in the *Mundialito* that year was FC Porto, the exciting Portuguese side that had won the European Champions' Cup the previous month. Under the noses of the most ambitious owners and coaches in Europe Gil persuaded the star of the Porto team, Paolo Futre, to join Atletico. The transfer talks lasted well into the night. Jesús Gil conjured up £1 million there and then and promised another £1 million in three months. In addition to a salary of £200,000 a year, Futre received a yellow Porsche. Gil returned to Madrid early on the morning of 26 June, the day before the election. The private plane landed in time for him to catch the morning news on television. As the cameras rolled, out stepped Gil smiling broadly and gesturing to the man emerging in his wake. Futre, perhaps the most promising winger in Europe, entered Spain to the kind of publicity usually reserved for film stars and royalty. The aspiring presidential candidate went on to ridicule the abilities of Atkinson and Hill and belittle the plans of Campano by comparing them to his own grandiose ambitions for the club.

The Futre incident was a propaganda victory of astounding magnitude. In the election the following day Gil swept to victory on a tidal wave of anticipation. And so the amazing Jesús Gil was unleashed on the football world. He launched into his term as president with a zeal rarely seen, and within days he signalled that his tactics in the election were no departure from his usual style. He demanded an investigation into the finances of the previous administration and within weeks had succeeded in upsetting most of the Spanish football establishment. Before his first year was completed Gil also managed to have public arguments with a variety of banks and the Madrid Society of Lawyers, to alienate his own players, dismiss two coaches and insult Atletico supporters in the grossest possible terms. Despite his outbursts, and the fact that his promise of success on the pitch was not fulfilled, Gil retained, and remarkably even increased, his support among the masses of Atletico members – the *Colchoneros* – to the extent that by the time of the standing ovation, when the players were in open revolt, over 60 per cent said in a survey conducted by *Diario 16*, a Madrid newspaper, that they would vote for him again. To understand this extraordinary situation it is necessary to explain what success means to the supporters of Atletico Madrid.

To most clubs in Europe qualification for a European competition is a prime target. Before English clubs were banned after the Heysel tragedy in 1985, success was measured by this yardstick. In England, clubs like Spurs and Arsenal, while striving for a Championship dominated by Liverpool and Everton, would nonetheless be satisfied with a place in one of the other competitions. The same is true across Europe, perhaps more so, because of a longstanding interest on the part of many continental football fans in their neighbours' internal competitions. In all countries of the continent, qualification for any European competition became a means of attaining respect and increasing revenue. Apart from the quest for championships and cups, local or traditional rivalry often assumes an exaggerated importance to both clubs and supporters, as any resident of Milan, Glasgow, Liverpool, London or Turin would testify.

In Madrid, the *Rojoblancos* – the red and whites – as Atletico are nicknamed, have always trailed mournfully behind the remarkable achievements of their exalted rivals Real. Everything about Real is bigger, better and more successful than anything Atletico have managed. Real's president, Ramón Mendoza, summed up the expectations of the club and its vast support when he said: 'We must always win, parity is not sufficient for us. We must win until we cease to be a club'. Even on the rare occasions when Atletico have produced a great side they have been overshadowed by Real. In the late 1950s, when Atletico's team was good enough to win the League, Real won the Champions' Cup five years running. To add insult to injury, Atletico are not even Real's true rivals: that position is occupied by Catalan giants Barcelona. When Atletico attempted to emulate the visionary concept of Santiago Bernabeu, who, through membership subscription, financed the construction of the beautiful Real stadium that bears his name (and in the process created the modern Real Madrid), the project almost ended in abject failure. The old Atletico stadium, The Metropolitano, had been sold to developers when the land beside the Manzanares was acquired in the early 1960s. Unfortunately for Atletico, the funds to finance the building work ran out before the new stadium was completed and the club was forced into borrowing the Bernabeu for its home games, the ultimate indignity. The situation was saved only by the intervention of ex-president Vicente Calderon, who persuaded, bullied and negotiated until the club's finances were rearranged and work on the new stadium could resume. That Atletico exist at all today is entirely due to the superhuman efforts of Calderon.

The magnificent stadium that arose in 1966 would probably be the primary sporting venue in most cities of Europe, but once again, the long shadow of Real is cast over the best efforts of the *Rojoblancos*. Compared to the majesty of the Bernabeu, Atletico's 70,000 all seated creation can only ever be number two. Furthermore, the Real club has announced its intention to refurbish its stadium, or even rebuild it completely. Such is Atletico's misfortune, it is known by the nickname *El Pupas* – the accident-prone. Thus for the *Colchoneros,* and by extension for Jesús Gil, success means one thing: to defeat, belittle and humiliate their mighty neighbours who do not even pay them the compliment of returning their hatred.

Perpetual second best then has been the fate of Atletico, despite the fact that they have had some wonderful successes of their own, especially in Europe, none more welcome than the 3–0 defeat of Fiorentina in a replayed final of the Cup-Winners' Cup in 1962. That same season, though, Real reached the final of the Champions' Cup where they lost 5–3 to Benfica in a thrilling game, and they also retained the Spanish League title. Four years later, when Atletico had won the League after an exciting climax to the season, the glory that should have been theirs was once again snatched away as Real won the Champions' Cup against Partizan

Belgrade. This tradition of coming second no matter what they do, and the tortured, persecuted personality of Jesús Gil were to prove an explosive mixture.

Gil is no stranger to controversy, in fact he has virtually made a career out of it and his methods, admittedly often successful, have always been unorthodox. It emerged, for instance, that Futre had not been signed by the club but was personally contracted to Gil and that Paulo's 'Uncle Gilito' had spent £130,000 on his 'American-style' election campaign, during which he promised the fans a League title, the construction of a sports city for the members, a casino boat on the Manzanares river to raise money for the club and the construction of a Formula One racetrack. The finance for all of this would come personally from Uncle Gilito's pocket which was filled with unimaginable riches, income from a lucrative property development on Marbella's Mila de Oro (golden mile), which is said to have realised revenues of £300 million by 1988.

Once installed as president, Gil began to bring in more star names. First to join Futre at the Calderon was Cesar Luis Menotti, the world famous coach who had guided Argentina to World Cup success in 1978. Menotti was quickly followed by Eusebio from Valladolid, Marcos from Barcelona, the infamous Andoni Goicoechea (dubbed 'the Butcher of Bilbao' after he broke Diego Maradona's leg), Zamorra from the Argentinian club Newell's Old Boys, Parra from Betis Seville and Lopez Ufarte from Real Sociedad. The new season, which had promised so much, got off to a bad start on and off the field. Performances were far from convincing, the team's away form was patchy and Menotti argued publicly with Futre over the latter's role in the team. Gil, shedding his Uncle Gilito role for the more recognisable persona of the 'Raging Bull', accused Ramón Mendoza, the president of Real Madrid, of being behind a robbery at one of Gil's country homes, presumably an allusion to Real's acquisition of the Atletico player Hugo Sanchez, the Mexican star who was top goal-scorer in the Spanish League when he made the short journey across the city to the Bernabeu stadium. In fact Sanchez had been sold to Real in the last days of the Calderon administration, partly to do something about the chronic financial difficulties, partly to help underwrite

Calderon's last transfer deal, the signing of Brazilian World Cup star Alemao from Botafogo. Gil's novel solution to the ensuing row was to challenge Mendoza to a horse race!

Gil also intervened in the delicate negotiations that were taking place between the Spanish federation and the television companies over a new television contract. Alleging that Real and Barcelona were being given preferential treatment he refused to recognise the federation's right to negotiate on behalf of all League clubs and banned television cameras from Atletico's matches. Next in the firing line was Josep Nuñez, president of Barcelona, who the Raging Bull claimed was 'interfering with other clubs' and 'using other presidents as the fancy takes him', after speculation in the press concerning the Catalans' interest in several Atletico players. The rest of the Barcelona directors were dismissed as 'a bunch of thieves'. Nuñez, according to Gil, 'never spent a penny of his own money' so he offered to buy the Barcelona president a pony in order that he could join the race with Mendoza to settle the matter.

Gil's real problem when he took over was the appalling state of Atletico's finances. There was the historic debt left by the previous directors plus the financing of the new arrivals. Gil also claimed that five years' income from ground advertising had been spent. In Spain, in a pre-season spectacular, the new season's signings are paraded in front of the fans who are invited to buy or renew season tickets. Gil hoped that his spending spree would result in 40,000 season ticket sales but had to settle for half that number. In desperation he turned to a variety of banks but was denied the credit he sought. Jesús Gil would have to use his personal fortune to keep Atletico going. Using possibly the most unusual collateral ever, the £5 million Internazionale of Milan had offered for Futre, he once again plunged into his own pockets. The banks' reluctance to provide Gil with credit provoked a furious public attack from the Raging Bull. Mariano Rubio, the governor of the Banco España, was called 'the cancer of the Spanish economy', after Gil accused him of 'doing everything possible to ensure that credit will not be granted'. In a sideswipe at Antonio Pedro Rius, Dean of the College of Lawyers of Madrid, Gil called the learned judicial officer an 'unrepentant prostitute', who had 'bought off a judge'. The two maligned individuals immediately filed a £5 million law suit against Gil for 'moral damages' and libel. Gil countered with more accusations, this time that Rubio had saved his friends a fortune by arranging preferential treatment for them when the Banco de Navarra collapsed. But perhaps the real reason for the banks' refusal to supply lines of credit had more to do with distrust of Gil's business methods and his operations in the construction industry which had collapsed in spectacular circumstances 20 years before.

Jesús Gil was not unknown to the Spanish public when he declared himself as a candidate for the presidency of Atletico Madrid. One of the first to recognise the coming Spanish building boom of the 1960s, Gil had switched from the transport industry to property speculation and made enough from two sites in Madrid to buy 1,200 hectares of land for £250,000 in the Segovian sierra from the sister of the Duke of Infantado. Here he set about constructing an urban development called Los Angeles de San Rafael. On 15 June 1969, a restaurant, part of an extension attached to a convention centre, collapsed as a large number of delegates to a sales conference were sitting down to lunch. Fifty-eight were killed. The subsequent enquiry showed that Gil, in order to cut costs, had used neither architect nor engineer when the extension was built. He was found guilty of criminal negligence and sentenced to five years' imprisonment and a fine of £2 million. In his summing-up the judge said: 'Forgetting the most elementary ideas and notions of stability of buildings, simply believing that from what he had seen during his professional work and his activities as a constructor he was capable of drawing up, directing and constructing [the project], overlooking any professional advice'. In the event, Gil served two terms of nine months in Madrid's notorious Carabanchel prison before being pardoned by the dictator Franco. Some years later, as if he were acknowledging a debt to his own past, Jesús Gil let it be known that he liked being referred to as *caudillo* – leader and guide – a title adopted by Franco on occasions when the more common *generalisimo* was not expedient.

As the 1987–88 campaign progressed Menotti, Futre and the other expensive imports did not make the impact expected, which was nothing less than a Championship-winning season. Menotti had coached in Spain before, at Barcelona in the early 1980s, but had failed to bring the Catalans the title that had eluded them since

the Cruyff era of 1974 despite the presence of his compatriot, Diego
Maradona. As the season progressed Atletico certainly had some
impressive results – 7–0 against Mallorca and a 2–1 away win at
Barcelona, for instance – but the pinnacle was undoubtedly the
memorable 4–0 away win in the Bernabeu in early November
when Atletico finally achieved a measure of dominance over Real
in their own lair with goals from Futre, Salinas and Lopez Ufarte.
However, the glorious victory over Real only presaged a slump.
Two weeks later Atletico lost the first of five home games then
went out of the Spanish knock-out competition, the King's Cup,
to Real Sociedad, a club from the Basque country that employs
only home-grown players. Worse for the *Colchoneros* was the awful
realisation that Real were yet again starting to forge ahead in the
Championship race.

Atletico's morale declined further in 1988 when they were
beaten 5–1 at Bilbao in January, beginning a run of four losses
that culminated in a 3–1 defeat at the Calderon by Real which
finally put paid to the *Rojoblancos'* fading title aspirations. It also
put paid to Menotti. The man who had arrived as Uncle Gilito's
crowning glory left ignominiously, described by Gil as 'all talk
and no tracksuit'. Menotti, for his part, blamed the relationship
between Gil and Futre for the failure. And failure it was because
Real, with Hugo Sanchez banging in the goals, were running away
with the League. Eventually, after a late surge under new coach
Maguregui, Atletico finished a creditable third in the Championship and qualified for the UEFA Cup after the game against Las
Palmas. But once again the team from the Manzanares trailed
behind its more illustrious neighbour, this time by 14 points. It was
Real's third consecutive Championship. Menotti, commenting on
his experience from the safety of Buenos Aires, said: 'At Atletico
the trainer must think, live and act according to the whims of the
president'.

Not long after he dismissed Menotti, Gil also got rid of his per-
sonal assistant, Francisco Bermejo, and surrounded himself with a
battery of legal experts who became known as 'the regular team'.
'I'm not at ease with him' was Gil's explanation for the dismissal.
The Raging Bull then began to turn his wrath on sections of
Atletico's long-suffering supporters. He had already angered many

at the start of the season by increasing prices by 50 per cent; now he decided to move a group of disgruntled season-ticket holders from their prime position on the half-way line to a far corner of the stadium. After criticism from members over the team's performance Gil, in his now customary manner, went on the radio to tell supporters to go on to the pitch and 'score some goals themselves'. Worse was to come. Atletico's members, Gil claimed, were 'layabouts' from the lower classes and 'a member who doesn't have a drug addict in the family will probably have a prostitute'.

Gil's tactics generated much publicity in Spain, where his out-rageous exploits fill voluminous column inches. Even the appoint-ment of a new coach was not straightforward. José Armando Ufarte, Menotti's assistant, was given a caretaker's role, then dis-missed and replaced by José Maria Maguregui, the coach of Celta de Vigo, even though Spanish League rules forbid a coach to work for two First Division teams in the same season. Although there was plenty of criticism of Gil's methods in the media, it served only to increase his popularity with the beleagured *Colchoneros*. Gil himself lost no opportunity to blame all and sundry for his misfortunes and it is this dogged ability to attack opponents, to back his professed undying allegiance for Atletico with a seemingly endless supply of cash, that endeared him to the fans. He was truly one of their own and they would defend him against all comers.

The close season of 1988 saw no let-up in Gil's campaign against those whom he saw as his enemies, or the enemies of Atletico Madrid. On 26 July he wrote to three players, including the captain Arteche, informing them that they were to be 'dismissed without compensation'. Arteche's sins, according to Gil, were that he was 'devoting too much time to his shoe business' and was 'smoking too much'. The two other players involved were Ramos, who had 'not trained hard enough', had 'disobeyed the club coach' and dared to 'criticise the president'; and Setien, who committed the supreme offence of staying single. Arteche was reinstated only to be fired again two months later, for criticising Gil in a radio interview. Gil initiated legal proceedings against Arteche for 'industrial sabotage' and employed security guards at the Calderon, ostensibly to keep the now ex-captain out of the stadium but surely designed as a flamboyant gesture for the media. The episode certainly contains all the hallmarks of one of Gil's stunts: the outrageous verbal attack; the resort to legal action; the display of power presented as a means of defence against a ruthless and unprincipled adversary. Meanwhile Alemao, who had never settled in Madrid, left for Napoli, to be replaced by another Brazilian, Baltazar from Flamengo.

As the 1988–89 season began Gil mounted a new offensive against the members. Prices were raised again, accompanied by more verbal abuse as attendances dropped following three straight defeats. After the second dismissal of Arteche the remaining players threatened another revolt. The first round UEFA Cup tie against Groningen of Holland was a disaster as the red and whites crashed out of the competition amid allegations that Gil had forced injured stars to play. After the game the club doctor and physiotherapist, who had been with Atletico for 25 and 18 years respectively, were fired for refusing to declare the players fit. Officially they were described as having 'mishandled injured players'. Maguregui was next to go, another victim of this tortured club. While assistant coach Antonio Briones took temporary charge Gil looked to the English game for his new supremo. Having been rejected by Terry Venables, the Englishman who had brought Barcelona its first League title for more than a decade in 1984–85 but was now manager of Tottenham Hotspur, Gil turned to another Englishman: Ron Atkinson, the very man he had denigrated on his return from Milan. He was to be the new saviour, after having been made, in Atkinson's words, 'an offer I couldn't refuse'. Atkinson's first game in charge ended in a 6–0 win against Español, prompting the new coach to remark: 'I've always had an ambition to manage in Spain. Having got here and experienced the ambience of the place I would love to stay and be successful. Madrid is a favourite city of mine. If we don't get the results, we'll get the tin-tack [sack]'. Gil's comment after that first game was: 'At last I have the Atletico I want'.

Atkinson lasted precisely 94 days in the Atletico job during which time he took the team from the depths of the First Division to third place. Notwithstanding this achievement and the fact that Baltazar was the Spanish League's top scorer, Atletico were still two places behind Real, with little hope of winning the title. Atkinson learned of his dismissal, not from Uncle Gilito, but from his erstwhile assistant Colin Addison, to whom Gil had offered the now vacant post. While Atkinson was taking a two-day break in Birmingham Gil informed Addison and the press of the latest developments but did not see fit to tell Atkinson, who was understandably upset. 'I loved the job and I wanted to stay', he said. 'Officially I don't know anything but I'll be seeing the president tomorrow so maybe I'll know more then. I've always said that nothing surprises me in football but when you've taken a team from 18th to third and then get the sack you've got to wonder what's going on.'

Jesús Gil, unable to restrain himself, launched into a ferocious attack on Atkinson's commitment to Atletico. 'Ron is too bossy. All he wants is to earn more money, have a good car and a villa on the beach. Otherwise he does not care. He likes to spend two days a week sunning himself in the Canaries. He made no effort to learn Spanish and did not know the players. If I have to sign 20 coaches until we find the right one for success then I will do it.' Strangely, Atkinson did not blame Gil for his exit, a testament to the kind of loyalty the president can inspire. 'The trouble', lamented Atkinson, 'comes from people behind the scenes who try to interfere in team affairs. There are a lot of monkeys employed here'.

Before Atkinson left, he was subjected to the depth of feeling at the club on many occasions. None more so than when Atletico lost 2–1 to Real in the Bernabeu on 4 December 1988. In the days before the game Gil stepped up his war of words on Real president Ramón Mendoza. He threatened to send the youth team to play the match, whereupon Mendoza said he would refuse to allow the game to be televised if Gil carried out his threat. Eventually, Uncle Gilito backed down when the League threatened to deduct points from the *Rojoblancos*. The game itself was one of the most violent Spain has ever seen. Seven players were shown the yellow card and three sent off while the Real goal-keeper, Buyo, was considered lucky not to have inflated the figures further after a display of histrionics that got Orejuela the red card. Once again the fanaticism of Jesús Gil and the tradition of hated inferiority had proved to be a powder-keg.

For the rest of the 1988–89 season, Colin Addison maintained the improved run of results which had begun with Atkinson's arrival. It was not enough, however. Real were heading for yet another Championship which left the *Rojoblancos* needing to win the King's Cup or achieve a high placing in the League to qualify for one of the lesser European tournaments. However, Atletico once again finished behind Real in fourth place and were knocked out of the Cup by the double-winners, the inevitable Real. Even qualification for Europe and the fact that Baltazar was top scorer with 35 goals were not good enough for Addison to have any prospect of keeping his job and sure enough, Gil announced a new coach for the 1989–90 season. Javier Clemente, at 38, was a dynamic personality who had taken Bilbao to two League Championships and one King's Cup triumph in the early 1980s, achieving the double in the process. Later, his Español team reached the UEFA Cup final. When asked what he felt about working for such a volatile president, Clemente said: 'He wants the same thing I do: to make Atletico Madrid the champions of Spain'. As if to upstage their neighbours, Real also took on a new manager for the 1989–90 season after Leo Beenhaaker had seen the team eliminated from the Champions' Cup at the semi-final stage in three successive years. Interestingly, Real chose Welshman John Toshack, who had enjoyed successful coaching spells in the European game at Sporting Lisbon and Real Sociedad. With Johan Cruyff completing his first season at Barcelona by winning the European Cup-Winners' Cup and finishing second in the League, Clemente clearly has his work cut out to achieve the objective set out by the president. So far, in chasing what seems an impossible dream, management changes at Atletico have cost over £1 million in wages and compensation.

Of course, events off the pitch continued to be as significant as events on it. The Superior Sports Council, a government agency which makes grants to a range of sports, opened an investigation into the financial arrangements between Gil and Atletico after the accounts of the *Rojoblancos* were called 'confusing and indecipherable'. The problems centred around the fact that Gil, since becoming president, had paid all the transfer fees himself but the wages and social security payments were apparently made by the club. What happened to any profit when a player was sold was a matter of dispute. The point about this episode is that the Spanish authorities had the power to order the investigation, and used it. In Spain, all professional clubs must submit their yearly budgets for scrutiny and all debts are examined in detail. Jesús Gil, using much of his own money, had failed to separate the transactions that were wholly related to his own business dealings from those of the club. When Atletico's accounts did not supply the required information, the investigation was started. The allegations against Gil were described by an anonymous source from within the Council. 'Gil is signing players as if it were a matter of a middle man granting permission to another firm to have the players. Apart from that, financial experts are asking why a certificate appears in the club's accounts, not signed by the president, that confirms the handing over to Atletico of players bought by the Gil enterprise. Nor is it clear which banks agreed to loans during the last season, nor whether the loans were granted to Gil or to Atletico, nor who endorsed them. Also unknown is the seasonally adjusted balance of accounts.' The matter was somewhat resolved when Gil presented new accounts, which showed that the president had sold off some of his property interests in Marbella to pay the social security bill.

In addition to the investigation, Gil lost his cases against the sacked players and the club doctors in the labour court and at present has no fewer than 21 law suits pending. It is hardly surprising that even the Raging Bull thought it prudent to impose a one-month media ban on the club's activities, although he found it ever more difficult to comply with the ban himself. In February 1989 the League announced that Atletico's total debt had reached £15 million.

It is interesting to speculate on what the rest of Spanish football has made of the Raging Bull's tumultuous period at the Calderon. The Spanish game inherited a certain dignity from the artistic and cultural framework of the bullfight, which it displaced as the major sport in the early years of the century. Real Madrid itself sprang from a group of aficionados who met at La Taurina, a bar and talking-shop adjacent to the plaza. This is not to say that there is any lack of scandal in the Spanish game; of course it has its fair share, but somehow matters of dispute seem generally to be resolved in a more orderly and amicable atmosphere than is generally appreciated. Football in Spain was patronised in the

1920s by King Alfonso XIII, who bestowed the title *real* (royal) on a number of clubs including Madrid FC. Football became a focal point as the game assumed an important place in Spanish culture and politics. In the Franco years, when the Catalan language and flag were banned, the only place where these symbols of nationalism could be openly displayed was at the Barcelona football stadium. After all, even Franco's police could hardly arrest the entire crowd. Football also fitted perfectly into the regional nature of Spanish society, a notion which came under attack from Franco's centralising ideology. This regional tendency can still be seen today as certain Basque clubs, such as Real Sociedad, play only Basque-born players, although the Spanish game generally has become cosmopolitan through an influx of top players and managers from all over the world. Through its diversity and its structure the game of football in Spain has always remained an important cultural influence. It is this balance that Jesús Gil has so flagrantly upset.

It would be easy to dismiss Jesús Gil as an anachronism, good only for media headlines and a cheap joke. It cannot be denied, however, that few Spanish club officials have used their own money to the same extent as Gil. Moreover, Gil gives another reason for the controversies he generates. 'My attacks against others are a deliberate strategy to break Barca and Real's overwhelming monopoly', he said. 'These two look like the Russians and the Americans.' He has also aligned himself with the traditional feelings of inferiority and persecution that have accompanied the *Colchoneros* throughout their existence. Gil articulates their defiance and their despair and gives the impression that he will fight to the end for Atletico Madrid. To Gil, Atletico is: 'me, and that magnificent and resigned group of supporters, which through its love for the club has had to put up with continual disasters and a lack of respect for their Atletico. I'm going to ensure they respect us. Nobody is going to make fun of us. I'm going to make sure the members are proud of their Atletico'. Perhaps the *Colchoneros* can perceive the parallel. Gil, like the club, knows from experience what disaster means. And, just like the members, Gil yearns for the respect that in his case was lost at Los Angeles de San Rafael. By delivering success to this, of all clubs, he sees the prospect of rehabilitation. When that day comes, the tormentors of Jesús Gil will undoubtedly suffer.

It is also true that, because he spends so much of his own money Gil's voice carries much weight with many supporters in Spain. With most clubs suffering from historic debts (even Real Madrid carries a debt of over £3 million and the collective debt of the whole Spanish game stood at £115 million in 1989), Gil's solution is obviously appealing. In Atletico's case the allegations of financial irregularities served another purpose. The only way to run a football club, according to Gil, is to make directors liable for their financial performance, rather than being able to hand on debts to the next administration, which is the case at present. The only way to do this is to bring in a system of companies based on the structure in Britain to replace what Gil sees as the outmoded Spanish model of club and members. With only one year of his tenure left to run, it need hardly be said that if this came about the largest, perhaps the only, shareholder in Atletico Madrid would be Jesús Gil.

In Spain, the affairs of clubs can be influenced by the members, who have the vote, by the central government, which makes grants to football clubs through the Superior Sports Council and the redistribution of pools income (the *plan saneamiento*), and by the League, which can reject a club's budget or accounts. For the year 1989-90 Spanish football will receive £5.5 million from the Council, almost 12 per cent of its budget. The tax on betting has been allocated to pay a percentage of clubs' debts and Real Madrid received £3.75 million from this source in 1987-88. Jesús Gil's campaign to usher in a British type of system was given a boost when the government introduced a white paper in March 1989 which would allow clubs to become limited liability companies. However, the proposed measures, which should become law by 1990, do contain some safeguards which are absent in Britain, including the establishment of a commission to oversee the financial affairs of clubs and draw up plans for the distribution of shares to the public and to members. The consensus of opinion is that the new law will stop clubs falling into an individual's hands in the first instance but might not prevent it in the future. If the development of ownership in England is anything to go by, it would appear to be a move which Spanish football fans may one day come to regret bitterly unless the best features of their current system – members, and their right to vote for the officers of the club – are retained. While Jesús Gil has won over the Atletico fans, he may also have started a process which will result in the death of democracy in Spanish football. For Gil, the rewards of success will be considerable. 'When we finish above Real', he said, 'I shall be the boss of all Spain.'

The story of football is littered with men who have seen themselves as saviours. Although his methods are more public and outrageous, and have provoked widespread opposition, Gil has sought to achieve much the same as Irving Scholar at Tottenham and David Dein at Arsenal: to lift relatively depressed capital city clubs to the heights of glory which they believe are theirs by right and to lead them into a new, commercially determined future. Essentially, these are personal revolutions, carried out by committed individuals. At Spurs, Scholar has ushered in a new corporate structure, a state of affairs Jesús Gil would dearly love to emulate in Madrid. However, across Europe the diverse administrations of the game are having to take on board new commercial developments, with many clubs becoming arms of larger, often international companies. In this brave new world, the roles of gifted organisers like David Dein, corporate predators like Irving Scholar and rich entrepreneurs like Jesús Gil are becoming subservient to the wider global interests of television and big business. And clubs like Atletico, Spurs and Arsenal, for all their pretensions to greatness, still have a long way to go to catch up with the truly big clubs of Europe. Meanwhile, events taking place in that most intense of soccer cities, Glasgow, a place that makes the rivalries of London and Madrid seem genteel, are beginning to show what is necessary for ambitious clubs actually to achieve greatness.

3
GLASGOW BELONGS TO ME

We have just enough religion to make us hate but not enough to make us love one another

JONATHAN SWIFT

It took only a second for the momentum to be interrupted, but it was enough. The surge was always dangerous, now it was about to become lethal. The critical moment occurred as an unstoppable force of 10,000 chanting, swaying bodies, densely packed and moving as one, flowed down the almost vertical stairway number 13. As long as everyone kept moving the descent was just about negotiable, but even under optimum conditions a person could be lifted involuntarily into the air at the top by the sheer pressure of the human mass and swept to the bottom without touching the ground until the crowd levelled off as it met Cairnlea Drive. Perhaps someone stopped to retrieve some lost article; perhaps boisterousness caused some to leap on the backs of others resulting in a build-up of pressure; or it could have been the drink and the intense last 60 seconds of the game during which Celtic took the lead, then miraculously, Rangers equalised with seconds remaining; maybe some had turned back in an insane attempt to re-enter the stadium. Whatever the cause, the surge was halted half-way along its length, downward pressure from the top of the stairway increased as more tried to join the exodus, and when it reached its peak, hell was unleashed on the streets of Glasgow.

First one, then more barriers gave way under the weight of human pressure. As the first victims fell, those behind were driven inexorably forward by the relentless pressure. The stairway was transformed into a seething black hole as hundreds tumbled into the abyss. The 66 who died were crushed amid twisted steel girders and the smashed concrete that had once been the steps. The injured spilled on to Cairnlea Drive where they lay until rescue vehicles fought their way through the crowds. At the time, it was the worst disaster ever to befall a British football game and it could, many say should, have been avoided.

Until that terrible moment on the Cairnlea Drive stairway everything had gone normally, if such a word can ever be used to describe matches between Rangers and Celtic, the two giants of Scottish football. It was 2 January 1971 and the crowd, passionate and committed in the inimitable manner of Scots supporters, was not unduly violent, although a good proportion had consumed large amounts of alcohol during the long New Year celebrations traditional in Scotland. In Glasgow, if not the whole of the country, the holiday was not over until the referee blew the final whistle at the end of the customary New Year meeting between the ancient rivals. On this day the air of normality was a bitter illusion. Something was seriously wrong with the old Ibrox stadium, home to Rangers since 1897. The capacity of the ground was fixed at 80,000 for the 1971 clash but this precaution failed to prevent the flow of people from the east terrace, many, according to a later judgment in the courts, anxious, even desperate to get away, emptying on to a stairway manifestly unfit for the purpose.

There had been three accidents on the notorious stairway 13 in the previous ten years. Two people had been killed in 1961 and the previous incident, in which more than 20 were injured, had taken place only two years earlier in 1969. When the first claim for compensation was decided in the Glasgow Sheriff Court in 1974, those charged with running Glasgow Rangers Football Club at the time of the disaster were severely criticised for their attitude towards safety. Awarding £26,000 to Mrs Margaret Dougan, whose husband Charles had been killed, Sheriff J. Irvine Smith accused Rangers' director David Hope of 'equivocation' and, commenting bluntly on the nature of Hope's performance in court said, 'the evidence here is such that it has to be read to be believed'. Of David White, Rangers manager at the time, the Sheriff was equally critical: 'He became increasingly unimpressive as his cross-examination progressed'. The evidence of Hope and White was rejected as 'wholly unreliable and untrustworthy', while a letter which had been sent by Rangers to the Scottish Football

Association (SFA) after the governing body had expressed concern over safety at Ibrox, was dismissed as 'blatantly untrue'. Rangers' administration generally was appallingly inept. 'Rarely', commented the judge, 'can an organisation the size and significance of Rangers Football Club have succeeded in conducting their business with records so sparse, so carelessly kept, so inaccurately written up . . . and so indifferently stored.'

Seventeen years after the disaster, David Holmes sat in the chairman's office of a new Ibrox, completely rebuilt and unrecognisable from the stadium of death that had occupied the same site in 1971. The dapper and confident Holmes, full of optimism for a revitalised Rangers, nevertheless displayed signs that the effects of the trauma lurked still in the majestic atmosphere of what is now the best football ground in Britain.

According to Holmes the impetus for the rebuilding of Ibrox came from the fateful happenings of 1971. After the disaster the decision was taken to completely modernise the stadium, to make it 'the safest, the most modern and the most comfortable possible'. At the time of the disaster Rangers were ruled by the towering personality of John Lawrence, a Glasgow joiner who built up a vast construction empire in the 1930s. Although he was still chairman in 1971, Lawrence was almost 80 years old and was exonerated on that basis from culpability in the disaster, but the deaths and the laxity over matters of safety could only have damaged his company's image. That company, John Lawrence (Glasgow) Ltd, exerted a profound influence over the years, not only on Rangers, but on the whole of Scottish football.

John Lawrence was brought up in the Govanhill area of Glasgow. He started a one-man business which soon grew into one of the largest house-building operations in Scotland. In the private sector housing boom of the 1930s the name became known through the slogan 'A home of your own by John Lawrence'. In 1954 the now influential Lawrence became a director of the club he had supported since boyhood. The building sector took off again in Scotland in the early 1960s as the slums and tenements began to be cleared and the Lawrence group once again took part in this rapid expansion. The company's image became further enhanced when John Lawrence assumed the chairmanship of Rangers in 1963. From that time Lawrence became synonymous with the club – to all intents and purposes he was Rangers – to the extent that ten years after his death he was described by the *Glasgow Herald* as a man who 'looked, walked and talked like a benign bishop and had a motto of keeping everybody happy'. However, there was a less benign side to Lawrence. He was unrepentant on the subject of Rangers' sectarian policy of refusing to sign Catholic players. In response to criticism in 1969 from the Rev Robert Bone of the Ibrox church, who complained of 'filthy language' and 'bigotry' at the stadium, Lawrence flatly admitted that discrimination had been in operation since the club's inception and that anyone coming to support Rangers did so in the knowledge of this policy.

After Lawrence died in 1977 it seemed as if the dynasty would die with him. One of his sons, Jack, died early and the other, Billy, had little interest in either the Lawrence empire or Rangers Football Club. The mantle fell upon the shoulders of the son of John's eldest daughter, Alice, the young Lawrence Marlboro. While Marlboro became a director of Rangers his principal concern was to build up the property empire which he diversified into transportation and oil and expanded into other areas of the world including the USA and Canada. He did, however, put into effect the decision to rebuild the stadium. Funded by Rangers' massive income from its football pools, work on the new Ibrox began in 1978 and by 1983 the transformation was complete. The finished stadium is a superb creation, though its capacity has been reduced to 44,000, including 36,000 seats. Gone is the vast bowl, replaced by stands on three sides of the ground, which has created over 20,000 square feet of rentable office space in the process. And gone forever is stairway 13.

However, the period of the building work coincided with a dramatic decline in Rangers' fortunes on the pitch and a corresponding drop in the number of paying spectators. The League Championship was beyond the team for almost a decade after the 1977–78 treble and in the same period the Scottish Cup was won twice. Those successes, plus four wins in the relatively minor competition, the League Cup, were clearly insufficient to satisfy either the fans or the directors. Behind the scenes the club was experiencing a series of the bitter disagreements that have, throughout its history, occasionally surfaced as ugly public arguments. The annual general meetings of 1976 and 1977 were characterised by raucous attempts to change the Board of Directors, led by local garage-owner Jack Gillespie, who eventually bought his way to a directorship in September 1977. Further changes occurred in 1983 when three new directors arrived: Tom Dawson, another garage-owner; Jim Robinson, scrap metal dealer; and Hugh Adam, who revamped the lucrative Rangers pools operation, the biggest in Britain. John Paton, formerly the owner of the largest taxi franchise in Scotland and a director since 1979, became chairman in another shake-up in 1984.

The acrimony and constant changes had a disastrous effect on morale both on and off the pitch. With crowds dropping alarmingly in a new stadium that had cost £10 million, Rangers were facing a serious financial problem. The comings and goings had dented confidence in the club and there was no figure like John Lawrence around to halt the slide. Moreover, the situation at Rangers was becoming a severe embarrassment to the Lawrence group as stories of sectarianism grew in the media and the club narrowly avoided an investigation into the problem by the world governing body, FIFA, in 1983, mainly due to the fact that the game's ultimate authority is as reluctant to delve too deeply into the internal affairs of clubs as the clubs are determined to keep FIFA out.

These developments must have rung alarm bells 8,000 miles away in Nevada, where Lawrence Marlboro was in constant touch with Rangers by computer link. The club was now the butt of comedians' jokes. The trouble with the new stadium, they said, was that the stands were built the wrong way – facing the pitch! Marlboro had built the John Lawrence group into an international organisation in which Rangers was financially insignificant, but in terms of public relations it was the group's most visible operation. The descendants of John Lawrence were now an extended family, many of whom owned shares in the club which were held in trust by Marlboro. Marlboro himself had left Glasgow by the end of the 1970s and moved permanently to Nevada where he lives in luxury at Lake Tahoe. He remained a director of Rangers although the position was more honorary than anything else. Marlboro is an intensely private man who shuns publicity, declining most requests for interviews and often flying into Glasgow in conditions of strict secrecy for business meetings. As barren seasons came and went, Marlboro watched the deteriorating situation at Rangers and became increasingly alarmed at what he saw. In November 1985 he acted. With the same single-mindedness he shows in all his business dealings, he decided to treat Rangers as a corporate entity that needed a complete shake-up and not as a football club run benevolently as an expensive hobby. In a boardroom coup which saw the demise of Dawson and Robinson, the reclusive Marlboro installed on the Board David Holmes, who was chief executive of the Scottish business, John Lawrence (Glasgow) Ltd, and who, like old John Lawrence himself, had worked his way up from a job as a joiner.

David Holmes' route to the chairmanship was unusual in the fanatical world of Glasgow football. Until his arrival in 1985, directors of Rangers were major shareholders and committed supporters. Many were self-made men who had followed the Blues since boyhood and had always dreamed of being involved in the club. Holmes was neither a Rangers fan nor a shareholder. He was there to take tough decisions to protect the Lawrence group's investment. At the same time, Marlboro also brought on to the Board Freddie Fletcher, the group's head of marketing. In 1986, after a hectic round of secret share deals, John Paton was forced out and Holmes was appointed to the post of chairman. Jack Gillespie became vice-chairman in an arrangement whereby he granted Marlboro an option to buy his shares in two instalments, in 1989 and 1990. The outsider Holmes was now in charge of the most lucrative football club in Britain, in a city which at best could be described as volatile.

The situation differed from that in Madrid in that the businesses of Rangers and Celtic benefited from the rough parity of the teams on the pitch over the years. Naturally, there had been periods of dominance by one or the other – Rangers were in the ascendant from the end of the First World War until the tables were turned in the 1960s – but even when one club was winning the League Championship, the other could be relied upon to win one of the cup competitions or to come up with something special for old firm games. However, when Lawrence Marlboro intervened to put David Holmes on the Board the pre-eminence of the old firm was under threat from the 'new firm' of Aberdeen and Dundee United, who had at last broken the stranglehold Rangers and Celtic had exerted on Scottish football for almost 100 years, and from the wider world, where sectarianism was increasingly coming to be seen as at best an anachronism, at worst a gross insult to the world of football, one that could not be tolerated in the sporting arena. Rangers' traditional policy of refusing to sign Catholic players was under attack while performances on the pitch were going from bad to worse. Now Holmes had to act. His installation by Lawrence Marlboro was the only way of ridding Rangers of the burden of its history. For the first time the club would be run, not by committed fans who happened to be rich, but by businessmen who in truth had little feeling for Rangers the football club (Holmes' allegiance was to Falkirk, Fletcher's to Morton), but who would bring the business methods of the Lawrence group to bear on what should have been a profitable part of the empire. As Holmes explained, 'I can be of greater benefit to Rangers if I can stand back from it all. I never looked at it as a football club, I looked at it as a business. You've got to stand back from it otherwise it would gobble you up'. Something of the task faced by David Holmes can be seen in the unique nature of Glasgow rivalry where, to paraphrase the great Bill Shankly, people don't make the mistake of believing football is just a game.

The basis of Rangers' success was built on the club's conflict with its Glasgow neighbour, Celtic. The clubs draw their massive support from the city's two distinctive communities, which are historically divided, as in Northern Ireland, on religious grounds. These entrenched social divisions, based on competing brands of Christianity, have elevated games between the clubs far beyond mere sporting rivalry to something which at times resembles a holy war. Rangers, representing the conservative Protestant establishment, have always held the dominant status socially and financially, whereas Celtic, whose identity is bound up with the Catholic minority, have traditionally been the under-dogs. Rangers' support has always contained an element of the militant Protestantism associated with paramilitary groups in

Northern Ireland, especially the Ulster Defence Force, and the ideology of violence which characterises such organisations has sometimes made its presence felt in the massed Ibrox crowd. As Celtic was originally formed as a club in 1888 by and for the Irish immigrant community, and traditionally flew the Irish tricolour over its stadium, meetings between the two teams inevitably became ritual encounters in which ancient battles could be re-enacted and traditional grievances voiced, often in the form of sectarian songs.

The religious divide in Glasgow has permeated every level of society. It encompasses education, housing, jobs and industry and has often found political expression in unionist and nationalist feelings. It is important to keep this in mind when the city's two great football clubs are discussed. They have not just attracted support from one or other of the religious communities, they *are* the communities; their roots lie deep in the fabric of the divide and they remain the focal point of an old religious argument. It is no coincidence that the reformation of 16th century Europe found far more acceptance in Scotland than it did in England, which became Protestant, not out of doctrinal disagreements with Rome but because of the personal and political interests of King Henry VIII. To this day the most fundamental Protestant churches on the British mainland are Scottish and opposition to a papal visit was nowhere stronger than in Scotland in 1982. Far from discouraging the unpleasant nature of these associations, the football clubs of Glasgow recognised early on that the intense rivalry had a positive side. It was good for business.

In the last 20 years, the media have devoted much attention to the sectarian issue and no doubt have sometimes put matters out of perspective, but fundamentally the situation today is little different from that of 50 years ago. As David Holmes recognised: 'There will always be rivalry between Rangers and Celtic, without it football in Scotland is a dead duck'. The problem, of course, is how to keep the situation under control so that healthy rivalry does not degenerate into mindless sectarian bigotry. In the harsh commercial world of the 1990s such a balance must, according to Holmes, be maintained. 'As a marketing tool', he explained, 'the atmosphere at Rangers-Celtic games is something all the money in the world cannot buy.' Holmes was not overstating the situation. Few games in the world can match the passion of an old firm derby.

From the earliest days of organised football in Scotland it was obvious that games between Rangers and Celtic were the real money-spinners. Celtic's share of the business has been owned and controlled for 90 years by three dynasties, an ironic development considering that the club was formed as a charitable institution in order to raise money for the impoverished of Glasgow's east end, which today remains an area of deprivation. The growing popularity of football in the late 19th century ensured increasingly large crowds and it did not take long for a section of the ruling committee to begin a campaign for the charity to become a limited liability company. After four years of manoeuvring Celtic finally became incorporated in 1897. The following year the directors decided to award themselves a 20 per cent dividend in the wake of the year's receipts, a British record at over £16,000, while charity received nothing. Since then Celtic and its finances have been firmly in the grip of the three families.

The largest shareholder on the first Celtic Board was James Grant, an Irishman who had emigrated to Scotland and made a fortune as a distiller. On his death in 1914 Grant's shares passed to his son John, who lived in Canada and had little interest in football. John's shares were eventually inherited by his sister, Felicia Grant, who, while taking no part in the day-to-day running of the club, was a keen supporter and actually acquired further shares. The Grant family interest is represented these days by Tom Grant, James' great-grandson and a director since 1985. James Kelly, a player in the first-ever Celtic team, also joined the first Board in 1897 and was chairman from 1906 until 1914. His son Robert took over in 1947 and ran the club until 1971. To complete the picture, the Kellys' latest addition to the Board is Robert's nephew, Kevin. James Kelly had been succeeded as chairman in 1914 by Thomas White, who ruled for the next 33 years. His son Desmond took over in 1971 and another member of the family, Christopher, grandson of Thomas, became a director in 1982.

These three families, the Grants, the Kellys and the Whites, have held effective rule at Celtic since the battle for commercialism was won in 1897. No longer as concerned with the well-being of the city's Irish Catholic community, the club under the three families became a profitable business, as can be seen from the early dividends paid to directors – as much as 25 per cent in 1907. With little financial scrutiny the three families ran Celtic as they pleased. Their reputation in Glasgow for being niggardly in financial matters, which has persisted since those early days, is in marked contrast to the amounts of money coming in during the boom years and the propensity with which the families continually voted themselves large dividends. In a community that suffered alienation because of its religion, the three families ruled without hindrance and early battles with the Protestants of the Glasgow Football Association and the SFA fuelled allegations by the directors of discrimination. The story was also current that the SFA actually tried to drive Celtic out of business and although no evidence has been produced to substantiate the charge it nevertheless helped to promote the 'us and them' mentality which, in turn, allowed the three families to do more or less as they liked.

In contrast to the cosy nepotism at Celtic, control of Rangers has always been subject to turmoil, intrigue and bitter arguments. Committee meetings in the early days were wild and riotous, as annual general meetings have often been since. Success was always accompanied by feuding with referees, the SFA and parts of the Glasgow press. The *Scottish Athletic Journal* accused the club of 'chicanery and trickery' and it was suggested that Rangers' affairs did not 'wear well in the wash'. Even the opening of the new Ibrox stadium in 1897 was marred by reports of cantankerous committee meetings and what the *Scottish Sport* called 'a vexatious lack of enterprise'. Following the example of Celtic, Rangers became a limited company in 1899, and ever since the business of the club has continually been the centre of disputes, not now in the glare of public meetings, but for the most part behind closed doors in secret with occasional overspills into the press or annual general meetings. By the time the die was cast, at the beginning of this century, the club was in the hands of merchants, businessmen and professional people, the *nouveaux riches* of Victorian Britain. It was solid, it was conservative, but above all else it was Protestant.

Whereas the directors of Celtic seemed to be interested mainly in the money that could be earned from football, Rangers were more concerned with success for its own sake. Failure for Rangers meant the failure of Protestant superiority; it was a blow against the collective dominance of the majority. Even the club's traditional refusal to sign Catholic players can be seen in this light. What use would success be if it were not achieved by a wholly Protestant team? For Celtic, success meant money, and since success could never be achieved by drawing players exclusively from the smaller, Catholic population, it mattered little whether Celtic's players were Catholic, Protestant, or anything else. The important thing was that the team performed well enough to keep the turnstiles clicking round. Jock Stein, the great Celtic manager of the 1960s and '70s is reputed to have said that given the choice between two good players, one Protestant, one Catholic, all things being equal he would go for the Protestant as he knew Rangers wouldn't take the Catholic.

The problem for David Holmes when he took charge in 1985 was that Rangers were not achieving the kind of results on the pitch that the fans demanded. The great era of Rangers dominance had ended with the arrival at Celtic in 1965 of Jock Stein, the Protestant manager who brought the club its greatest success, the European Champions' Cup in 1967. After the emergence of Stein's Celtic, Rangers' success was sporadic, two great seasons under manager Jock Wallace in the late 1970s, when the club won all three domestic competitions, being the highlight. When Wallace left in strange and unexplained circumstances in 1978, former captain John Greig took over. Under Greig, Rangers declined further as first Aberdeen, then Dundee United produced Championship-winning teams. Wallace returned in 1983 to stem the tide but the decline had gone too far. In fact things had got so bad before the return of Wallace that when Rangers approached Alex Ferguson, manager of Aberdeen, and Jim Maclean, manager of Dundee United, they both did the unthinkable and turned down the biggest job in Scottish football.

Holmes' first few months at Rangers were traumatic. Performances had hit an all-time low and the fans were deserting Ibrox in droves. The club finished an appalling fifth in the League, behind champions Celtic, had lost in the semi-final of the League Cup to Hibs and were knocked out of the Scottish Cup at the first hurdle by a newly-emergent Hearts of Edinburgh. All this stretched Rangers' finances to the limit. David Holmes outlined the strategy he devised to turn the situation around. 'When I came to this club,' he said, 'it was a sleeping giant. My job was to wake it up. It had potential but it didn't have cash. Contrary to what many people think Rangers do not have lots of money, the club has to survive on what it earns. I went to the bank with a business plan and, on the basis of my track record with the Lawrence group, asked them to loan the club £2.5 million.' On 7 April 1986, with a positive response from the bank and after a series of secret meetings and phone calls, Holmes pulled off what was to prove his master stroke when he dismissed Jock Wallace and appointed Graeme Souness as player-manager. The courteous, mild-mannered David Holmes was displaying the hitherto concealed toughness that had evidently been acquired in the transition from joiner to hard-nosed business executive. Graeme Souness had distinguished himself as an uncompromising midfield player with Liverpool and Sampdoria of Genoa. Holmes thought that Rangers' profile was too low for such a big club and he saw the signing of Souness as a way of bringing the Rangers name to a world-wide audience. Director Freddie Fletcher, Rangers' head of marketing, emphasised what the signing meant to the supporters. 'Acquiring Graeme Souness was the first thing that happened to excite the fans. It indicated to them that the new administration at Ibrox was serious about making Rangers one of the foremost teams in Europe.'

The arrival of Souness also signalled to the club's supporters that the days of sectarianism were drawing to a close. Rangers' constituency would have to extend beyond its traditional confines to reach lucrative world television markets. Souness himself was married to a Catholic but this was not the only departure from tradition that the new manager instigated. In a series of remarkable transfer deals that changed the face of Scottish football, Souness overturned a century of tradition and began buying English players. The English contingent did not come cheaply. Rangers were now paying some of the highest salaries in Britain and the outlay in transfer fees alone stood at over £7 million by 1988. Having built a magnificent stadium, the club was now turning its attention to the creation of a team fit to play in it. Rangers, the big club, were now acting the part and the crowds came flocking back as Souness began to mould a successful team.

Those first moves of Graeme Souness were sensational. He signed the English players Colin West, Chris Woods and Terry Butcher, the latter two being English internationals, for over £1 million. Over 36,000 turned up at Ibrox for a pre-season friendly against Bayern Munich and by the time of Rangers' first League match under Souness expectation had reached fever pitch. The game is remembered, however, not for the 2–1 defeat Rangers suffered at the hands of Hibernian of Edinburgh, but for the dramatic sending-off of the fiercely competitive Souness after just 36 minutes for an appalling foul on George McCluskey, which was followed by fighting among the rest of the players. Souness's tackles had been legendary in the game for many years but in the goldfish bowl he now inhabited together with the managerial responsibility he now shouldered the incident assumed disastrous proportions, prompting David Holmes to remark that he could see 'all our good work disappearing'. The controversy that has always travelled with Rangers had struck again. The team recovered quickly, though, and August finished with a win over Celtic.

Problems of discipline on the pitch have continued throughout the Souness era, one of the worst incidents coming in a fight with Celtic players during the 'old firm' game on 24 October 1987 that led to Woods and Butcher of Rangers and McAvennie of Celtic being sent off. Another English import, Graham Roberts, naïvely began to conduct the massed Protestant choir on the terraces in sectarian songs and the incident resulted in all four being charged with incitement of the crowd to breaches of the peace. The judge at the subsequent trial remarked that he was well aware of the atmosphere of hate that surrounded games between the two clubs. It was as though the present Rangers were unable to shake off the ghosts of past misconduct, the bad behaviour that had always been a part of the club since its earliest days and had been epitomised in recent times by lengthy suspensions for misconduct meted out to several Rangers players, notably Willie Johnstone and Gregor Stevens. After the new manager was again sent off in the penultimate match of the season at Aberdeen for another dreadful foul, a quick drink in the pubs and clubs of Glasgow became known as a 'Souness' – 'one half and I'm off'.

The unique pressures and high media profile of the two Glasgow clubs, coupled with Souness's 'win at all costs' philosophy, has taken its toll. Ted McMinn, Robert Fleck and Graham Roberts all left Rangers after disagreements of one sort or another and Jan Bartram, the Danish player who was signed by Souness in 1988, claimed that the manager was 'the world's worst loser' who 'kicked in a television set' after one particular defeat. This side of the Souness reputation was enhanced when it was discovered that he had, legally but surely unethically, narrowed the Ibrox pitch for a Champions' Cup match against Dynamo Kiev in order to bemuse the Russians who had trained on the full-size pitch the day before.

After the dramas at the start of the 1986–87 season Rangers' fortunes on the pitch began to change dramatically. The League Cup (now the Skol Cup) was won in October with a stormy 2–1 defeat of Celtic and although the club went out of the UEFA Cup to Borussia Moenchengladbach of Germany when two Rangers players were sent off, and lost remarkably to Hamilton in the third round of the Cup, by the start of 1987 the club was ready to mount a serious attempt on the Championship. As the push for the title gathered pace, Ibrox once again began to pull in the crowds. When the Championship was won in May, Rangers had played host to over a million spectators, earning the club the largest receipts in its history at just under £4 million.

Off the field the team's success allowed the new administration to implement the long-term business plan. Lawrence Marlboro had realised that parochial concerns could no longer serve Rangers as they had for so long and David Holmes claimed that his target was to make the club 'the biggest in Europe'. Like many of their English counterparts, the Rangers administration has pulled in new sources of revenue from the business community and has created new breeds of season-ticket holder: the affluent, independent young and the family. But, as Holmes explained, the commercial policy is interdependent with the success of the team. 'The best money we can get is through the turnstiles but the more money I can get through commercial ventures, the more I take the pressure off what is happening on the park.' Accordingly, Freddie Fletcher set to work on the commercial potential and income from that source went from £239,000 in 1985–86 to £2.2 million in 1987–88. Today, only 30 per cent of the club's income comes from gate receipts. David Holmes sees the future of Rangers in Europe but the 'end product' he wants is for Rangers to be 'world-wide'. Aware of the growing importance of television, the club began its own television service to exploit the support of second and third generation expatriate Scots all over the world who Holmes describes as 'never having been to Scotland but who know Ibrox. It's their vision of Scotland and we want to take it to them'. Rangers have since expanded into other areas, even buying a professional basketball team and a franchise from the Admiral sportswear company.

This emphasis on the international nature of the audience is uncommon in England although in Scotland there has been more of an historic affinity for British football's European dimension. The Champions' Cup contained Scottish clubs from its inception, whereas the English League refused to let champions Chelsea take part in the competition's first season, 1955–56. The event that truly instilled the ideal of Europe in Scottish hearts occurred in a game in which no Scottish club took part. The German side Eintracht Frankfurt had utterly demolished Rangers in the semi-final of the Champions' Cup in 1960, winning 6–1 in Germany and 6–3 at Ibrox, where a crowd of 70,000 turned up despite the first leg drubbing. Rangers themselves had beaten such teams as Anderlecht of Belgium, Red Star Bratislava and Sparta Rotterdam of Holland en route to the semi-final. On a magical evening in May, 135,000 spectators (a record for any European final) packed Hampden Park to see the Germans do the same to Real Madrid, winners of the competition every year since it began but now believed to be past their best. What the vast crowd witnessed was one of the most skilful displays of the pure art of football ever seen as Real won 7–3 with four goals from Hungarian Ferenc Puskas and three from Argentinian Alfredo Di Stefano.

These events fuelled an appetite for European action in Scotland. The culmination of the efforts of Rangers and Celtic in Europe came in 1967 when both clubs contested European finals. While the 2–1 victory of Celtic's 'Lisbon Lions' over Internazionale of

Milan is legendary, Rangers, in a largely forgotten final of the Cup-Winners' Cup six days after Celtic's triumph, lost 1–0 to a Franz Roth goal for Bayern Munich, the emerging German side which would later dominate the Champions' Cup. Victory would have been remarkable, as no city has provided two winners of European competitions in the same season. This made Rangers and their fans even more determined to win a European trophy but the Champions' Cup has always eluded them. When the club finally did win a European competition, the Cup-Winners' Cup in 1972, the victory was marred by crowd trouble in the so-called 'Battle of Barcelona', and Rangers were forced to accept the presentation of the trophy in a small underground room, instead of in full view of the crowd as tradition dictates.

The European perspective has obviously occupied the thinking of the new administration at Ibrox. When David Holmes said 'I would not take Rangers into a British League – our future is in Europe', the statement had a ring of truth about it. He did not seem to be indulging in wish-fulfilment. The Rangers fans obviously agree with him; 2,000 were locked outside a full house for a pre-season friendly with Bordeaux in August 1988.

As the upheavals got underway at Ibrox, the big question was, how would Celtic react? Despite being current champions Celtic had rarely paid large sums for players and were not in a strong position to compete. The three families had over the years paid themselves the highest dividends in British football and had sold exciting young players, sometimes against their wishes. As the glare of publicity focused on Rangers, Celtic tried to keep a low profile in the belief that Souness was spending recklessly and would fail. Tom Grant summed up the view of the Celtic Board in an interview with the *Glasgow Herald* in December 1986 in which he ridiculed Souness's spending and explained that Celtic would not 'splash out outrageous sums of cash, just because people see Rangers do it'. The fans were not satisfied, however, and they had good cause for complaint. By the end of the season Celtic had sold four of their top players, McInally, McClair, MacLeod and Johnston, for over £2 million. In the wake of Rangers' Championship victory, manager David Hay, who had pleaded with the Board for cash to buy new players and secure the continuing services of those whose contracts were due to expire, was fired. Many were of the opinion that the refusal of the Board to react positively to events at Ibrox was more responsible for the relative failure than any shortcomings on the part of the manager.

A change of heart came over Celtic in the close season of 1987 amid growing public demands for a wider share ownership. Billy McNeill was appointed manager after a disappointing time in England at Manchester City and Aston Villa, where he suffered the ignominy of managing both clubs to relegation from the First Division in the same season. McNeill had been captain of the great Celtic team of the 1960s and had won championships with the club in a previous spell as manager. At last the purse strings loosened and Celtic splashed out on new players: £500,000 for Mick McCarthy; £800,000 for Frank McAvennie from West Ham; and £650,000 for Joe Miller from Aberdeen. Souness also bought in more imports, including his old Sampdoria team-mate and England international Trevor Francis; another English international, Ray Wilkins from Paris St Germain, his former colleague at Liverpool; the Israeli defender Avi Cohen and the black winger Mark Walters from Aston Villa. But as a bewildering array of players came and went at Rangers, Celtic won both the League Championship and the Scottish Cup that season, the club's centenary year. Although Rangers could only manage to win the Skol Cup in 1987–88, and were eliminated from the Champions' Cup in the quarter-finals by Steaua Bucharest, average crowds were still significantly increased. David Holmes wrote in the 1987–88 annual report: 'It would be foolish to pretend that this has been anything other than a traumatic season . . . the supporters have stood by us and we by them . . . the object of Rangers Football Club is not to make huge net profits but to maximise the potential of the club and provide success on the field of play . . . [my objectives] as chairman are to make Rangers the premier club in Europe and to establish Ibrox as the number one football centre in Scotland. We are well on the way to the second objective, the first may take a little longer'.

Meanwhile, problems were beginning to upset the equilibrium of the Lawrence group. Rangers were playing to capacity crowds but the massive outlay on transfer fees still left the club in a large amount of debt – £1.9 million in 1987–88 – and there was rumoured to be dissension in the large Lawrence family. Marlboro was becoming more committed to building projects in the USA and the group sold its plant and transport division to haulage contractor W.H. Malcolm in April 1988. When Marlboro flew to Scotland in October 1988, ostensibly to watch the Skol Cup final between Rangers and Aberdeen, he opened secret negotiations with Edinburgh-based businessman David Murray, a friend of Souness, to sell the Lawrence interest in Rangers. Four weeks later, the dynasty which had been identified with Rangers since John Lawrence came to the club in 1954 was gone. Lawrence Marlboro, in a short statement, claimed that it was too difficult to run the club from the USA, although this had never bothered him before. It was more likely that a need for cash on the part of some members of the family led to the decision to sell the group's most liquid asset, although other family members stated that they did not know what was going on. There is also the matter of pure business profit to consider. In his share-buying spree of 1985–86 Marlboro had paid £12.50 per share. Three years later David Murray paid him £20.00 per share, giving Marlboro a handsome profit and Rangers an official valuation of £8 million when the club's fixed assets alone were valued at £23 million. In the same deal Graeme Souness acquired a 7 per cent stake in the club. Since David Holmes was to remain as chairman a delicate situation arose: the manager owned more shares than his nominal boss, the chairman. This was soon rendered academic when in June 1989 David Murray replaced Holmes, becoming Rangers' youngest-ever chairman at 37.

David Murray, a man of great ambition despite having lost both legs in a car crash when he was 22 years old, was said to have a personal fortune of £35 million. He formed Murray International Metals and by 1982 was a millionaire. The basic core of the business is steel but diversification has seen the company move into materials testing, electronics components, medical and offshore industries, office equipment and the ever-present property development. Murray bought Rangers amid rumours, later denied, of an impending bid by Robert Maxwell. As owner of the MIM basketball team Murray already had connections with sport and had earlier been thwarted in a bid to purchase Ayr United, his home town club. His first announcement was of a plan to redevelop the one remaining stand that had been left as the centrepiece of the ground during the rebuilding of the 1970s and '80s, the famous Archibald Leitch-designed south stand, the exterior of which is protected from change by holding listed status. For Graeme Souness, the purchase of 7 per cent of the shares displays what he calls his 'lifelong commitment to Rangers Football Club'.

Lawrence Marlboro, in one of his few public statements, commented on the sale: 'Obviously, severing my connection with Rangers makes this a sad and nostalgic day. However, I'm delighted that the new custodian . . . is Scottish based and a genuine Rangers supporter'. David Murray announced his determination to go one better than any previous regime, saying, 'that means to win the European Cup. It is the only thing Rangers haven't done. Football is what this club is all about and it is now in Europe that it must be done'.

In March 1989 Murray brought Alan Montgomery into the club as chief executive. Montgomery was previously the financial director of Scottish Television and had turned a £7 million overdraft into a £14 million credit. A Rangers supporter since boyhood, Montgomery had worked his way up to senior management, through his expertise in financial matters. He was employed to turn around the £7 million overdraft that had built up during Souness's spell as manager and plan for the club's development as a leisure industry. First Freddie Fletcher, then David Holmes had left. The two had been responsible for a revolution at Ibrox but had been left high and dry by the change of ownership, two more victims of the upheavals and boardroom changes that have been a characteristic of the club since its inception. The fact that the new chief executive came from a background in television led to speculation that Rangers may bid for the Scottish Television franchise when it is put out to tender in 1991. Given that the Rangers Television Service is expanding and that the new owner wants to pursue the European dream, with its lucrative television interest, it would be surprising if the club did not seek a wider involvement in the media. Both David Holmes and Alan Montgomery have indicated that a bid is a possibility. Montgomery said: 'If we are interested in any of the new media possibilities . . . we will make our decision and go for it'. He added that it would not be difficult for Rangers to raise the necessary £100 million. In addition to his involvement in any possible diversification into the media, Montgomery is also a keen supporter of Murray's European ambitions. 'Clubs no longer live on their gate money', he said. 'That is only 30 per cent of Rangers' income. So we cannot run a business this size purely for domestic reasons . . . the future of Rangers is in Europe.'

The upheavals off the pitch actually seemed to galvanise Souness and the team imposed itself again on the 1988–89 season. Although they went out of the UEFA Cup to Cologne, and lost 1–0 to Celtic in the Cup final, Rangers took both the Championship and the Skol Cup. As usual, the season did not pass by without controversy: Souness was banned from the bench after arguing with an official. Later the ban was extended and the manager was fined £2,000 for attempting to coach the team from the touch-line during the Cup semi-final. Once again, the club is ready to mount an assault on the Champions' Cup, this time with more than ever resting on the outcome. And once again Celtic have been forced to respond. A disappointing season for the team was saved when they beat Rangers in the Cup final and qualified for the Cup-Winners' Cup. Billy McNeill attempted to bring new players to the club using the £1.2 million Celtic received from West Ham for Frank McAvennie.

Celtic showed that they too were now prepared to break the million-pound barrier when McNeill tried to buy back Maurice Johnston from the French club Nantes. However, the deal broke down, allegedly because Johnston believed he would lose much of his income to the Inland Revenue. After returning to Nantes, he was approached by Rangers. In a deal which rocked the whole of Scotland, Souness whisked Johnston off to Ibrox to become the first Catholic signing under the new regime. The tax problems that had been a sticking point with Celtic were pragmatically surmounted by Rangers and were not allowed to prevent the historic move. Introduced to the press in Rangers' Blue Room, Johnston revealed he was 'delighted to be here', the same phrase he had uttered when he was paraded round Parkhead some weeks earlier. Within hours a crowd had gathered outside Ibrox, shirts were burned and some fans vowed to cease following Rangers, showing once again that it is not so easy to rid Glasgow's football of its sectarian influence. The media, however, hailed Souness's dealings as a bold step forward, one that should have been taken years ago. David Murray said: 'We look on this as a sporting signing and nothing else. We are only too well aware of the historic feelings in Glasgow, but we want the best football side in Europe'. Whether the voluble Johnston can withstand the inevitable pressures of being the first Catholic player of any significance to join Rangers remains to be seen. In response, the Celtic Board for once dug deep into its coffers to compete, signing a number of players, including Paul Elliot from Pisa, Dariusz Dziekanowski from Legia Warsaw and Mike Galloway from Hearts for a total of £1.5 million.

The Marlboro revolution at Rangers forced the Scottish game generally into a higher profile throughout the football world. Changes had been taking place for some time, as the rise of Aberdeen, Dundee United and Hearts has shown. While English clubs continued to lose support, attendances in Scotland increased every year from 1981. The Scottish first division, which was reorganised as the ten-club Premier Division in 1976, gives some credence to the argument for superleagues by minimising the number of inconsequential games and keeping interest alive throughout the season with a corresponding benefit to attendances and playing standards. At Ibrox in 1987–88, average crowds were 39,000, 90 per cent of which were seated, a far cry from the 19,000 which was the average when Holmes arrived and a world away from the attitudes towards the paying customer which were current on that terrible day in January 1971.

The new attitude towards supporters became even more apparent when plans for the further redevelopment of Ibrox were made public. The listed south stand is to have its roof removed in order to add two new tiers, one of which will house executive boxes, to be financed through an issue of Rangers bonds. The terraces that remain are to be upgraded and new heating and lighting is to be installed. The completed stadium will be a multi-purpose facility with a stage beneath the ground that can be raised for concerts. The Govan stand, part of the redevelopment of the 1970s, is also to be changed to incorporate new offices, a conference hall, exhibition suites, restaurants and boxes. The total cost will be £14 million, but the new stadium is expected to add in excess of £20 million to the club's valuation. David Murray said of the proposals: 'What if one day it [Ibrox] is the national stadium? I am trying to build a business structure that is not dependent on results. We can see the time when an average week at Ibrox could comprise a rock concert one night, a boxing show the next and football the night after that'.

Holmes, Murray and Souness have transformed Glasgow Rangers. Under John Greig and Jock Wallace the team had to be winning to pull in the crowds, unless it was an old firm game. In 1987–88, an unsuccessful season for Rangers, crowds were up to the highest average since the new stadium was completed and commercial income had gone through the roof. These developments have not killed the bigotry of the old firm's support, nor have they widened the participation of supporters in the administration of the game, although this has become an issue at Celtic. But with a European outlook, the Scottish League no longer has to play second fiddle to England and a realistic assessment of the future can take place. For Rangers that assessment is simple. When Lawrence Marlboro sold out his holding, the club was without doubt the biggest in Britain. Richard Gough, who was transferred to Rangers from Spurs, put it this way. 'Tottenham of course was a big club, but there's no doubt in my mind that this is the biggest. The expectations here are so much higher than they were at White Hart Lane or anywhere else for that matter. The fans in London enjoyed watching their football and obviously liked to see their team win but it wasn't the life and death thing it is in Glasgow. Here every match means so much to so many.'

It has been a transformation achieved on the back of a commercial revolution that has allowed Souness to spend vast amounts of money since his appointment. Such an international outlook and so great an ambition were once, however, the preserve of another: a club which once embodied the very qualities now in evidence at Rangers. It was once the biggest club in Britain and arguably the most famous in the world. Now, it has become a prime example of the failure of the English game to keep up with the rest of the world.

4
A TALE OF TWO CITIES

To treat sport like sport is to fail to understand the seriousness of your business

ROY HOFHEINZ
Owner of Houston Astros (baseball)

On 17 May 1988, as on any other Tuesday night, the British sat down in front of their television sets in their millions to watch the goings-on in a fictitious working-class district of London. The twice-weekly soap opera 'EastEnders' regularly tops the television ratings chart and is unlikely ever to have to make way for anything, let alone a football match. Meanwhile, across Europe the attention of millions of European television viewers was drawn to another working-class district of England, in this case the Old Trafford area of Manchester, which that night played host to a football game that had captured the imagination of a number of continental television programmers, who had been only too keen to accommodate the match in their schedules. It is not an unusual situation, however, for European television to show more commitment and excitement over a game of football than does its British equivalent, which has always assumed that the public in Britain only really wants to see British sides. This parochialism was accurately mirrored by the teams on the pitch. Manchester United, once the greatest club in world football, now sadly not even the biggest club in Britain, has been run for years in the manner of a local business by the Edwards family, while the club's opponents that night, AC Milan, now occupy a minor but precise role in the grand design of their owner, Silvio Berlusconi. This grand design involves nothing less than the whole future of European football and its integration into a master plan of big business, television networks, publishing, computers, property and supermarket chains.

The match received hardly any build-up in Britain and was not shown on any UK television channel. This was in marked contrast to the 21 other European countries that thought the game of sufficient importance to be worth screening, reflecting the widespread interest in Milan's exciting blend of quality Italian players and foreign imports, especially the Dutch duo of Ruud Gullit and Marco van Basten, the last of whom had made only a handful of appearances after spending much of the season side-lined through injury.

That 37,000 people turned out on a typically chilly May evening for the end-of-season friendly was remarkable given the circumstances and remains a testament to an awareness of European football often underestimated in the corridors of power. It did not quite recall the glorious nights of the past but at least it was something. David Dein, the Arsenal vice-chairman, made the trip from London to see the game, because he 'missed seeing continental teams play in England' but other English administrators and managers were notable by their absence. If any evidence were needed, the sad regression of English football in general and Manchester United in particular was exposed for all to see by the new Italian champions. While the optimism for England's forthcoming European Championship campaign was out of all proportion to the side's true prospects, those who saw the team that finished second in the English First Division in 1987–88 brushed aside with consummate ease on its own ground, could not help but reflect on the widening gap in talent, technique and tactics that has opened up between England and the rest of the football world since 1985.

The situation behind the scenes also exposed the gulf between those English clubs that imagine themselves to be on a par with the big European outfits and the true giants of the world game like AC Milan. The match had been organised on the initiative of Milan president Silvio Berlusconi, one of the new breed of European media entrepreneurs, to boost the football output of his television stations in Italy and France. Martin Edwards, the chairman of Manchester United, appeared bemused as Berlusconi's organisation swept into town, backed up by a large European media circus based at the Ramada Inn in the centre of the city. He openly professed 'amazement' that Milan had offered to play a friendly 'for a much smaller fee than we would contemplate' and went on to reveal that the Berlusconi organisation 'were doing it for the television rights in Europe', a concept obviously alien to English football directors who had for years been operating under a television system that placed little value on such games.

When the Italian Second Division team Atalanta of Bergamo played a Cup-Winners' Cup tie against Welsh non-league side Merthyr Tydfil earlier in the 1987–88 season, the Welsh part-timers really went to town, turning the whole week of their home leg into an Italian extravaganza. The community put on the equivalent of an Italian trade fair. The hospitality at Old Trafford for the visit of Milan might well have been prepared for Bolton Wanderers or Wigan. Pork pies and cheese sandwiches were the order of the day, with no concessions being made to the Latin tastes of the visitors. Incredibly, there also seemed to be no one on the Manchester staff who could speak any Italian, which led to an embarrassing scene in the lounge as the Italians sat on one side of the room while their Mancunian hosts remained on the other, communicating only when one of the numerous English-speaking officials of the Berlusconi organisation appeared.

Watching the United team, which included the England captain Bryan Robson, trailing 3–0 to the attacking verve of the Italian champions after an hour's play, one could not help turning one's thoughts to the glorious Manchester teams of years gone by. Teams that had delighted fans of football far and wide; teams that had won the admiration, even love, of the nation with scintillating performances against the best opposition the world could provide. If Glasgow Rangers were now the biggest club in Britain it was only because Manchester United had somehow lost the heritage that had seen them become one of the top clubs in the world in the 1950s and '60s. It was somehow symptomatic of the way the game in England has lost its way. We wondered what the greatest of United heroes, Bobby Charlton, now a director, made of the evening. When he was waylaid by enterprising representatives of the charity Sport Aid to use his influence to enlist the support of players, it was not one of Manchester United's stars they sought, but the dreadlocked Dutchman Ruud Gullit.

Manchester United were the first English club to enter the European Champions' Cup, against the wishes of the Football League, which was led at that time by the dictatorial Alan Hardaker, the man who had been instrumental in stopping Chelsea from taking part in the inaugural competition a year previously. He had said: 'The Management Committee felt that additional fixtures might be difficult to fulfil' – the Scottish League, being at the time marginally more open-minded, at least nominated a team to take part, Hibernian of Edinburgh, although the club were not champions of Scotland. Hardaker did not possess the vision to realise that games between European clubs would eventually become at least as important as domestic encounters, even though huge crowds were already flocking to see friendlies against foreign opposition as early as the 1940s and '50s and television exposure brought the games to the attention of the whole nation. From that first season, 1956–57, when United reached the semi-final before going out narrowly to the great Real Madrid side, the quest for European glory became an obsession for the club and its inspirational manager Matt Busby, a man who did have the wider perspective that those in charge of the League so obviously lacked. After the terrible disaster of the Munich air crash in 1958, which destroyed the young side that Busby had created, a tidal wave of emotion propelled the club to great achievements. The instinctive sympathy felt for United grew as Busby recovered from his own injuries to put together what was arguably an even better side than the one which perished in the snow of Munich, a team which reached its peak ten years after that tragic event when United and Busby finally won the Champions' Cup, the first English team to do so.

The day after the Munich disaster a man who would shape United's future for the next 20 years joined the Board. Louis Edwards had been recommended to the directors by Matt Busby. As the owner of a successful family business in Manchester, he was brought in for his 'business acumen'. The early Edwards years at Manchester United coincided with the club's rise from the ashes of Munich and it soon became a very profitable concern. It seemed that Edwards had the Midas touch. In the year of the disaster, 1958, United became the first British club to make a profit of £100,000 and in a series of share deals in the 1960s, later exposed by the television programme 'World In Action' to be of questionable legality, Edwards became the club's chairman and majority share-holder.

Louis Edwards was born in Salford in 1914 and made his fortune from the wholesale meat trade during the Second World War. By the 1970s the company he built, Louis C. Edwards & Sons (Manchester) Ltd, supplied or owned 70 butcher's shops in the north-west and had concessions at over 100 Woolworth stores. In 1973, when the company was at the height of its profitability, turnover reached £22 million with pre-tax profits of £360,000. The organisation was tightly controlled by members of the Edwards family, principally Louis, his brother Douglas and their four sons. While Louis pursued his interest in Manchester United, Douglas became a grandee of the local Conservative party, serving a term as Lord Mayor of the city. Five years later, however, the financial position of Louis C. Edwards & Sons was in a completely altered and disastrous state, as a result of allegations that the quality of the meat the company supplied was poor. Losses for 1978, following a series of fines for contravening the Food and Drugs Act, were put at £344,000. In 1979, the Scottish financier James Gulliver bought 20 per cent of the shares and control of the management for £100,000. Under Gulliver, the family firm that had been brought to the brink of bankruptcy expanded aggressively into the food industry with a series of take-overs, finally emerging as the Argyll food and supermarket group.

Meanwhile, Louis Edwards had managed, by 1978, to acquire over 75 per cent of Manchester United's shares on behalf of himself and his family. On 24 November he wrote to the few remaining shareholders who were not part of the family with a scheme that could only be described as audacious considering the parlous state of Louis C. Edwards & Sons. A million new shares would be issued, valued at £1.00 each. The new shares would not be offered to the general public, far from it. For every one share already owned, a total of 208 new shares were available. Presented as a means of raising cash to buy new players, the actual result of the share issue was to increase the Edwards family wealth at a time when it was going through a rough patch by securing over 700,000 new shares at £1.00 each when all the financial analysts were saying that they could be instantly resold at £4.00. At this stage though the family did not need to realise profits on the shares. To pay for them they eventually sold their remaining stock in the once worthless Louis C. Edwards & Sons to James Gulliver, who claimed that the Edwards family had 'something like £8 million in aggregate from our [the Gulliver Food group] involvement. They couldn't believe their luck'. The 'luck' Louis Edwards attracted to his own finances did not extend to Manchester United, despite the fact that he brought his saviour, James Gulliver, on to the Board in 1979.

A small number of disgruntled shareholders, angry at the new share issue, accused Edwards of feathering his own nest and the local television company, Granada, began an investigation. The findings were screened on 28 January 1980 by the award-winning current affairs programme 'World In Action' under the title 'The Man Who Bought United', and were a detailed and potentially damaging exposure of the links between Edwards' companies and the share purchases of the 1960s which, according to the programme, produced large profits for the Edwards family as well as a controlling interest in the club. Louis Edwards never got the chance to present his side of the story. He died of a heart attack four weeks later. His eldest son, Martin, who had been on the United Board since 1970 took over, claiming that the television programme had 'contributed to Father's death'.

For the fans, the last years of Louis Edwards' rule could not match the days when, with the meat business in full cry, United had conquered Europe. The quality of football produced by the Busby team in the 1960s, coupled with the natural sympathy that Munich still engendered, ensured massive support for the club, not just in Manchester, but throughout the country and the world. Programme sales alone at home matches in the 1960s would often total over 60,000. In the season of the Champions' Cup triumph, average gates reached almost 58,000 (an English record) and crowds everywhere came to see the team that produced three European Footballers of the Year – Bobby Charlton, Denis Law and the mercurial George Best – an achievement unequalled to this day. However, after the Champions' Cup it seemed as if all that could be achieved had been achieved. The dream that had sustained Manchester United and its supporters had been accomplished and it became increasingly difficult for the ageing Busby to motivate great players who had seen it all before. In the season the club won the Champions' Cup United finished second in the League, but the talk in Manchester was now beginning to turn to the football played by the town's other team, Manchester City, who carried off the title with a superb footballing side put together by Joe Mercer and Malcolm Allison. Defending the Champions' Cup the following season, United managed to reach the semi-final before they were knocked out by the eventual winners, AC Milan. In the League, United slipped out of the top three and the downward slide began.

Busby retired from management in 1969 but his shadow has loomed large over the efforts of subsequent managers. Since the Championship-winning season of 1966–67, United's domestic success has been limited to three FA Cup wins and the club qualified for European competitions on only six occasions up to the ban on English clubs in 1985. Under Busby, United won the Championship five times and came second on seven occasions, were victorious in two FA Cup finals and were a regular qualifier for Europe. The nadir came with relegation to the Second Division in 1973–74, a fate that was decided in the most ironic of ways. Denis Law, a United man through and through, had been transferred free to Manchester City amid some acrimony by manager Tommy Docherty. In the 82nd minute of a derby game in April 1974 Law calmly backheeled the ball into the United net to score the only goal of the game. Recognising the enormity of what he had done, he could only grimace through clenched teeth as his team-mates celebrated what proved to be the winning goal. Although the team bounced back the following season under the managership of the inimitable Docherty, the glory days would be few and far between. Docherty, after building a stylish but ultimately inconsequential side, was fired in 1977 as a result of his affair with Mary Brown, the wife of the club's physiotherapist. The two later married. Docherty was replaced by the quiet Dave Sexton, acknowledged as a first-rate coach but also known to be a poor communicator. Sexton's teams, and those of his successors, Ron Atkinson and Alex Ferguson, sometimes looked as if they might do something, but their achievements have rarely matched the expectations. Despite the changes in management, until Brian

McClair managed the feat in 1987–88, no United player had scored over 20 League goals in a season since George Best 20 years before.

In 1984 it was reported that media tycoon Robert Maxwell had made a £10 million bid for United. With negotiations conducted mainly through the press, Martin Edwards flirted with the idea of selling to Maxwell, while Manchester United supporters looked on, horrified that the Edwards family could contemplate disposing of the club with which it had become synonymous. Eventually, with Martin Edwards holding out for £15.00 a share – the same shares that had cost him a maximum of £1.00 each – the deal collapsed as Maxwell withdrew. Later, Edwards surprisingly claimed that the bid was 'complete nonsense. He [Maxwell] never actually made an offer'.

James Gulliver quit the Board in 1985, expressing 'misgivings' about the way the club was being run and alleging that Martin Edwards could not control the spending, then running at over £6 million, of manager Ron Atkinson, who had arrived at Old Trafford in 1981 to replace the studious Dave Sexton. 'I think', said Gulliver of Edwards, 'he has got some toughness, but he's just not able, for various reasons, to handle Ron Atkinson'. In fact Edwards finally found the best way to control Atkinson in 1986. He fired him and lured Alex Ferguson to Old Trafford. Ferguson was the Aberdeen manager who had turned down a desperate Glasgow Rangers in 1984. In a secret deal five days after Gulliver's resignation from the United Board, he sold his shares to Martin Edwards' wife, Susan, for over £400,000. Some of these shares were later sold to Syrian businessman Amer Al Midani, the son of one of the world's wealthiest men. Midani has since become a director of United and has been touted as a possible buyer should Martin Edwards decide to sell.* But even total control could not halt the downward trend. From another British record profit of £301,000 in 1975–76 United's finances slumped to a loss of over £3 million in 1981–82 and £1.3 million in 1987–88.

If such a catalogue of decline had befallen, say, Glasgow Rangers, all hell would have broken loose in the press and at annual general meetings. Strangely, through all the misfortune, criticism of the way the United administration has allowed the team to slide has

*As we went to press Edwards did in fact agree to sell his shares to a consortium headed by Michael Knighton, who was due to replace him as chairman in November 1989, Edwards remaining as chief executive.

been muted to say the least. At the 1988 AGM, after United finished a distant second in the League, nine points behind an all-conquering Liverpool, it was assumed by the press that the Board would get a rough ride but in the event the directors' reports, including a salary of £85,000 for Martin Edwards, were passed on the nod with little dissent. In 1989, many of the earlier allegations were substantiated in a book called *Manchester United, The Betrayal Of A Legend*, by journalist Michael Crick and an ex-employee of the United Supporters Association, David Smith. The true magnitude of Manchester United's decline, however, can only be seen in the context of European and British football. Like many United supporters, Crick and Smith still cling to the old myth of United's superiority. They write: 'No other club in Britain can boast such consistent and world-wide support as Manchester United'. While this may once have been the case it is a measure of their failure that United's support can no longer compare with that of the European giants and has slipped behind that of Glasgow Rangers, and Liverpool now have a higher average home attendance in the English First Division. On 3 May 1989, Old Trafford saw its lowest League attendance for 18 years, 23,000 for the visit of FA Cup holders Wimbledon, and a few days later only 26,000 turned up for a game against Everton. Even in Manchester, for the last few games of the season Manchester City drew bigger crowds than United as they pushed for promotion from the Second Division.

In the great days of Busby, United rarely had to resort to the transfer market, such was the quality of young players coming through from the reserves. Between 1952 and 1957, the seasons of the 'Busby Babes', only one player was bought. The situation was the same in the heyday of the Best/Law/Charlton side – between 1964 and 1967 only goal-keeper Alex Stepney arrived from another club. The final ignominy almost arrived in 1989, when the Manchester United reserve team, containing over £3 million of talent, including Robson, Hughes and McClair, went down 3–1 at Leicester City and faced relegation to the Second Division of the Central League. Needing to win their last game by a considerable margin to avoid the drop, United packed the Central League team with nine first-team players and duly saved the day by winning 4–0 at Coventry City. But it had been a close-run thing and it was a salutary reminder to those who thought that Ferguson should use more home-grown youngsters that the quality of United's youth system was not what it once had been.

It is barely conceivable that, in common with Rangers, AC Milan and their fans would allow such a decline to happen without taking drastic action to put matters right. In fact Milan did suffer from a similar slump but the new Italian champions had come back in spectacular style. President Silvio Berlusconi took over the club in 1986 following a period of turmoil that makes events at Manchester United, Glasgow Rangers, Spurs and Atletico Madrid seem like models of serenity and calm. It was not building work that caused the upheavals in this case. Milan share the San Siro stadium with local rivals Internazionale, thus removing one of the biggest causes of financial hardship in football, especially in Britain, by utilising the stadium every week during the season and sharing the cost of its maintenance, the bulk of which is paid for by the city council which owns the stadium. This system, common in Italy, once stood a chance of taking root in Manchester when Old Trafford was bombed in the Second World War and United had to play its games at Manchester City's ground, Maine Road. The arrangement did not last for long, however, and United were soon back at their traditional base, reflecting the conviction of many English fans that their identity is bound up with the home of their club. Nevertheless, United drew some large crowds to Maine Road, including the club's record attendance of 84,000. To be fair to Louis Edwards, it has to be said that the improvements which took place at Old Trafford during his reign made the stadium the best in England, although in relative terms this is no great accolade – the average English First Division ground is among the worst in the world.

The problems for Milan began in 1980 when the club which had reached six European finals was relegated on the orders of the Italian Football Federation's disciplinary commission for involvement in a bribes, betting and match-fixing scandal, of which there are many in the exotic world of Italian football. The Milan president, Felice Colombo, was one of many officials and players suspended from the game and the club went through three traumatic seasons when no one was visibly in command. Promotion was followed by immediate relegation again in 1982, this time for finishing third from bottom of Serie A, the Italian First Division. At this point Colombo's stake in the club was purchased for the ridiculously low figure of £1 million by Giuseppe Farina, a millionaire landowner and lawyer who had been driven out of the Italian game two years previously after he had wrecked the finances of the modest Serie A club Vicenza in a disastrously botched attempt to hang on to the goal-scoring prodigy Paolo Rossi. Vicenza, a club which had been in the top flight for 20 years, ended up dropping out of the professional League altogether when relegated to Serie C a year after Farina had committed his blunder. The supporters of Milan could have been forgiven for experiencing a shudder of apprehension when they heard the news of Farina's arrival.

Sure enough, within two years Farina's profligate management style had all but bankrupted Milan. Income tax, which had been deducted from the players' salaries, had not been paid to the treasury and the club was a staggering £12 million in debt. Farina fled the country in 1986 and now lives in exile in South Africa. By 1986, then, the way was open for AC Milan to be acquired by the suave, high-profile Silvio Berlusconi, who immediately insisted on a complete clear-out of the old administration. He filled the club with executives from the business empire he owns and controls, which is based on the Fininvest corporation, the third largest private company in Italy. Berlusconi described the take-over as almost an act of charity when he said: 'I took over because it was necessary to do so and because many people put pressure on me to do so. My friends, politicians, football people. There was an intense press campaign to encourage me . . . I look at it [this way], for me it was a duty. I went to the heart of the matter. I changed the structure and transformed the Milanello [the club's training facility outside Milan], which everyone says is now the most practical sports centre in Europe. I changed the technical team and I searched out the best players in Europe'. Despite the original reasons for Berlusconi's involvement, AC Milan was now to become an integral part of his plans to dominate whole sectors of the Italian economy and a large slice of the European television market.

Silvio Berlusconi, like so many others of the new breed of football club owner, had originally made his fortune from property development. Born the son of a bank manager in Milan in 1936 he studied law at the city's university before working as a tour guide, then a photographer and sometimes a singer in the coastal resort of Riccione. It was during the north Italian building boom of the 1960s that Berlusconi first came to the attention of the Milanese public when he constructed large-scale housing projects such as 'Milano 2', a complex of futuristic design where traffic and pedestrians never intersect. Since expanding into television in 1980 he had taken on the traditional Italian broadcasters on a number of fronts and emerged victorious, so much so that by the time he bought AC Milan in 1986 he already owned the three largest independent television networks in Italy, based on Canale 5 in Milan; had recently expanded into French television; and would soon hold significant stakes in the television industries of West Germany and Yugoslavia, the last of which can be received in Italy. The parent company, Fininvest, which is entirely owned by Berlusconi and his family, also controls the largest advertising sales organisation in the country, a record company, film and television studios in Milan, Rome and Madrid, a publishing company which produces among other publications the daily newspaper, *Il Giornale,* a film library said to be worth over £1.5 billion and the largest supermarket chain in Italy, La Standa.

From his palatial 250-acre home, the Villa San Martino in Arcore, just outside Milan, the man *Fortune* magazine has called the richest individual in Italy, ahead of Gianni Agnelli, the boss of Fiat and Juventus, keeps in touch with his television ratings by computer link. Berlusconi, whose 143 companies cover such diverse products and services as insurance and aerospace materials, clearly now sees his future in the electronic media. He said: 'I am a television entrepreneur but I'm not just a television financier. I create television – at least I try to'. This growing empire poses a serious threat to RAI, the Italian public service broadcaster which has enjoyed a virtual monopoly in the country for over 30 years.

Like David Holmes at Rangers and Jesús Gil at Atletico Madrid, Berlusconi recognised that it was necessary to create a team capable of winning the Championship, which last came to Milan in 1979.

In this, his ambition coincided with that of the Milan faithful, though for entirely different reasons. For the fans, winning the title was a matter of pride, expectation and realising the possibility of putting one over on their eternal local rivals, Internazionale. But for Berlusconi it meant he would become directly involved in the lucrative rights to televise the club's European games, and would strengthen his hand in the ongoing battle with the Italian state broadcaster RAI for the right to screen domestic football. It would also put him in a powerful position with the European governing body, UEFA, in trying to implement his long-term strategy, the creation of a European superleague.

Milan's first season under the Berlusconi presidency, 1986–87, was not to have a fairy-tale ending. The club finished a disappointing fifth in Serie A. The seriousness of his intent, however, can be judged by the wholesale changes which took place on the playing side in the close season and his call for 'lovely football'. Berlusconi got rid of Swedish coach and ex-player Nils Liedholm and the British players that had been brought to the club, Ray Wilkins to Glasgow Rangers via Paris St Germain and Mark Hateley to Monaco. In their places came a coach from the small Serie B club Parma, Arrigo Sacchi, who had no playing pedigree and only a modest coaching record; Argentinian boy wonder Claudio Borghi, who scored two of the goals in the friendly against Manchester United, and the exceptional Dutch duo, Gullit and van Basten, who were later joined by their compatriot Frank Rijkaard. The cost of the imports was over £8 million of which £5.7 million was a world record transfer fee paid for Ruud Gullit to PSV Eindhoven. This brought Fininvest's total investment in AC Milan to something approaching £20 million, including the initial buy-out and subsequent recapitalisation, estimated to have cost £12 million.

After a slow start to the new season, during which van Basten suffered the injury which kept him out for months and the club saw a victory against Roma turned into a defeat by the federation because of crowd trouble in the San Siro when a firecracker exploded at the feet of Roma goal-keeper Tancredi, Milan turned the corner at the beginning of 1988 with a 4–1 home win over defending champions Napoli, the early-season pacemakers. That victory was the catalyst that started the team on an unbeaten run which they maintained until the end of the season, overhauling Napoli in the best possible style by defeating Maradona's side for the second time with two matches to go. The club that had won the Italian Championship ten times, all before the problems of 1980, were back. Not only that, the team played a brand of exciting, attacking football rarely seen in the Italian game, a style described thus by coach Sacchi: 'I believe that football should be considered like an opera. You must assign a role to a player and it's up to him to interpret it. My players must have physical, technical, artistic and cultural qualities in order to carry it out'. That the revival should have happened in such a planned and calculated fashion surprised no one who knew how Silvio Berlusconi operated. This, after all, was just another piece of the jigsaw in Berlusconi's grand design, which stretched way beyond the fortunes of AC Milan.

The success of Milan should certainly provide a lesson for those who run Manchester United. At the start of the 1988–89 season the club sold 66,000 season tickets, producing revenues of £10 million. Jacques Thibert, the editor of *France Football*, said of Berlusconi's contribution: '[He] is a man central to the Milanese phenomenon. Without him, the club would exist, but it would not be what it is and would not be what it is about to become, that is one of the two or three strongest clubs in the world. Berlusconi has built up his AC Milan on the concept of image. He cares deeply about his own and he would not want to see it brought down by a football team so he has provided the means to achieve the team he wants, with the style, spirit and conviction that he demands. What is impressive is that he has succeeded'. Berlusconi himself put it another way. He said: 'I don't think solely in terms of image. I gave a mission to Milan: to become the most important club in the world. When I do something, it is important for me to do it well. I put my heart, my intelligence and my soul into it because I always set myself ambitious goals. I am number one in Italy in construction, in television, in distribution. I am number one in Europe in broadcasting and advertising. In football I want to try to be number one'.

Football enjoys a special relationship with Italian society, similar to that in Spain. The great and powerful like to be seen at matches and involvement in the running of a club can bestow on a person immense status. The game in Italy, as Sacchi made clear, is elevated to the level of opera and art – the performers are often highly-strung as well as highly-paid and the owners great patrons like those of La Scala and Venice. In this environment all commercial aspects of the game are greatly prized. The most prized of all, and therefore the most lucrative, is the right to screen matches on television.

Berlusconi already knew the value of football. The event which really established Canale 5 in Italy occurred in 1981 when RAI turned down the chance to screen an international tournament from Uruguay, the *Mundialito* (the 'Little World Cup'). Berlusconi stepped in to pick up the rights, at which point RAI realised its mistake and very publicly tried, and failed, to get the tournament back. The Canale 5 network cleaned up in the ratings and Berlusconi's television empire was up and running. Soon afterwards RAI failed to renew its contract with the makers of the American soap opera 'Dallas' after showing the first 13 episodes. Berlusconi immediately bought up the next 64 and the show became the highest-rated on Canale 5. Berlusconi's attempt to buy Italian League football for his networks forced an auction with RAI, which ended with the state broadcaster having to pay a massive £40 million to screen matches in the 1987–88 season.

This was the reason Milan were in Manchester. Having failed to wrest domestic football from RAI, Berlusconi instituted a prestigious annual close season tournament in Milan featuring clubs from Europe and South America, the format obviously designed for Canale 5. With tongue in cheek, Berlusconi called the competition the Mundialito. After the 1987–88 season the San Siro stadium was due to undergo extensive building work for the 1990 World Cup, increasing its capacity from 77,000 to 85,000, all seated, so the Mundialito could not be contested. Instead Milan, far from celebrating the Championship which had been clinched only days before, played two prestigious friendlies in three days against Manchester United and Real Madrid, both designed to maximise television income and help Berlusconi keep up the pressure on RAI. As Robert Reeves, the sports co-ordinator of Rupert Murdoch's Sky channel, which was carrying the game against United on its satellite service to 16 countries, remarked: 'The mechanics of it are that if the match is not sent to Italy, it is off'. If any further evidence were necessary, a look around the perimeter advertising at the Manchester game provided it – 42 of the advertising boards were Italian.

For most presidents and chairmen the winning of championships and European competitions is an end in itself. For Berlusconi, football is only a means to an end. All elements of his business empire are inextricably linked, all mutually interdependent, giving the impression of almost total self-sufficiency. The Standa supermarket chain, purchased in 1988 for £425 million, is set to form a two-way partnership with the television operations. Berlusconi described the thinking behind his actions in terms of achieving a 'symbiosis between Standa and our television channels'. Giovanni Belingardi, spokesman for the Standa project, was somewhat less obscure, revealing: 'Clearly, with our resources in terms of television advertising, we will be in a position to give a tremendous boost to supermarket sales'.

In the new order, the Standa stores would not only push those products advertised on the Berlusconi networks, but would be redesigned, offering a range of goods and services produced by Fininvest companies, from insurance and travel to cinema and football tickets. Personalities and star names from Canale 5 television shows and the Milan football club would make in-store appearances to increase the glamour quotient for special launches and promotions and giant video screens would transmit pictures of the guest appearances to other Standa stores. The television network already helps the football business by screening anti-hooligan advertisements. When Berlusconi's operations are examined in detail, each acquisition emerges as one part of a grand design to create a global conglomerate, based on the electronic media, which will be a world leader and powerful political voice when the European internal market is instituted in 1992.

Televised football delivers an important audience in most European countries but the most lucrative games of all are those in the latter stages of European competitions. For Berlusconi these competitions represent both a marvellous opportunity and an unacceptable risk. As owner of Milan, rights to televise the club's European games are his, but the knock-out format of these competitions means that income and budgets cannot be worked out beyond the first round, which in turn means that revenue can be guaranteed for only one home game. Milan possesses a proud European pedigree, having reached the semi-final of the Champions' Cup in its initial season and going on to become the first Italian club to win the trophy in 1963, beating the great Portuguese side Benfica 2–1 at Wembley. The club won the Champions' Cup again in 1969 after knocking out Manchester United in the semi-final, the Cup-Winners' Cup twice and reached the semi-final of the UEFA Cup in 1972 which they lost to Spurs. But ominously, like Manchester United, the days of glory lay in the past. Milan had made no significant impact on Europe since 1974, when they were beaten 2–0 in Rotterdam by the East German club Magdeburg in the final of the Cup-Winners' Cup.

It is the arithmetic produced by these facts which provided the impetus for Berlusconi to present a blueprint for a European superleague to UEFA in 1987. But after gaining no response he encouraged his advertising agency, Saatchi and Saatchi, to submit a recommendation to UEFA for the implementation of the new League in 1989. Berlusconi's director of television sports promotions, Giovanni Branchini, explained: 'The costs of bringing the best players to a club like Milan is astronomical. It is difficult to justify such spending if it does not bring a successful season in Europe. This makes instant success necessary but such a thing cannot be guaranteed. We need to play to capacity crowds in every game and each match must be an event worthy of television. If Europe were arranged on a league basis all the competing clubs could be guaranteed a basic number of home fixtures against top European opposition'. Although the idea was rejected out of hand by UEFA it is unlikely that Berlusconi will leave the concept alone. The economic arguments for the superleague are certainly powerful and it is doubtful whether UEFA will be able to withstand the pressure for very much longer as more and more clubs come to accept the fiscal logic of the idea. The inexorable march of technology makes the bandwagon appear unstoppable as football clubs in Europe look enviously at the amounts of money flowing from continent-wide television to the gridiron teams of the National Football League (NFL) in the USA. How such a development would affect the majority of fans in the countries of Europe is a subject that has never really been addressed, though Branchini was certain that supporters in Milan would be 'enchanted' by such a development.

In 1988–89 the Milan team, which lost the services of Ruud Gullit through injury for long periods, suffered the kind of reaction that had set in at Glasgow Rangers after the Championship-winning season. Europe, though, was another matter and the side reached the Champions' Cup final after scintillating displays against Real Madrid, who were held 1–1 in Spain and beaten 5–0 in Milan. The final in Barcelona produced, if anything, an even better display as Steaua Bucharest were beaten 4–0, the Dutch imports Gullit and van Basten scoring two each. It was perhaps the most exhilarating performance in a Champions' Cup final since that great night in Glasgow almost 30 years earlier when Real Madrid showed the rest of Europe just how good they were. Trevor Francis of Queens Park Rangers, one of the few English managers that bothered to attend the game (Francis had played in Italy for Sampdoria and Atalanta), said of Milan's play: 'The first hour was as near perfection as I've seen. The pressing of Milan's players made it impossible for Steaua to do anything. Their work-rate was as impressive as anything we see in England. It should be compulsory for our managers to see these matches'.

Berlusconi outlined his own thoughts on the club he had taken over. 'The policy that we are in the process of developing at the heart of Milan is to consolidate the osmosis of the club with its environment and its public. The game they play is that of a team which must always win and always give entertainment at San Siro and away. Milan plays to give the public one and a half hours of sheer pleasure. We have spread our youth-recruiting policy to all Milan and Lombardy. All things being equal we would prefer local talent. But, as you know, to play the leading role in Europe, we must also hire the best from outside.' The Champions' Cup performances were more than consolation for the fact that Milan had to give up the Italian title to local rivals Internazionale.

The president of Inter, restaurant-chain owner Ernesto Pellegrini, had seen what had been achieved by Berlusconi and put some of his rival's ideas into effect himself, particularly the signing of top foreign players from the same country, in this case Matthaus and Brehme from West Germany. The two presidents have now achieved a unique feat in the history of European competitions. In 1989–90, for the first time since Manchester in 1968–69, one city will have two teams competing in the Champions' Cup and both will play in the same San Siro stadium. Berlusconi's 'big show' proved to be no idle boast. With Pellegrini as a powerful ally, the culmination of the 1988–89 season may in future come to be seen as the beginning of the European superleague.

The economic crises that have afflicted many of the big clubs in Europe have occurred at a time when the continent is experiencing massive changes in the economic sector. It was as if the old guard, men such as Arthur Richardson at Spurs, could no longer survive in the game that for them had been a 'rich man's hobby'. The Edwards family at Manchester United had always been sharp operators in the insular world of Mancunian commerce and politics but the transition from local phenomenon to international business has been pursued on the strength of past glories. Money has been spent at United, sometimes in recklessly large amounts, £17 million on players since the last Championship-winning season of 1966–67. But most of the spending has been piecemeal, and there has been little evidence of any overall strategy to claim the League title or become a big club off the field in the European sense. Commercial income has risen, but it is the commercialism of a provincial club rather than an international name and does not produce the same percentage of total income that is provided by Glasgow Rangers' commercial operations.

Money has also been spent on facilities: a new administration block, private boxes, more seats and, ironically, a Manchester United museum, but this expenditure has to be set alongside the fact that most of the improvements have been to the advantage of the corporate or wealthy supporter. The chairman's salary and the other methods by which the Edwards family still manages to make more than a healthy profit from the club have also drawn criticism. Although United's accounts claim that no director is 'materially interested in any contract that is significant in relation to the group's business', it was reported by *Business* magazine in

1986 that the company which supplied the club with most of its printing, Dawnprint, had included on its Board none other than Martin Edwards (between 1981–83) and his brother Roger (1981–85). Dawnprint's parent company was Edwards Printing (Manchester), and the majority shareholder was Roger Edwards. Martin Edwards denied any wrongdoing: 'I wouldn't favour anybody on the grounds that I knew them. When Roger approached me about doing the printing I said, "You must never approach me. I will never instruct anybody in this company to give you the business. You've got to get it yourself. If you do, you'll get it on price".'

It is interesting to speculate on what might have happened to United if Robert Maxwell's bid had been successful in 1984. The Maxwell record in football is certainly impressive. The achievements of steering a small club like Oxford United into the First Division and returning Derby County to top flight respectability are feats of which the Maxwell family can be justifiably proud even if the methods used have not always met with universal acclaim. Perhaps Manchester United needs a world-wide operator like Maxwell or James Gulliver to ensure that the club plays on its true stage. Whatever view is taken, it cannot be denied that until someone at United can produce the atmosphere to nurture a winning team, the title of the 'biggest club in Britain' will recede further into the fading memories of those fortunate enough to have witnessed any one of Busby's teams.

As the truly big clubs of Europe move towards a European superleague, Manchester United have shown little comprehension of what they need to do to place themselves in a position to participate. While English clubs remain out of European competition the business of European football is undergoing a huge transformation, led by television and deregulation. Inexorably, the future looks more and more likely to be dominated by the small screen and the superleague. If English clubs such as Manchester United continue to act as they have in the past, the country that invented the game may well end up a backwater.

When Milan's League position failed to live up to Berlusconi's expectation he was not prepared to wait. The grand design would not permit it. 1992 cannot be put back. His involvement was certainly no 'rich man's hobby'. The imperatives that drove Berlusconi to spend £20 million on a football team are the same as those which saw him purchase La Standa supermarkets for £425 million. Each will contribute its share to the empire and expand its activities. Television for Berlusconi provides another means to the same end. 'Enterprises must have another medium to sell their products and commercial television is the most obvious medium when it comes to products for family consumption', he said when bidding for La Cinq in France. 'We must not think of the European market as static and unchanging; the market will develop naturally when private television arrives.'

Owning a football club, of course, means satisfying customers who feel a passionate sense of loyalty and who possess a deep emotional attachment to their team. Silvio Berlusconi has skilfully channelled these feelings in Milan and elsewhere to boost the prospects of all parts of his empire. An all-conquering AC Milan would bring the European superleague closer but would also begin to realise for football sums of money so staggering that even the NFL might gaze upon the old game with envy. The Champions' Cup final is just the beginning of Berlusconi's 'big show'. The roots of this development are not to be found in Italy but in France, the most international of all footballing nations.

5

THE FRENCH REVOLUTION

I try not to break the rules but merely to test their elasticity

BILL VEECK
Baseball owner

The conversation was the culmination of a frantic three days for Claude Bez, president of Girondins de Bordeaux Football Club. The controversial Bez had spent the previous 36 hours on the phone to the presidents of other clubs and negotiating with the authorities to gain acceptance of his audacious plan. There would never be a better time to act than now. Those pressmen that were around were more interested in filing their copy on the result of the match being played that night, which meant that Bez could approach his man secure in the knowledge that here in the old city of Budapest, far away from the media pressure of home, the dialogue could be kept secret, unofficial, and if necessary, deniable.

Michel Platini, the greatest of all French footballers, was on a routine assignment in Budapest to cover the UEFA Cup game between Ujpest Dozsa and Bordeaux for Canal Plus, a French television channel for which he worked. He later described his reaction to the question put to him by Bez. 'You could have knocked me down with a feather . . . I had expected anything but that.' What Bez had asked Platini was whether the recently retired captain of France, who had no previous experience in management, would be interested in the job of manager of the national team. Without the slightest hesitation, Platini agreed, despite the fact that the team already had a manager, the beleaguered Henri Michel, who had been under increasing pressure to go following a 1–1 draw with Cyprus in a World Cup qualifying match the previous Saturday. It was this result which precipitated Claude Bez's skilful manoeuvring for Michel's replacement by Platini, though Bez had for some time been one of the manager's most vocal critics.

A meeting was arranged for the following Monday, 31 October 1988, between Platini, Bez and the president of the French federation, Jean Fournet-Fayard, at the luxurious Georges V Hotel in Paris, to work out the details of the new appointment. As Michel Platini flew to New York for a veterans game to celebrate FIFA's decision to award rights to host the 1994 World Cup to the USA, Claude Bez returned to Bordeaux a happy man. It had been a most profitable trip; he had seen his team make further progress in the UEFA Cup by beating the Hungarians 1–0, he had single-handedly secured the next manager of France, but perhaps most important of all, he had moved himself to the centre stage of the French game. By becoming the powerbroker of the national team Bez was now in the most influential of positions within French football, his title of National Team Director being vague enough to allow him to oversee all aspects of the team's operations.

The choice of the recently retired Platini, let alone the way he was appointed, might appear strange to British eyes. However, French football had undergone a remarkable renaissance in the years since Michel Platini had first emerged as an exciting young player with Nancy in the 1970s. Moreover, the game now inhabited a new commercial environment where the performance of the national team was the most important consideration of all, with large sums of money depending on the side's results. The charismatic Platini would revive public interest after a poor run of results and the failure to qualify for the 1988 European Championships under Henri Michel. And he might just be the man to guide the team to the World Cup finals in Italy in 1990. Platini's playing record speaks for itself. The second most-capped Frenchman, he played in 72 internationals and scored a record 41 international goals. He played in two World Cup semi-finals, and when the country won the European Championships in 1984 he was top scorer with nine goals including two hat-tricks. He won championships with St Etienne in France and Juventus in Italy, and during his sojourn in the Italian League he was top goal-scorer three times and was in the winning side in the Champions' Cup, the Cup-Winners' Cup and the World Club Championship. He was European Player of the Year three times in succession, an unequalled achievement. Perhaps the most flattering accolade is the fact that the word *platini* is entering the French language, meaning an act of genius, something out of the ordinary.

The choice of Platini surprised the French as much as it did the rest of the football world, although Franz Beckenbauer had already trodden the same path when he was appointed German team manager after a glittering career at international and club levels. Coincidentally, Beckenbauer's position was also announced after a meeting at the Georges V Hotel. Nonetheless, the idea of offering the job to Platini was hardly likely to have occurred to the conservative French federation. It took someone with a unique vision of the game, someone who had shown that bold action achieved results – someone like Claude Bez. The man who would play a major role in reshaping French football after many years of decline was born in Bordeaux just months after the German invasion of 1940. Bez's family owned one of the biggest accountancy businesses in France which managed to survive the war intact. The young Claude Bez was insulated enough from post-war austerity to be able to devote his time to classical studies and sport, gaining a regional cup-winners' medal as a junior footballer. His motto even then was 'the ball may pass but the player may not'. This belligerent streak has remained with Bez ever since. Like Jesús Gil, he is a master of the provocative statement, and is a natural target for the media. A workaholic, Bez is suspicious of those who do not think like he does but his philosophy and actions can be unpredictable. He has said, for instance: 'Clubs will always find a way to break the rules. Me, I have three million ways'. Then again, he donated the receipts from a friendly match against the Spanish team Real Sociedad of San Sebastián to Basque schools and spent £60,000 of his own money to take care of the family of a badly injured reserve goal-keeper.

The coach Bez brought to Bordeaux, Aime Jacquet, said of him: 'He appears determined to always give the worst impression of himself'. Perhaps what Jacquet had in mind were some of the more controversial incidents involving Claude Bez. Like the time the intransigent Bez suspended the veteran French international Alain Giresse for appearing on a television channel, Antenne 2, with which Bez had a dispute; or the time he publicly brawled with a disgruntled customer at the Avis office in Lyon, where Bez was trying to convince Jean Tigana to join Bordeaux.

Colourful would be a polite way to describe Bez, a man not usually given to subtle diplomacy or quiet reasoning. But it was precisely these qualities Claude Bez needed when he joined the executive committee of Bordeaux in 1974. French football had reached its lowest ebb, success was a thing of the past, at home and abroad. The domestic League was mediocre to say the least, attracting small crowds with little interest from sponsors, advertisers or television. The last anyone could remember of the French internationally was the team of the 1950s, which finished third in the 1958 World Cup, and the club side Stade de Reims, which in the same decade contested two European Cup finals against Real Madrid, losing narrowly in the first-ever final in 1956 by 4–3. Two World Cups came and went – in 1970 and 1974 – without French participation. It was a sad turn of events for France and one with which all lovers of sport could sympathise. It was even sadder for a country which has a history of visionaries who were in large measure responsible for the internationalisation of sport, going back to Baron de Coubertin, the founder of the modern Olympic Games in 1896. If the British spread football geographically it was France that cemented the bonds which nurtured the game's international progress. The world governing body FIFA was formed on a French initiative and held its first meeting in Paris; the World Cup itself was conceived by Frenchmen, Jules Rimet, after whom the first trophy was named and Henri Delaunay, who subsequently also founded the European Nations Cup; and the concept of European competitions first took root in France under the auspices of Gabriel Hanot of the sports newspaper L'Equipe. Claude Bez despaired at the sorry state the great game had reached in the country which had given it so much.

The emergence of a St Etienne side that could match its domestic success on the European stage in the mid-1970s provided Bez with the incentive to begin his push for similar results in Bordeaux. Suddenly the quality of French football was set to improve in dramatic fashion as a succession of gifted players made their mark, none more so than the young Michel Platini, who scored on his debut for France in Michel Hidalgo's first match as manager, against Czechoslovakia in 1976. The goal came from a Platini free kick, which was to become his trademark. The job of taking free kicks was normally Henri Michel's but Platini took over the role after that goal and soon assumed Michel's position in midfield. Like a mysterious nemesis, Platini's career seems to have stalked Michel's, advancing in direct relationship to Michel's decline, first as dead-ball specialist, then as central midfielder and captain, and lastly as manager of France.

Michel Hidalgo had been assistant to the Romanian coach Stefan Kovacs who, if he did nothing else during his term as manager of the national team from 1973–75, did instil into a number of French coaches a belief in the inherent talents of French players. St Etienne reached the Champions' Cup final in 1976 where they were narrowly beaten by a Franz Roth goal for Bayern Munich – the same Roth who had scored the goal against Rangers in the Cup-Winners' Cup final almost a decade before. The following year the club reached the quarter-finals before going out to Liverpool. In the same period the national team's results under Hidalgo were beginning to improve and there was real hope of qualifying for the 1978 World Cup finals in Argentina. With the game in France decidedly on the upturn Bez was asked to be president of Bordeaux in 1977.

Until then Bordeaux had been known as a rugby town, despite being home to the country's second oldest football club, Girondins, which was formed in 1881. Bez set out to make it famous for football. Looking at its history, this was not going to be easy. The club had won the French Championship only once, in 1950, and had made little impression since. Bez realised that in order to achieve his aim, a new, revitalised Bordeaux would have to be European in orientation and would need to capture the imagination of the Aquitaine public and the financial support of the region's politicians. As a member of a committee Bez had found his revolutionary ideas difficult to implement in the conservative environment which had so retarded the French game. As president he would be in a position to realise his dreams but he would still need substantial backing from other quarters.

Accordingly, before accepting the presidency, he sought out the one man in Bordeaux who could deliver the necessary support, the Mayor and Prime Minister of France, Jacques Chabon-Delmas. Bez had grandiose plans which, if they came to fruition, would serve both men admirably. For Bez, they would provide the chance to lead the way to a new future for French football; for the populist Chabon-Delmas, the opportunity to record another significant achievement for posterity, this time for his own people, for Bordeaux, for Aquitaine. Chabon-Delmas gave Bez the assurances of financial support he needed. How crucial the relationship between the two became to the subsequent development of Bordeaux can be seen from a Bez aside some years later. Asked about the contribution of Chabon-Delmas, Bez replied: 'If he wasn't there, we would not be there'. For his part, Chabon-Delmas pointed to the positive contribution he considered the football club to have made. 'The club is one of the strongest economic assets of the region', he asserted. 'Our subsidy has been more than covered by the dividends of our investment.'

The concept that Bez outlined to Chabon-Delmas would have been commonplace in Italy or Spain but in France it was nothing short of sensational. Chabon-Delmas provided the finance and low-interest loans, Bez spent the money on bringing the best footballers in France to Bordeaux and promoting the Bordeaux club's name through a series of business ventures, all of which quickly became self-financing. Bernard Lacombe, Albert Gemmrich and Gerald Soler, all French internationals, were the first arrivals but *la politique des vedettes* – 'the policy of stars' – was a continuing process designed not only to achieve (many said buy) success, but also to bring glamour and excitement to an apathetic public. The general manager, Didier Couécou, later to become caretaker coach when Aime Jacquet departed, remembered the feeling at the time. 'It was the first time that a consistent policy had been implemented in France so if we wanted any good player we could have him. We could be more certain of success with great players than with unknowns.' Something of the Bez style can be seen in Gemmrich's account of the conversation that took place between them when he signed for Bordeaux in 1979. After the two had verbally agreed terms Bez suggested they drink to the deal. 'But we haven't signed anything yet', Gemmrich said.

'We have time', was the Bez response.

'What if I sign for someone else?'

'I would be delighted', said Bez. 'It would prove you're a bastard, and I don't want bastards at Bordeaux.'

Aime Jacquet was hired as coach in 1980 and Marius Tresor, the great international sweeper who had won over 40 caps while playing for Marseille, joined the club soon afterwards. Although success was by no means immediate – progress was steady rather than spectacular – the stars kept arriving. Nordine Kourichi, the Algerian international, was followed by the gifted French international midfielder Jean Tigana, who was signed in 1981 for a French record fee of £200,000, a figure which reflected the low financial base of the country's football at a time when transfers in excess of £1 million were commonplace elsewhere in Europe. The signing of Tigana also underlined Bez's high-profile style. Until then, the amount paid in a transfer deal had not been published in France, but Tigana's capture was too good a public relations opportunity to miss. Bez made sure the record fee was known to the country's media, breaking the unofficial code of confidentiality that had existed for some time. He was not about to let protocol stop the Bordeaux publicity machine.

For many years, true to the country's international outlook, a large number of overseas players had plied their trade in the French League. Although some of these were European, the vast majority were South American and African. Bez, in another startling series of moves that was the second phase of the 'policy of stars', began to bring some of the top players in Europe to Bordeaux. The most successful of this new breed of expensive import was the German international striker Dieter Müller, who was signed from Stuttgart in 1982, and he was later followed by his countryman Uwe Reinders, the Portuguese international Fernando Chalana from Benfica and Zlatko and Zoran Vujovic, the Yugoslav twins from Hajduk Split. As other presidents looked with envy at what Bez was doing, so they also began to loosen the purse strings and France was set to become a major consumer of the world's football talent.

For most of the 1970s Bordeaux had languished in the bottom half of the First Division. After Jacquet's appointment, however, the team's performances began to improve significantly. After finishing 16th in Bez's first season as president, the club began to climb: they were fourth in 1981–82 and second in 1982–83. In 1983–84 the pinnacle was finally achieved as Bordeaux won the first of three Championships and two French Cups in four years. In 1986–87 Bez saw his creation reach the ultimate domestic heights by winning both League and Cup, the first team to have done so since the great St Etienne side of the 1970s.

If St Etienne had signalled the revival of French football the Bez revolution at Bordeaux extended it to encompass large areas of French life. On the commercial front, Bordeaux expanded into other businesses, including a downtown office block, six shops, a local radio station, the Merignac hotel, a travel company, a country chateau which has been turned into a training centre, a tennis club and a summer camp for children. With help from Chabon-Delmas the Bordeaux stadium, the Parc Lescure, was completely redeveloped by 1986, financed by the regional, local and city administrations. More importantly, £5 million was given to the club to build, according to Couécou, 'the best sporting complex in Europe', which would permanently house 30 junior players, 'with the hope that in time they may make the club less reliant on the policy of stars'.

Other ambitious men saw that Bez was becoming a power in both Aquitaine and the French game generally and set out to emulate him. The most important of these was Bernard Tapie, a businessman with political ambitions who took over Olympique Marseille in 1986 after a plea by the socialist mayor to 'remake Marseille into a big club'. Tapie also spent heavily on domestic and overseas players, including Alain Giresse from Bordeaux – he was tempted after a glorious career as a one-club man by Tapie's financial inducements – and the Germans Karl-Heinz Forster and Klaus Allofs. Marseille was a football city that had been in the doldrums for a number of years but after Tapie brought in Michel Hidalgo to be the club's general manager following his retirement as coach of the national team the crowds returned and another rivalry was born, between Bez and Tapie. Marseille pushed Bordeaux all the way in 1986–87 but eventually finished second to the Girondins in the League and the Cup, prompting Tapie to say: 'We haven't won a title since I have been president but we have the biggest away crowds of any team. We don't always win but everyone wants to see us. We stir emotions and our club is dynamic. The rest is secondary'. While Monaco took the title in 1987–88, Tapie finally received his reward the following year, when Marseille won its first Championship for 17 years. In June 1989 Marseille added the Cup to the League title when they beat Monaco in the final. At about the same time Tapie made a serious attempt to buy Diego Maradona, a natural consequence of his conception of Marseille as the 'Napoli of France'. When the Maradona affair ended inconclusively Tapie, desperate to win the European Cup, bought Chris Waddle from Spurs for a staggering £4.25 million. Other arrivals for 1989–90 included France's undisputed world-class players Amoros and Tigana.

Other French clubs had already got the message and the influx of foreign players had begun. The Monegasque Royal Family, the Grimaldis, are committed to their football team and determined to use it to promote Monaco around the world. 'My father is truly the number one supporter of the club', Prince Albert declared. To this end they bought Englishmen Mark Hateley from AC Milan and Glenn Hoddle from Spurs to play in the magnificent newly-built Louis II sports complex. Montpellier managed to land the South American Player of the Year of 1987, Colombian Carlos Valderrama. As the glamour quotient increased with the standard of play, so also did the income from commercial sources.

In eight years of European competition from 1981–82 Bordeaux has performed patchily. Despite reaching the semi-final of the Champions' Cup in 1984–85, where the club was knocked out 3–2 by Juventus after winning the home leg 2–0, and the same stage of the Cup-Winners' Cup in 1986–87, the Girondins have suffered some embarrassing defeats, including a first round exit from the Champions' Cup in 1985–86 at the hands of Fenerbahce of Turkey. It seems as if the club has suffered from a strange affliction, a jinx almost, which has been a companion of the French game for many years. The nation that founded and promoted the concept of European competitions, that did more than any other to

ABOVE: Irving Scholar.

LEFT: David Dein.

Jesús Gil and Ron Atkinson.

(Left to right) Lawrence Marlboro, Jack Gillespie, Graeme Souness, David Murray and David Holmes.

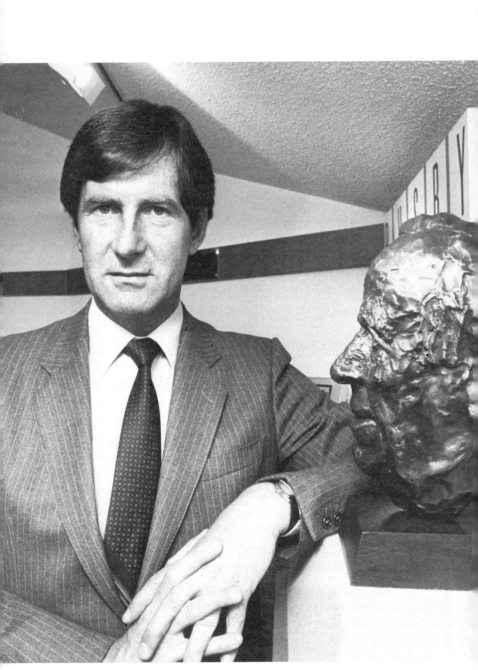

Martin Edwards.

OPPOSITE: Silvio Berlusconi.

ABOVE: (left to right) Jacques Chabon-Delmas, Claude Bez, Jean Fournet-Fayard and Didier Couécou.

LEFT: Michel Platini.

Philip Carter.

Graham Taylor.

Jack Dunnett.

internationalise the game, has never won any European club prize. The great St Etienne team notched up some notable victories in Europe and reached the final of the Champions' Cup in 1976, when the side won the hearts of the Glasgow public but not the match. The jinx had been operating since at least 1955–56 when Stade de Reims were unluckily beaten by Real Madrid in the first-ever European final.

True to French history, after defeating Ujpest Dozsa Bordeaux went out of the UEFA Cup in the third round to Napoli, albeit after a bumper pay-day from the home leg. Although the standards of play in France had improved, crowds remained low in many cases, with average First Division attendances of 11,000 in 1987–88. However, Bordeaux's attendances were healthy enough and gates of over 40,000 could be guaranteed for games against attractive opposition, especially the revitalised Marseille of Bernard Tapie and Michel Hidalgo. Average gates at the Parc Lescure in 1987–88 were almost 20,000. The big revenues though came from European matches. Bez had already broken a 30-year arrangement whereby the television companies of Europe got together to hold down artificially the cost of screening games from European competitions. That deal had involved Canal Plus. For the match against Napoli at the Parc Lescure, which Bordeaux lost 1–0, there was consolation in the fact that the visit of Maradona and company had swelled the coffers of the club by more than £1 million.

In France, for those clubs without rich benefactors like the Grimaldi family, much of the finance comes in the form of subsidies and grants from local and regional governments, many of whom regard the provision of football as the administration's duty. As the Mayor of Strasbourg, M Rudloff put it: 'I don't think a 35 million franc [£3.5 million] deficit is anything to worry about as football is essentially a public service and the municipality should pick up the tab'. In fact clubs are forbidden to make a profit by a law of 1901, passed not long after the headlong rush by English and Scottish clubs to become limited companies. Nonetheless, even a moderate size First Division club such as Toulouse can plan for an income which cannot be matched by any English club, including Manchester United. In the 1987–88 season the Toulouse turnover was £6.2 million on an average of 12,000 spectators. Of this, over £1 million came in the form of municipal or regional subsidy. Bordeaux is given £600,000 a year, while Lyon, when in the Second Division, received £800,000. The total turnover of Bordeaux in 1988–89 was £12 million.

This concept of direct municipal involvement in a professional football club must seem alien to those steeped in the British model. In France it is not at all uncommon. In most cases, clubs play in stadia (usually designed for multi-sports and community use as well as football) provided by the municipality and it is interesting to note that building problems do not seem to have caused the upheavals that they have done elsewhere. The idea of supporting the local football team is based on the same philosophy as support for the arts. It does not make a profit for individuals but rather acts as a kind of flagship for the region, attracting business, tourism and an international profile. Jacques Chabon-Delmas claimed that the subsidy to Bordeaux football club had been recouped by the effect the club has had on the Aquitaine region. It had 'helped in the expansion of our economic plan', while, according to Chabon-Delmas, it would have taken 'ten years . . . to achieve the same result with a more conventional policy'.

Nowhere is this approach more apparent than in the principality of Monaco, where the football club, Association Sportive de Monaco, is virtually an adjunct of the state, financed, sponsored and supported by the Grimaldi family, particularly Prince Rainier and his heir, Albert, who can often be found training with the team. With Hoddle, Hateley and the African stars Weah and Fofana, the Monaco version of the 'policy of stars' paid handsome dividends as the club won the Championship in 1987–88. With the new high profile of French football, the team in Monaco is now as important as the famous Formula One Grand Prix motor race. 'I believe that professional football, as it is today, is almost a necessity,' said Prince Rainier, 'especially in Monaco, where there are a large number of events aimed at a specific public and a few . . . which are popular events. In Monaco, the football team is part of the everyday world. It is a relatively important part of our budget – on the same level as the Philharmonic Orchestra. These are normal costs for us as we don't have, for example, military expenses.'

The problems French clubs encountered in Europe did not extend to the national team during the period in which Bez was building the new Bordeaux. Michel Hidalgo harnessed the emerging French talent to marvellous effect and built his team around the man who became one of the greatest footballers of all time, Michel Platini. Under these two France not only became a formidable force in world football, but did so with a style of play that was always attractive and at times breathtaking. After qualifying for the World Cup in Argentina in 1978, France finished third in Spain four years later. The greatest performances of all were in the European Championships in 1984, when Hidalgo's team swept to victory in their own country, amid a torrent of Platini goals.

Hidalgo retired from the international arena after the European Championship success of 1984, handing over the reins to Henri Michel, who had guided the French Olympic soccer team to the gold medal at the Los Angeles games. In the Mexico World Cup of 1986 the team that Hidalgo had built finished third, but by then it was clearly past its best. A number of players, including Platini, ended their international careers at the end of the Mexico finals but those taking their places could not live up to their illustrious predecessors. Meanwhile there were other moves afoot in France which were to give the game further impetus and a lot more money, but the performance of the national team was central to their development. Most important of these were the French Government's plans to deregulate the nation's television services.

The coincidence of national success and the raising of standards in the domestic League would significantly increase football's revenues from sponsors and from television. With Bez in the forefront, French football negotiated a new contract with television at the beginning of the 1987–88 season which saw each First Division club receive a minimum of £500,000 per year. Apart from Italy, where the special circumstances of Silvio Berlusconi's competition with RAI had led to an auction for football, the French deal was the biggest any football federation had ever signed with the small screen. The contract resulted in a huge increase in sponsorship and other commercial income making many French clubs cash rich. The outcome of Bez's policy regarding television would alter forever the relationship between the game and the small screen in France and would open the door to new, more lucrative television deals all over Europe. For French football clubs it provided the opportunity to finance the upsurge in transfers that followed the Bez revolution and it elevated the French game to the first rank of European leagues.

Michel Platini bowed out of first-class football after playing in a memorable send-off match between a French XI and a Rest of the World team in his home town of Nancy in May 1987. His much-publicised plans to host a television talk show ended amid recriminations with the newly-privatised TF1 television network which Platini had chosen ahead of Silvio Berlusconi's Canale 5 in Italy. The idea had been for Platini to talk to leading world figures, including politicians, royalty and Hollywood stars. Unfortunately they did not exactly beat a path to the great man's door and the show was cancelled. In December Platini appeared on the Italian World Cup draw jamboree and by January 1988 he was working for Canal Plus as a football analyst.

In the absence of Platini and the rest of the great generation of French players, the national team under Henri Michel suffered. The country failed to qualify for the 1988 European Championships in West Germany when they were left trailing in third place in their group matches by the eventual finalists, the Soviet Union. In the draw for the 1990 World Cup France were placed in a tough, but by no means insurmountable group from which two teams qualified. The main threats appeared to come from Yugoslavia and Scotland with Norway as outsiders and Cyprus as the sacrificial lambs.

Michel, however, was beginning to face the kind of intense pressure from the public and the media that seems unique to international management. Unable to get the best out of those veterans that were left he started to put his faith in a younger group of players, many of whom came from his victorious Olympic squad, who were more amenable to his disciplined style. There was a public argument with one of the old guard, Luis Fernandez, in August 1988 after Fernandez was left out of the side and it was only resolved after the intervention of the president of the French federation, Jean Fournet-Fayard. This was quickly followed by an astonishing incident involving the French League's most expensive player, Eric Cantona, for whom Marseille had paid Auxerre £2.1 million. Cantona was omitted from the team to play the friendly against Czechoslovakia and immediately went on radio to blast Michel as the worst manager of all time. Again Fournet-Fayard had to intervene, and this time he exerted some much-needed discipline by banning Cantona from internationals for the whole of the season. In the meantime Fournet-Fayard appointed a new national director of coaching in what many saw as a move to undermine the authority of the manager. The man hired by the president was Gerard Houllier, who had achieved considerable success in the French League including a Championship win with Paris St Germain in 1985–86.

The World Cup campaign got underway with a narrow 1–0 win against the Norwegians on 28 September 1988 but the closeness of the result did not augur well for the next game, away to Cyprus, supposedly the sacrificial lambs. On 22 October the 1–1 draw, France's worst international result for many years, sealed Michel's fate. On the day of the match against Cyprus it was announced that the television station Canal Plus had won a six-year sponsorship deal with the French national team worth £1.5 million a year – if the team qualified for the World Cup in 1990 and the European Championships in 1992. The deal had been negotiated by Jean-Claude Darmon, head of Mediafoot, a sports marketing company, but it was the new commercial climate created by Claude Bez that made football so attractive to potential sponsors. Darmon spelled out the importance of success: 'The economic opportunity is 10–13 million francs [£1–1.3 million] for sponsorship, which I can get every two years for qualification for a major competition'. Canal Plus had already won the rights to televise the lion's share of the French League and this was the company's first opportunity to be involved with the national team. In a related move, Darmon also announced that an income in excess of £1 million could be gained from perimeter advertising if the team qualified for the World Cup.

It was thus vital for the whole of French football that the team achieved the necessary results on the pitch. The Cyprus outcome was disastrous and made qualification for Italy that much harder.

Bez offered his help to the manager but the proud Michel did not respond. Visibly agitated at the rebuff, Bez began to work out a strategy for the future that did not include Henri Michel. What better way was there of cementing the new commercial relations with Canal Plus than installing the station's own man, Platini, as manager. The fact that Platini did not possess the necessary coaching qualifications had been taken care of by the appointment of Houllier, who could fulfil the coaching role while Platini picked the team and fronted the operation as manager. After the Cyprus result Fournet-Fayard finally became convinced that Michel should go but the manager's replacement was suggested by Bez, who spent the weekend contacting as many other club presidents as possible. When he flew to Budapest he was armed with sufficient support to effect the downfall of Michel and the installation of Platini.

By Monday 31 October Michel Platini was manager of France. By Tuesday morning the news had been leaked to the press and the chase was on to verify the story. Bez went to ground while Fournet-Fayard issued a statement: 'All this talk of Platini is just press talk, without foundation'. It later emerged that Fournet-Fayard had that same day cleared Platini's path by telephoning the Under-21 team coach, Marc Bourrier, to forestall any bad feeling he may have had about being passed over for the job himself. Platini was cornered by the news-hounds in the dressing-room of the Stadio Communale in Turin after the testimonial game but he denied all knowledge of the national manager's job: 'I've only just returned from the United States and I know absolutely nothing about what's been going on in France. I haven't talked to anyone there at all. As for being national manager I say again I know absolutely nothing about this. I haven't even given it a thought'.

The following day the news was official. Fournet-Fayard, under overwhelming pressure from journalists, confirmed that: 'Everything was sorted out at that lunch. He [Platini] assured me of his interest and desire to take over the national team'. In direct contradiction of his earlier statement he went on, 'I realised after the disastrous match against Cyprus that we could not go on as we were'.

The coup was complete. Claude Bez had procured the new manager of the national team and had been able to accomplish this feat because of the platform he had created in the French game at Bordeaux. He had been instrumental in raising the status and income of French football to unimagined levels and the deals with Canal Plus were signed. Bez even felt confident enough to switch the national team's travel contract from the traditional Wagon-Lits company to Bordeaux's own travel operation.

The importance of the national team to Bez's plans became more apparent as Bordeaux's League progress began to falter after the system of play was changed at the beginning of the 1988–89 season to accommodate the expensive purchases of Clive Allen from Tottenham Hotspur, Yannick Stopyra from Toulouse and Enzo Scifo, on loan from Internazionale of Milan. The 'policy of stars' had become a vicious circle. At the beginning of each season the president had to come up with an expensive new signing, preferably a forward. The public now demanded no less. To make way for the newcomers Zlatko Vujovic was transferred but Allen was injured for much of the time while Stopyra and Scifo failed to fit in, and the club slipped into the bottom half of the table. After the Girondins went out of the Cup to Second Division Beauvais, Aime Jacquet was temporarily replaced by Didier Couécou and results gradually improved, although the club still finished the season without a trophy and out of Europe. Bez's answer for 1989–90 was to bring back the Belgian coach Raymond Goethals, who had previously managed Bordeaux in the 1970s.

The idea of a League club chairman intervening to appoint a new national team manager while the incumbent was still in his chair would horrify the all-powerful men of the Football Association in England. It is universally recognised in France, however, that the fortunes of everyday domestic football, at all levels, are bound up with the performance of the national side. Even so, Bez's actions drew criticism. Guy Roux, manager of Auxerre and the vice-president of the union of managers, was the first to express disquiet over Bez's role and Bernard Tapie accused the Bordeaux president of using the national team to advance his own position. Bez's replies were full of his usual grandiloquence: 'The world of football must understand that the general interest is paramount'.

Of the president of Marseille Bez said: 'Tapie sees conspiracies everywhere, he doesn't believe anyone could work in the general interest'.

Claude Bez had built a club at Bordeaux which could now stand comparison with the biggest in Europe and in the process had, with the success of the national team, dragged the whole of French football from its lowest depths to new heights of affluence and popularity. When Glenn Hoddle and Mark Hateley went to Monaco there were many in the British press and the game who were generally disparaging in their comments on the quality of French football. The insularity of the British had surfaced again. It was as if 1984 and Michel Platini had never happened. Of course, as England failed to qualify for the 1984 European Championships, less interest was shown in the competition, but even so some of the remarks were little short of insulting.

Hoddle himself has little doubt as to the standard of play in France. 'All clubs have impressed me', he said, 'including those in danger of relegation. Mark Hateley and I were knocked out with the play of a Second Division club we met in the Cup. Only five or six teams in England have sufficient technique not to play kick and rush. The average Englishman is a limited player. I am made for Latin football, if I had been born in France or Italy I would have enjoyed my career more. It is a paradise for the technician.' If evidence were needed of Hoddle's words, Monaco's progress in the Champions' Cup should be proof enough of the new standards in France. Hoddle himself starred in a memorable performance against Bruges when he made five goals in a 6–1 win, prompting one journalist to report: 'If dream football exists, it was here in Monaco this evening. Hoddle destroyed them'. However, the quarter-final tie against Galatasaray of Turkey saw the old French jinx return. After being out injured for some time, Hoddle returned for the second leg, played in Cologne because of crowd trouble in Turkey, but Monaco lost 2–1 on aggregate and went out of the competition.

There can be no question that the French League is now among the strongest in Europe and much of the credit for the improvement must go to Claude Bez. However, it became clear that Bez had overstretched himself in his dealings with Canal Plus, Platini and the authorities after a row with the French federation. Bez's sense of honour forced him to resign from his role with the national team and the League Management Committee. Worse still, there were grave financial problems at Bordeaux due to the poor performances on the pitch. Expressed with his usual candour, Bez's trenchant analysis reached the heart of the problem. 'With my involvement in the national team and the commercial diversification the players believed a top team was no longer essential to the club . . . we are therefore going to refocus the club on the team.'

In France, football has once again come to be of national significance after spending many years in decline. The revival of the national team has now been entrusted to the philosophical Michel Platini. Despite the loss of his first match as manager by 3–2 to Yugoslavia in Belgrade, Platini was able to shrug his shoulders when asked how he was enjoying his new role: 'You explain when you win,' he commented wryly, 'and you explain when you lose'.

But in the new, harshly commercial world of French football it was more vital than ever that the national team qualified for the World Cup finals in Italy in 1990. Bez, with support from Jean-Claude Darmon, who had helped persuade the French federation that a change was necessary to secure the funds from sponsorship, was no longer prepared to jeopardise that objective, even to the point of taking the huge gamble that Platini's appointment represented. Like Silvio Berlusconi, Bez had for some time been involved in the televising of football and understood perfectly the new importance of the small screen, but to maintain public interest, not to mention the sponsorship deals he had helped to negotiate, it was absolutely essential that the French team was seen in the major championships of the world game. However, when a defeat by Scotland and an uninspiring home 0–0 draw against Yugoslavia effectively meant non-qualification for the World Cup for the first time since 1974, Platini did not have to suffer press headlines of the genre 'en nomme de Dieu, partez!' or 'vous êtes un plonker!' as has befallen the England manager, Bobby Robson. On the contrary, it was accepted that football success at international level is often cyclical and the French team was just not ready for the 1990 World Cup. Platini's reaction struck a chord with the public. 'If we don't go to the World Cup, it will not be a national disaster. We must rediscover the will to win. Players, managers and presidents must rekindle the passion of the game.' In a survey before the Yugoslavia game, it was asked whether Platini should go if France failed to qualify for the World Cup. Over 70 per cent of the general public and 84 per cent of football supporters thought he should stay.

Far from seeking to find a scapegoat in the new manager, French football took a long hard look at itself in the wake of the failure. The League, which comes second to the interests of the national team, will be reduced from 38 games to 34 and two-leg cup ties are to be replaced by sudden-death matches in the 1990–91 season. This reduction has been instituted in the belief that part of the national team's problem is that too many games are played. In England, ever more games are being played by top footballers. In 1989, amid talk of a return to a 22-club First Division, it was even suggested that all First Division clubs be forced to enter the meaningless Simod Cup.

The attachment to international competition has deep roots in the French game. Although the British invented football and took it to other countries, it was the French who founded the game's institutions, the French who instigated all the great international competitions, and the French, led by Bez, who broke the old traditions in televised football that had held the game back for so long.

6

INSIDE THE BOX-PART ONE

When it comes to advertising, it is the mind-boggling $1.1 million minute for Super Bowl XX that people talk about. It's become as much a phenomenon as the game itself

ROBERT RAISSMAN
Advertising Age

Silvio Berlusconi's battles in Italy with the state run RAI television network were watched with more than a little interest in the other countries of Europe. Numerous aspects of the Canale 5 network were debated, written about and analysed as media-watchers tried to glean some scrap of information which might be relevant to their own countries. But while the level of discussion in Britain focused on Berlusconi's scantily clad female stars, the outrageous game shows and the entertainment spectaculars, which were presented as the shape of things to come in Britain once television was deregulated, the rest of Europe looked to other, more serious areas of Berlusconi's operations.

When Berlusconi began to bid for the right to screen Italian League football the prospects for success were slight. In a country where the importance of football to society and culture is large (television audiences for big matches can reach 70 per cent), RAI were devoting vast amounts of airtime to the game, with a football programme transmitted virtually every day, mirroring the voluminous output of the Italian football press. It was impossible for Berlusconi to make a similar amount of time available on his Canale 5 network but it is extremely unlikely that winning the rights to football was his sole intention. If he couldn't win the rights then he could at least force up the price of the game so that RAI would be less willing to compete in other areas. This was achieved when the state broadcaster had to pay a mammoth £40 million to the Italian League for the exclusive rights to show action from the 1987–88 season alone. Meanwhile the Berlusconi network could still keep the pressure on RAI by screening the Mundialito, other friendly games, such as the one against Manchester United, and whatever overseas action could be acquired.

One of Berlusconi's companies in the Fininvest group is Publitalia, whose business is to sell advertising space on commercial television, particularly on the Berlusconi network. It was becoming increasingly obvious that with a proliferation in the number of channels available, the make-up of an audience was just as important as its number. This concept is necessarily alien to purely public service broadcasters like the BBC, which does not have to sell advertising and therefore is by its very nature less responsive to such information. Sport in general and football in particular deliver a specific audience to television (especially young, free-spending males), making them extremely attractive to advertisers of cars, beer, financial services and so on. And for important matches, both the absolute numbers and the demographic composition of the audience make football one of the most profitable areas of television programming.

Throughout Europe the appetite for football was being fuelled by new investment in cable and satellite technology and a growing realisation on the part of governments that their traditional stranglehold on the structure of television systems must be loosened. The result of this has been wholesale deregulation across the continent, even in those areas such as Germany and Scandinavia which have in the past jealously guarded their restrictive practices. With the level of competition rising with the increase in channels, football authorities in Europe sought to exploit the situation. The future of the game was looking increasingly as if it would be inextricably linked to the growth of the small screen and the band of media entrepreneurs who are beginning to control it.

In France these developments fired the imagination of Claude Bez. Political decisions had been taken in the Elysée Palace which gave Bez the impetus he needed. The traditional public service broadcaster TF1 was to be privatised as the main measure in a liberalising policy that would see vast changes to the staid and somewhat conservative nature of the French broadcasting system. In the meantime a new force had arrived on the scene in 1982, in the shape of Canal Plus, a subscription-based television channel. Canal Plus began broadcasting a mix of feature films, general entertainment and soft porn but did not reach the level of subscribers necessary to make it profitable. In fact the station was virtually bankrupt by 1985. The outlook changed for the better as the channel started to show occasional live football matches from the improving French League. As the great media powers of Europe, including Silvio Berlusconi and Robert Maxwell, were queueing up to buy a stake in the new privatised sector, Canal Plus, with its football coverage to the fore, began to attract subscribers in droves.

As the timetable for privatisation was set for 1987, Bez looked closely at what it meant for French football in general and his club, Bordeaux, in particular. At the time television paid little for the game; even the French Cup final was sold for a mere £80,000, and some disastrous programmes had been made, none more so than the strange 'Multifoot', which covered a number of live matches simultaneously. Bez realised that it would be a long haul to bring the French League the kind of rewards enjoyed by the Italians and that it would require a co-ordinated effort on the part of the whole of the French game. Accordingly, he started to push the rest of his co-presidents, and the French federation, into considering a long-term strategy. In the meantime, Bez queried another practice of European television which deprived the game of income, the outcome of which would have repercussions across the whole continent, and would be of immediate benefit to his Girondins of Bordeaux.

We have already seen how games in European competitions have become the real events of the football world at club level, attracting large crowds and revenue from advertising and sponsors. However, television companies in most European countries had blanket contracts that allowed them access to all competitions. This meant that only a nominal fee, if any, was paid for the rights to European ties. In addition, the television companies, through their collective organisation, the European Broadcasting Union, operated a policy based on what they called the principle of reciprocity. The mechanics of this were simple. The television company covering the home leg of a European tie would make the pictures available free to the station which was to screen the return match and in return would themselves gain free transmission of the second leg.

For instance, if Manchester United played Atletico Madrid, the game in Manchester would be covered by ITV or BBC who would give the pictures to Spanish television. At the return match in Madrid, the Spanish company would similarly give the pictures to ITV or BBC. This effectively gave the television companies two premium matches for the price of one, or often for no price at all. They could do this because world football had until then been extremely amateurish in its dealings with television. When the blanket contracts were signed no account was taken by football administrators of the extent to which they had signed away many technical but lucrative rights, such as the right to show the match anywhere in the world and as many times as the television company liked without any extra payment. When Claude Bez realised he could challenge this situation, the relationship between the game and television changed overnight.

Bez reasoned that European games did not fall under the national agreement and that selling a home match to a French television company did not mean he had also to include international rights. This argument – the selling of pictures not rights – meant that Bez could negotiate a separate agreement with a television service from the opposition's country. The first game in which this was tested was the 1–1 draw against Dnepr of the USSR in a Champions' Cup tie in 1985, which Bez sold to Canal Plus in France. The huge pay-off for the new policy came later, however, first in a Champions' Cup quarter-final game against PSV Eindhoven in 1988, which netted Bordeaux £300,000 from television, then early the following season in a bonanza against Napoli, worth £500,000 for the home leg alone. The French station which won rights to screen most of these matches because it was prepared to pay significant amounts for the games was Canal Plus. By 1988 Canal Plus had increased its subscribers to 2,000,000, close to the station's capacity, mainly on the back of its football coverage. The policy of reciprocity was broken, not just in France, but throughout Europe. In Italy RAI paid £10 million for European matches alone in the 1987–88 season, even though champions Napoli were knocked out of the Champions' Cup in the first round by Real Madrid. RAI, desperate not to lose glamorous European games to Berlusconi, agreed a system of payments that guaranteed the clubs a fixed amount at the start of the season no matter how far they advanced in the competitions. In return RAI were given rights to all home ties played by Italian clubs up to and including the semi-finals (the finals of the two main European competitions are controlled by UEFA, which sells the television rights itself). Under the terms of this arrangement the champions Napoli received £2 million for one home game against Real Madrid. RAI also paid £300,000 to the Madrid club for Italian rights to the away leg, which was played behind closed doors because of crowd trouble at the Bernabeu. Cup-winners Atalanta were paid £1.5 million and each UEFA Cup entrant £1.2 million. After Napoli's first round defeat, RAI were less keen to pay out large sums of money in advance to Italian clubs in Europe and the deal was not renewed for the 1988–89 season. Having forced RAI to part with £10 million for one season's European games, Berlusconi could now bid for the best ties himself and had the added advantage of owning AC Milan, the team that would be the Italian representatives in the European Champions' Cup in 1988–89. In April 1989 RAI announced an exclusive four-year deal to televise the national team's games for which they will pay £30 million.

While all this was going on in Italy, Canal Plus began radical changes in the way football was filmed and presented, using far more cameras than had ever been seen before and sophisticated lenses to concentrate on close-up shots of the action. Using ABC's 'Monday Night Football' programme in the USA as its example, Canal Plus built a television spectacular out of a previously mundane diet of weekly League games. The company devoted more airtime to the programmes with analysis and replays, and was quick to recognise the potential of Michel Platini as an analyst. It was Canal Plus that showed the rest of the television networks in France and Europe how backward their coverage had become. For years the guiding principle of televised football had been to provide the viewer with the equivalent of a seat above the half-way line and games in many countries were filmed with just two half-way line cameras and possibly another behind the goal. The style of coverage had been virtually the same since it was established in the 1950s. The innovations brought in by Canal Plus included a multiplicity of pitch level cameras, replays from a bewildering number of angles and cameras often detailed to follow one particular player throughout the match. The French channel also experimented in other areas, by taking out large amounts of advertising at stadia for instance, and, in the games shown live on the station, using every spare centimetre of space to promote the Canal Plus name, even to the extent of incorporating its logo into the goal nets.

As these changes began to bring in more viewers the French federation set up a high-powered committee under the president of the League, Jean Sadoul, and Jean-Claude Darmon of Mediafoot to find ways of exploiting the approaching privatisations. The federation had been advised that legally, if ownership of TF1 and the other channels changed, as it must under the new broadcasting legislation, the contracts football had agreed with those stations would be rendered null and void. Armed with this the federation began negotiations with all networks and channels for a new contract for the whole of French football. Darmon spelled out the federation's approach thus: 'In my new way of canvassing the channels, I don't say "How much are you offering?" I haven't even talked about money, I leave that to the presidents. My message is different, I present to them what one could call a list of demands'. The list of demands included on-screen promotion to increase attendances, the sale of pictures not rights and participation in advertising and subscription income.

TF1 eventually fell to the consortium of Robert Maxwell and property tycoon Robert Bouygues while Berlusconi won the regional channel La Cinq. Neither of them, however, won the Grand Prix. The victor in the war of football and the new premier partner of the game was to be Canal Plus, which would screen 20 live games from the French League, some cup matches including the semi-finals, and a small number of live foreign games. Part of the reason the French federation chose to deal with Canal Plus was that it reached a limited number of subscribers, thus ensuring that widespread live coverage did not adversely affect attendances. TF1 retained a highlights programme, 'Telefoot', the rights to most internationals featuring the French national team and the Coupe de France. The first deal between football and television in France, signed in 1977, had been worth a mere £45,000. With a spread of games across the channels, including women's and youth matches, French football concluded a deal for the 1987–88 season worth £20 million. It escaped the notice of most people in England, including the League and FA, who did not know what was happening less than 200 miles from London.

At the same time a new television deal was being negotiated in Spain, where deregulation had been slow in its development, despite government policy encouraging a measure of competition. In this environment the Spanish football federation could only really deal with the state broadcaster TVE, but nonetheless after some wrangling over payment for the highlights programme 'Estudio Estadio', which TVE claimed should be free of any payment as it was essentially news coverage, a deal was struck which recognised the principle of payment for all football coverage, worth £7 million a season for two years. TVE and the regional independent stations would alternately screen a selected live game each Saturday night and TVE would continue to transmit 'Estudio Estadio' on Sundays, featuring every First Division match, goals from the Second Division and an international round-up. In a country with a relatively small population and little competition the deal was good for football, especially since 'Estudio Estadio' is one of the most technically accomplished of all football programmes and TVE deploys considerable resources in its making and presentation, even to the extent of inviting referees to the studio to talk about their decisions. However, one person in Spain had been following events in Italy and France and felt aggrieved that Spanish television paid so little by comparison. But worse still, he was annoyed that the lion's share of television income went to Real Madrid and Barcelona, the result of a system of grading in which more was paid for a game featuring one or other of the two giants. Jesús Gil attempted to rectify this situation the only way he knew how, by all-out attack.

At the start of the 1987–88 season the Raging Bull issued a statement declaring that the Spanish federation had no right to negotiate on behalf of Atletico Madrid and that cameras would not be allowed to film the *Rojoblancos,* at home or away. When the legal position was clarified it was clear that Gil was within his rights. Events in three countries had now shown that the balance between football and television was irrevocably changing. Where television had once called the shots, paying little and devoting few resources to the game, now football was in a position to demand favourable treatment. Gil recognised that without Atletico's games, coverage in Spain would be less than comprehensive, and a hastily-agreed compromise left him with a larger share of the cake and the right to negotiate Atletico's European games himself.

Within a year, the television contract in Germany would also be up for negotiation and already the Germans were taking on board what was happening across their borders in the rest of mainland Europe. With a complicated and restricted television industry, the German football federation would have to tread very carefully, but already it had shown what could be achieved. When the international friendly against Italy was played in Cologne in 1985, the Germans made an unprecedented £333,000 through an on-screen sponsorship by Agfa films. The access fee paid by the television company ARD was reduced from £100,000 to £75,000 for an agreement allowing the sponsorship. With perimeter advertising bringing in £167,000 and gate receipts £500,000 the German federation grossed over £1 million from this one friendly match.

A measure of deregulation was taking place in the Federal Republic although its pace was uneven across the country due to the fact that in Germany the individual states exercise a large degree of control over their television systems. Nonetheless, new private stations had appeared, mainly in the large cities. The most important of these private stations are RTL Plus, in which the principal stake is owned by UFA, a subsidiary of the giant Bertelsmann media group, and Sat 1, controlled by a consortium of newspaper and magazine publishers. Traditionally, football had been screened solely by the two public service networks, ARD and ZDF, who between them paid £5 million to the German federation for rights to the 1987–88 season. The stranglehold of the public service networks was broken when UFA made an offer worth £15 million per season for a three-year contract. UFA maintained that it was prepared to resell some of the rights it would gain under the proposed deal to the other networks, but the lion's share of glamorous matches would go to RTL Plus. ARD and ZDF countered with an

£11 million bid and a propaganda campaign which sought to bring pressure on the federation from the large numbers of people who were unable to receive the private stations.

As the war of words hotted up, the matter became a political issue which concerned the whole future of the German television system. The residents of some states where private television had either not been allowed or was discouraged, became angry at the prospect of being unable to watch regular football – so angry that Herman Neuberger, president of the federation, even received threats to his life. Eventually, the offer from UFA was accepted, although for at least the 1988–89 season the company would have to share the rights with ARD and ZDF. As live football was not part of the deal, the issue became one of scheduling. Which channel would screen what matches and when would they be transmitted? The compromise, under which ARD and ZDF alternately screen a Saturday evening highlights programme of half the League games while RTL Plus and Sat 1 show the other half, has not worked particularly well, resulting in falling audiences and a large amount of discontent. However, the pull of football can still be seen in the audiences for the 1988 European Championships, held in Germany, which drew massive numbers of viewers despite a lack of German success in the competition. Three games drew over 15 million viewers and one, the 2–1 defeat by Holland, pulled in 57 per cent of the audience.

In the space of two years, the income from television increased beyond the wildest dreams of administrators in most European countries, and now represents one of the most important sources of revenue to the game. In country after country, as privatisation and deregulation become the order of the day, the lessons of Italy and France are being applied. Even a small country like Portugal can expect to receive increased income from television, prompting Jorge Goncalves, a property developer who made a fortune in the United States and is known as the 'Portuguese Berlusconi', to invest £5 million of his own money in Sporting Lisbon, confident in the belief that it can be recouped from the emerging private television sector. Yet in virtually all of these countries money is not the only issue in the debates about television. Just as important are the matters of live televised football, its effects on attendances and other commercial income and the way the game is portrayed.

The debate in Europe found an echo in Scotland, where the Scottish authorities were reviewing their television policy. Constrained by reliance on BBC and ITV, the Scots had managed to weather a potentially damaging split in their ranks over the issue of live football which some clubs wanted to extend. In 1988, a deal for £1.75 million was concluded, but the main element was not money, rather expanded coverage in the form of highlights programmes. Also, the Scots began to market their game overseas – the Skol Cup final in 1988 was sold to 49 countries. When Scotland played France in a World Cup qualifying game in 1989, the Scottish Football Association were aware of developments across the Channel and demanded £800,000 from French television for rights to screen the match live. Even French television bosses were taken aback, but after some hard bargaining that went on well into the night before the game, a deal was struck which was not far short of the Scots' demands. In May 1989, the Scots announced a three-year deal with English satellite broadcasters BSB worth £12 million. Ernie Walker, secretary of the SFA, said of the deal: 'The Scottish authorities have always guarded the game against over-exposure and many bitter battles have been fought in public. It follows that we are conscious of where we are going and it seemed to us the time was right to harness this new technology. To have stood back and done nothing would have been dangerous and it would be folly to think that this medium would not pose a threat'. While the bigger clubs can expect to make over £400,000 each from the arrangement with BSB, their smaller brethren will also receive substantial amounts, possibly providing the finance to raid English clubs for players. BSB will, of course, broadcast the games to England as well as Scotland.

The television revolution had spread beyond Europe to the wider world. Even in the United States, one of the few countries in the world where football is not the number one sport, there was renewed interest in the game from television when FIFA announced that the USA would host the 1994 World Cup. In recent years the World Cup has begun to realise television and sponsorship income that is now rivalling that of the NFL, which has the benefit of operating in the most sophisticated television environment of all. The 28 teams of the NFL receive $1.4 billion from American television networks in a partnership that has been nurtured since the early days of the professional game. NFL Films was established to control pictures from stadia and the company produces high quality images, makes programmes and utilises the medium to the full as a promotional tool for the game. With admission prices aimed at a middle income market, television takes the game to the masses. Undoubtedly the pinnacle is the Superbowl, which has achieved eight of the ten top audiences in US television history. All games are played in advertisement-free stadia, thus television income from commercials, which often use ex-players, is vast: over $1 million for a 60-second spot during the 1989 Superbowl. The NFL has also utilised television to the full in its overseas expansion. In the UK television has managed to popularise an alien sport by building awareness through detailed explanations of how the game works and using the most up-to-date presentation techniques. One of the reasons the NFL can operate in this way is that all its negotiations are carried out by one man, the commissioner. The disparate nature of the world's soccer authorities make similar arrangements more difficult but the experiences of an increasing number of bodies have led many to believe that the NFL provides the model for the future.

In Brazil, where catastrophic organisation saw over 300 top level players leave the country to ply their trade abroad after the 1986 World Cup, and where crowds and interest were declining alarmingly in the face of a complicated, not to say unintelligible system of fixtures, the whole Brazilian league structure was revamped in 1987 under the name of the Copa Uniao ('Union Cup'). Although the new competition faced initial problems because it was instigated by the top ten clubs rather than the Brazilian federation, the direct participation of the television network TV Globo in the form of sponsorship and marketing shows how even in Brazil, where huge, passionate crowds have traditionally been the lifeblood of the game, it is now recognised that football's future is tied to the deals it can negotiate with the small screen. And in other parts of the third world, where foot-ball has become increasingly important, the process has followed a similar pattern. Television rights to prestigious African club competitions, for instance, and the African Nations Cup have recently been sold to a Nigerian media company, the Degue Broadcast Network, which, while obviously generating much less revenue than is the case in Europe, nevertheless represents a realisation of the part television can play in strengthening the African game's position in the global marketplace.

In Italy, Berlusconi's intervention started the process as he recognised the unique ability of football to attract a particular audience. In France, where clubs are not allowed to make a profit, the concept of live football on the main channels was a non-starter, yet still the French managed to achieve an unprecedented increase in income through the use of a professional, Jean-Claude Darmon, and thorough preparation of their case. In Spain, Jesús Gil showed that football could take on the television companies and win, while Germany proved that even in a country with restrictions on television advertising and a federal communication system football is still central to a successful schedule. All these countries inhabit a media environment whose decision-makers have come to realise the true value of the game to the small screen. They have learned from one another's experiences and consequently created a domino effect as each nation's television networks in turn have fallen in the face of the new reality. As far as the English supporter and television viewer was concerned, however, these events were unknown, unreported by the media and those in charge of the game. The 20 miles that separate England from the mainland of Europe might as well be a gulf of light years across interstellar space for all the impact the revolutionary changes of Europe and beyond have had on football and television in the United Kingdom.

7

INSIDE THE BOX-PART TWO

Few men have virtue to withstand the highest bidder

GEORGE WASHINGTON

At the end of the 1987–88 season, fully one year after the radical changes in Italy, France and Spain, and at the same time as the Germans began to negotiate a new television contract, the deals that the football authorities of England had made with television expired. Unbelievably, the revolutionary moves in Europe had barely penetrated across the Channel and nobody in the administration of the English game, whose League was about to enter its centenary year, knew anything about them at all.

Perhaps the one exception to this state of ignorance was Irving Scholar. Having spent time in Monaco he had followed what happened in France and Italy with interest. Although Scholar had failed in his bid to get himself elected to the Management Committee of the Football League in 1984 and had no official role in negotiations with television after 1985, this did not prevent the Spurs chairman from becoming closely involved as the unofficial leader of the 'big five' clubs – Tottenham, Arsenal, Liverpool, Everton and Manchester United – who were linked, not for the first time, to a possible breakaway from the League. As for the rest of the members of the football establishment, they knew they were not receiving enough money from television, but they had no idea how to change the situation.

Irving Scholar's awareness of the opportunities in television dates back to the 1983–84 season when regular live matches began to be shown for the first time in England. Fearing that the advent of live coverage would drive down attendances which were already in a serious, long-term decline, the Tottenham Board brought in the advertising agency Saatchi and Saatchi as part of a £100,000 marketing plan to boost crowds. When Spurs reached the UEFA Cup final at the end of the season, Scholar tried to cash in by offering television rights to the game at White Hart Lane to the highest bidder. Unfortunately, neither the BBC nor ITV were prepared to bid against each other and the income from television for the game turned out to be negligible. This rebuff obviously rankled with Scholar, who made it his business to find out as much about the medium as he could in the subsequent months and years, so that come the day when the BBC/ITV monopoly could be challenged, he would be ready.

Live League matches on television in England did not start because the clubs thought they were a good thing for the game. On the contrary, in their view live television was something to be resisted as it was thought that it would reduce crowds throughout the League. It was also believed that attendances at televised games would suffer adversely. Furthermore, a number of clubs had been approached by companies who were willing to pay large sums of money for the right to display their names on the shirts of footballers. Television would not allow these advertisements on screen and the ludicrous situation developed where clubs would wear their sponsor's logo only if the cameras were not present, which rather negated the value to the sponsor and seriously retarded the revenue potential of the sponsorship. This happened because previous League negotiators had blithely signed away the right to control their own advertising and by 1983 the shirt advertising ban had become a convention for televised football, though all television channels were quite content to display advertising in other sports, particularly motor racing. So the clubs of the Football League conceded what in the long term would prove to be their most valuable asset – the principle of live football – to television, for nothing more than short-term commercial income that should have been theirs in any event. Even this was only achieved after the intervention of Robert Maxwell, then chairman of Oxford United, who recalled: 'I went to see the BBC bosses and I said you must allow shirt advertising. They said we can't under the charter. I showed them that they could do it under the charter. And so they gave in'. If the process was as simple as Maxwell claims, it is even more remarkable that football gave live games to television for such a minor concession.

A compensation scheme was instituted to recompense televised clubs for any loss of spectators, although the knock-on effect, that is, gates declining at other games because a live match is on television the following day, was never addressed. Cliff Morgan, then the BBC's head of outside broadcasts, said of the football authorities: 'When the League offered us 31 matches live, we said "Can you deliver?" The answer was "Anything can be delivered so long as the money is right". I was shattered that they could believe that money is more important than the welfare of the game'.

The 1983 deal, made jointly with ITV and BBC, had been negotiated by the League's Television Committee which was chaired by Sir Arthur South of Norwich City and included Peter Robinson, secretary of Liverpool, Robert Daniel of Plymouth and Philip Carter, who had been chairman of Everton for two years but was not on the Management Committee. Robert Maxwell had been on the original Committee but had resigned after a disagreement with Philip Carter during which Maxwell had advocated a more confrontational approach to the television companies. The contract was eventually agreed amid rancorous publicity which resulted in ominous noises emanating from the television companies to the effect that football could not expect regular increases in access fees in future, and that anyway the game was declining in popularity. Summing up television's view, John Bromley, ITV's head of sport said: 'We want football to tell us exactly what they would like in an ideal world and then, I assume, we will tell them what they can have'.

It was certainly true that by 1983 television audiences for football in England had been in decline for five years or more. But the same period had also seen a general downturn in traditional television audiences for ITV and BBC due to competition from video and the recently established Channel 4. Television across the board was devoting more and more hours to different sports such as snooker, darts and American Football which competed for the sporting audience. Furthermore, criticisms were made of English television's football coverage which many said had become stale and outdated and had not been substantially changed for 20 years.

The game was also a victim of its own success, having drawn massive audiences in the 1970s. Thirty million watched the 1970 Cup final between Leeds and Chelsea and the BBC highlights programme 'Match Of The Day' regularly attracted over 10 million viewers. These figures clearly could not be sustained forever but it is significant that when audiences started to fall as television diversified, those charged with presenting football on the small screen did not try to attack the situation with a new format or a change in presenters but simply attempted to acquire the game for less money in real terms than had been the case previously. Moreover, the 1983 deal was due to run out in two years and television executives, thinking ahead to the possibility of delicate negotiations in 1985, began a campaign of denigration, which portrayed football as an old-fashioned pastime, one that could no longer bring in the mass of viewers it had attracted in earlier years.

The campaign was allied to a deliberate policy of devaluing the product on the part of at least some of the television contractors by exploitation of the small print in the contract that football's negotiators had overlooked. The time a football programme is transmitted, for instance, is crucial to its success. Football had left this matter entirely to the television companies. London Weekend Television, for instance, scheduled its Sunday highlights programme 'The Big Match' at lunchtime when a large proportion of its target audience was bound to be otherwise engaged at the local pub. The onset of live football also saw a cut-back in the number of edited highlights programmes which meant that lucrative sponsorship deals would become concentrated more and more on the small number of teams which television decided the public wanted to see live. They could do this because, once again, football's negotiators had failed to ensure either an adequate balance between edited and live games or any say in the decisions about which teams would be screened. To listen to those in television, football should have been grateful for any coverage at all.

The initial offer from ITV and BBC in 1985 was a four-year contract worth £4.5 million per year for 19 live games with highlights programmes as and when the television companies saw fit. The bid drew qualified support from the South committee and the

Management Committee and both bodies recommended acceptance, but it was subject to some vehement hostility at a meeting
of all 92 club chairmen. The main opposition came from Irving
Scholar, Robert Maxwell and Ken Bates of Chelsea, who all
thought the money on offer was far too low. Maxwell claimed
that the impending satellite revolution could force the price of
football through the roof: a deal worth at least £10 million a
season was the figure he had in mind. 'The game has sold itself
too cheaply to television in the past', he asserted. 'Football fills a
lot of time on the screens. We must be run as a business and not
kill our own audiences.' Swayed by the opposition, the meeting
rejected the offer but reorganised the Television Committee and
mandated it to talk further with the television companies on
the basis of 13 live games only and an increase in the financial
terms.

The composition of the Television Committee was now Sir
Arthur South, Peter Robinson, Ken Bates, Irving Scholar, League
secretary Graham Kelly, administrator Lee Walker and Robert
Maxwell, who returned to bring his obvious expertise in the
media business and to add some much needed weight to the
negotiating team. Maxwell had originally been horrified when
he discovered the small amount television was paying for the
game and immediately began to use his influence to push for a
radical change in the way football was sold to the small screen. In
this Maxwell drew support from Irving Scholar, who understood
the subject better than most, and the representatives of Saatchi
and Saatchi, who were retained by the Football League on a six-
month contract following the success of the marketing campaign
at Spurs.

The competition Maxwell sought, however, simply did not
exist in negotiations for football. Since 1978, when Thames Television's Michael Grade concluded an exclusive deal for the ITV network (known as 'Snatch Of The Day') to screen League matches
and which was later overturned by the Office of Fair Trading
because of the League's failure to register the correct documenta-
tion, the two major companies in British television, ITV and BBC,
had negotiated together as a cartel. As long as the two corporations
remained solid there were no other outlets to which football could

turn for extra money. For large clubs like Liverpool, of course, sponsorship hinged on television exposure on one of the two main channels, which may have accounted for Robinson's opposition to the Maxwell strategy of open confrontation. Saatchi's advice to the League was twofold. First, the cartel must be broken and second, the true worth of the product to television, based on advertising revenues, must be worked out in depth. The company's analysts later put the value of the game to television at £6 million for the 1985–86 season.

In the past, normal practice had seen straightforward talks between the League and the two heads of sport, John Bromley of ITV and Jonathan Martin of the BBC, which normally led to a speedy conclusion, mainly because Bromley and Martin refused to compete with each other. In 1985 the new committee's first move was to refuse to meet with Bromley and Martin together, but rather invite them to put forward a tender bid for the exclusive right to televise the game. Predictably, ITV and BBC refused to bid independently, knowing that there was no other organisation which could muscle in on their traditional territory. Instead, two polite letters arrived at Lytham St Annes stating that, while they were not interested in tendering, both companies would like to sit down in the usual way to negotiate a contract. It was the first set-back of many in that fateful year.

Bromley and Martin had prepared the ground well as Irving Scholar realised. 'For years football and television have been very good for each other but I feel at the moment there is an imbalance in favour of the television companies', he said. Scholar was soon proved right. In a decision that smacked of a powerful patron teaching a greedy dependent a lesson, Bromley and Martin decided that football would disappear from the screens until such time as the League came to its senses and accepted the deal on offer. No one would miss it, the viewing figures proved that, and anyway there were any number of exciting sports waiting in the wings to fill the vacuum. Jonathan Martin put television's case. 'Football rates itself far too highly and has no God-given right to be on television. It is not our job to underwrite and subsidise the game. We don't depend on football and if it loses its slot there is no knowing if it will ever get it back.' John Bromley sang a similar song. 'League action is not the be-all and end-all of soccer on television. There is lots of other stuff we could use.' Martin was also quick to point out that over 18 million viewers watched the World Championship snooker final between Steve Davis and Dennis Taylor, more than attended an entire season of League matches. It was the first of many times this argument would be deployed, generally in the form of the oft-repeated slogan 'snooker is the most popular sport on British television'. The counter-argument, that you can only compare a World final in snooker to a similar event in football such as the World Cup or FA Cup final, and that programme for programme, football consistently attracted more viewers than any other sport including snooker, was never propounded by the football authorities. Neither did they succeed in convincing Bromley of the true value of live football to the ITV schedules.

A compromise may well have been worked out had not fate and the perennial problem of hooliganism reared their heads. The terrible fire at Bradford City, in which over 50 died, the appalling riot at an FA Cup game at Luton by Millwall fans, both captured by television cameras, and a fatality at Birmingham when a wall collapsed brought home to the public once again that football grounds were unsavoury and unsafe places to visit. But it was the 39 deaths at the European Cup final between Liverpool and Juventus of Turin at the Heysel stadium in Brussels that sickened many football supporters and dealt a terrible blow to the game's image.

It may be a harsh judgment, but football had contributed to its own demise. Hooliganism was a problem that had been worsening for many years, and there had been little positive action by the governing bodies to put matters right. The Bradford fire, like the Ibrox disaster, could have been avoided had basic safety procedures been followed. At an annual general meeting of the Football League in the wake of these developments, the main item of discussion was the size of the sponsor's logo on the shirts of players. Unbelievably, measures to combat the game's decline were not on the agenda. Not until the complete ban on English clubs taking part in European competitions was imposed by UEFA did any football authority begin to take any meaningful action to force the English game to put its house in order. In the climate created by these events, both ITV and BBC (which had screened the match from Brussels despite the deaths that had occurred before the game) became holier than thou, now claiming that football was as good as dead in the country that had invented it.

So followed one of the most traumatic periods in English League history as the new season started with no televised football. Attendances had been dropping alarmingly in the first half of the 1980s and the vast majority of League clubs carried large debts which made most of them technically insolvent. Sir Arthur South resigned from the Television Committee while Robert Maxwell, disillusioned by Heysel and the inability of any single person no matter how powerful to bring about the radical change of attitude he advocated, bowed out of the negotiations as he had in 1983. Saatchi and Saatchi's contract was not renewed. In the cumbersome world of the Football League's system of committees and sub-committees, even a seasoned operator like Maxwell had to admit defeat through the sheer frustration of it all. Some within football, notably Brian Clough, thought that the lack of television coverage would bring the crowds flocking back to League games but this view soon proved to be sadly mistaken.

In the 1980s, television has assumed a position of supreme importance to all sports. The medium can make or break an event and has infused into the public the idea that if an event is important enough for the television cameras to be present, then it is also something worth attending in person. Television can turn a live football game into an event of international significance. Indeed, the medium even enhances live games for large numbers of people who want to be able to say 'I was there'. By taking the negative approach, that television can only harm attendances, few clubs have really capitalised on the benefits that being the focus of attention can bring. Gates did not recover, in fact they slipped back further, as any analyst could have predicted.

Meanwhile another spectre appeared. If the 92 chairmen could not agree a deal, the big First Division clubs would go it alone by breaking away from the Football League to form their own 'superleague'. Then they would no longer need to be concerned with small-town teams, especially those in the Third and Fourth Divisions, which were, according to the big clubs, holding back progress by their ability to outvote the First Division when it came to general meetings of the League, the only forum where major decisions could be taken or ratified. The prime mover in the superleague discussions was Irving Scholar. One who at this time hardly knew him, but who shared his views, was David Dein.

The split had been caused by a basic conflict of interests which is inherent in a League consisting of so many members. The big names were attracting higher levels of sponsorship, commercial income and increased revenue from perimeter advertising. And the payments from television had traditionally been divided equally between the 92 clubs. This resulted in a feeling within the elite that since it was their matches that television wanted, it was bad business practice for the income derived from the small screen to subsidise small clubs who really should go to the wall if they could not survive on their own merits. After the money was divided, the income to the big clubs was negligible. What was vital to them was to maintain a presence on television to keep their profile high and the sponsorship cash rolling in. The small clubs, on the other hand, did not make large sums from sponsorship and advertising so for them the income from the small screen was a lifeline. As Douglas Alexiou, the vice-chairman of Spurs, remarked, 'I'm sure the top clubs would be magnanimous and give some of the money to the small clubs but it is essential that we keep the lion's share'. The problem for the big outfits was that numerically the small clubs were superior and would always vote to preserve the status quo.

Reaction to the threat of a breakaway on the part of the media, the fans and the players' union, led by Gordon Taylor, was generally unsympathetic to the arguments of the big clubs. Gradually it became clear that the superleague spectre had been raised to force the small clubs to agree to a restructuring of the League's voting procedure, which would leave far more power in the hands of the First and Second Divisions. At the same time the breakaway clubs wanted to change the way gate money was allocated so that the home team kept all match receipts, thereby denying the also-rans of the First Division the chance of a few big pay-days each season when they visited Old Trafford or Anfield. But most of all they desperately needed to get back on television, since the European ban was costing them dear.

Moreover, the lack of television exposure was causing rumbles of discontent from Canon, the Japanese company that had become overall sponsor of the Football League with the advent of live televised football in 1983. Meetings with ITV and BBC continued, but always ended in deadlock as positions became more and more entrenched. One meeting was over in five minutes, which led to Ken Bates calling Bromley and Martin 'the tea boys'.

By December 1985 football had been off the screens for half a season, the big clubs were getting desperate and the rumblings of discontent from Canon at the lack of exposure led many to conclude, rightly as it turned out, that the company would not renew its sponsorship at the end of the season. There could be no doubt that television now held the whip hand. Alternatives to ITV and BBC had not emerged, despite attempts by the football authorities to generate interest elsewhere. These included an approach by FA secretary Ted Croker to Cheerleader Productions, who packaged American Football for Channel 4, through his son Andrew, then an executive with the independent production company. None of these initiatives came to anything, however, and the scene was set for one of the most inglorious episodes in League history, one that would have repercussions far beyond the immediate concerns of the big clubs.

Philip Carter, who had not been elected to any official League post but had become spokesman for the First Division clubs and representative of the breakaway group, met with Bromley and Martin and on 20 December concluded a television deal for the second half of the 1985–86 season. The complete capitulation on the part of the League can be seen in the financial terms of the deal. Having already turned down £4.5 million for the whole season when the clubs voted down the original offer, Carter now had to accept a paltry £1.5 million for the remaining half season. When a two-year extension was signed the following July for £3.1 million per season, the debacle was complete. From his weak negotiating position, Carter also had to concede free access to any League game for edited highlights purposes as and when the television companies chose, yet there was no promise of a regularly scheduled highlights programme, and in fact both channels began to severely cut back their edited coverage in the mistaken belief that the television viewer only wanted to see live action. England is the only European country to have this imbalance between live and recorded programmes. In continental Europe, and in Scotland, highlights are the mainstay of football coverage. In France, if you want a live League match, you have to pay for it on the subscription channel.

The FA, which was always in a stronger position than the League because of the glamour of the FA Cup, signed a deal soon afterwards. It was Ted Croker's policy to wait until the League had agreed a deal before concluding one of his own and throughout the dispute the FA had publicly backed the League in its stance, although cracks began to appear in the relationship as the third round of the FA Cup, traditionally played in early January, approached. Eventually Croker agreed a deal worth approximately £1.5 million a year for the most prestigious domestic football competition in the world. International games would continue to be negotiated on a match by match basis. To be fair, the FA had tried to support the League as much as possible and Croker had been left in a weak position by the ineptitude of League negotiators and the in-fighting and bad publicity caused by the threatened breakaway, although he was an advocate of League reform himself. He probably achieved all that was possible given the climate at the time and the fact that the FA Cup final itself was not allowed to be sold to television on the open market: an anachronism which had persisted since the inception of ITV in the 1950s.

The trade-off between the breakaway clubs and the rest of the League was eventually agreed at the end of the 1985–86 season. In a deal hammered out by Gordon Taylor, secretary of the players' union, the big clubs would stay in the fold only if major changes in voting procedures and the number of clubs in each division were agreed by the lower division clubs. In addition, sponsorship and television money would be shared out differently, with more going to the First Division, and the Management Committee was to be changed, with president Jack Dunnett and the old guard moving aside to make way for a completely new team. The new Committee, led by Everton's chairman Philip Carter and later joined by David Dein, would seek the power to initiate major changes in the way the League operated. If all this were agreed, there would be no superleague.

The abject defeat of 1985 left some bitter resentments within English football. Unfortunately, there was little anyone could do about the situation. That would have to wait until the television contract expired at the end of the 1987–88 season. In the meantime Robert Maxwell's predictions about satellite television were nearer to being realised and deregulation was at last on the agenda. Given the problems that football had suffered, it is surprising that no one from the League bothered to send a fact-finding team to Italy or France to gather information from those countries on how they had increased their income so substantially. It was also the case that during the term of the 1985 contract television coverage on both channels became ever more focused on big clubs and live games. Weekend highlights programmes were now few and far between and some notable omissions appeared in what was supposed to be comprehensive coverage. The last Saturday of the 1986–87 season, for instance, when a third of League clubs were involved in crucial promotion, relegation and play-off matches, was completely ignored by ITV and BBC. It was symptomatic of the belief that the public only wanted to see a handful of the biggest clubs. The fact that on this particular Saturday the nation's attention was centred on Fourth Division Burnley, a small-town club with a glorious past who were in danger of dropping out of the League altogether, was entirely dismissed by television.

Then in November 1987 salvation appeared on the horizon when a new satellite service, one that had not even started transmissions, became the first-ever broadcasting body in the country to recognise the value of football to television and to back its interest with hard cash. British Satellite Broadcasting (BSB), which had been awarded the contract to launch and manage Britain's most powerful civilian communications service, the high-powered Direct Broadcast Satellite system, approached Trevor Phillips, the League's commercial director, and expressed serious interest in purchasing exclusive rights to League football. BSB was planning to introduce four new channels of which one would be devoted entirely to sports and the company was of the opinion that without football, any sports channel was a non-starter. At last a measure of competition was to be injected into the process and football would soon be wooed in a freer market. The first serious offer from BSB was presented by its chief executive Anthony Simmonds-Gooding in January 1988. The proposal included an annual payment of £5.5 million, over £2 million more than ITV and BBC were paying together.

Two days later Phillips had briefed Philip Carter, David Dein, Irving Scholar, Martin Edwards and Peter Robinson on the substance of the BSB approach. Although pleased at the breakthrough the five were not entirely satisfied with the amount on offer and asked Phillips to continue negotiations with a view to raising the price. Ten days later BSB upped its offer to £7.5 million per season, but the company wanted the contract to run for ten years. At a meeting the following day BSB proposed a radical departure from anything previously offered to football in any country. In essence the concept outlined by BSB called for the formation of a joint company, owned by the League, FA and BSB, which would produce football programmes for the new satellite company and would receive favourable consideration if it were to bid for the full BSB sports production contract, which was due to be put out to tender in the near future.

The stakes had now been significantly raised. With its own production company entirely funded by BSB, the game would at last be able to control its own product and would not even need to go out and sell the finished programmes, which would be broadcast by BSB. In addition, by bidding for the full sports production contract, football could become involved in the televising of other sports. This could lead to a new era for all British sport by creating a common institution which would pool the resources of each for the betterment of all. As the most important spectator sport by far, football's size and experience would have made it the natural leader of the enterprise. At last the prospect of independence from the traditional two channels was a realistic possibility and it looked as if 30 years of subjugation might soon be over. Even the French and Italians would have been envious of the possibilities this kind of arrangement could open up.

There was nothing altruistic in the offer made by BSB. The company was well aware that it would soon be in the midst of a cut-throat battle with both the traditional television services and its rivals in the satellite business, notably Rupert Murdoch's Sky channel. In order to become attractive to advertisers, satellite channels would have to be able to offer exclusive elements in their programming. BSB could only be received by the purchase of a dish and decoding device, both of which would have to be marketed to an already confused public and football was seen as a prime vehicle for achieving mass dish sales. With League clubs in 92 cities and towns across the country, BSB could create an instant marketing opportunity if it bought the rights to football. This meant that suddenly, lower division clubs were just as important as the big outfits, and an integral part of the BSB concept was that a wide range of teams should be televised, including those from Divisions 2, 3 and 4. At the very time when ITV and BBC were saying that no one wanted to watch these lesser lights, here was a new company proclaiming that the very opposite could provide it with the means to penetrate the mass market.

The immediate problem with the BSB offer rested on the response to it from ITV and BBC. The BSB channels would not be broadcasting until late 1989 and even then the number of receivers capable of picking up the new service's signal, and therefore the number of viewers, would be small. This created a dilemma for football. On the one hand BSB's initial market was likely to be too small for the game to maintain its mass television profile and thus might adversely affect sponsorship and advertising income; on the other BSB was prepared to put its faith and its money into televised football as a strategy to increase the number of viewers and become competitive with the terrestrial channels. While John Bromley and Jonathan Martin had spent years telling anyone who would listen how football was in decline, the positive nature of BSB's view of the game can be seen in a comment from the company's new head of sport, Andrew Croker, who said: 'I don't think we can be taken seriously as a sports channel unless we have football. Football is the biggest sport by any measure'. BSB even had an answer to the big clubs' short-term need for immediate exposure while subscribers to the satellite service built up. It was proposed that its coverage need not be exclusive to the extent that the other channels would be denied all access to League football. The company put forward the possibility of complementary scheduling, along the lines of the French arrangement, where ITV and BBC retained some football although the lion's share would go to BSB. After all, two of the ITV regional companies, Granada and Anglia, owned a stake in BSB, so there should have been little objection to the proposal in principle.

As the negotiations with BSB had been kept secret, the first meeting with ITV and BBC took place as usual on 22 February 1988 at FA headquarters in Lancaster Gate, London, with the two companies, as always, presenting a common front. No offer was made but both sides agreed to meet at a later date when the television companies had examined football's demands. These were a considerable increase in rights fees to £7 million; a guaranteed weekly highlights programme; and a maximum of ten live matches per season. BSB then proposed that some football matches, especially the big games, should be transmitted on a pay-per-view service. If approved, a proportion of the revenues from these games would go direct to the League, the FA or the clubs involved. In addition, a percentage of football-generated advertising income would also be paid to the League. This development represented the possibility of huge revenues to football as these services built up year by year. Forecasts put the possible income at £200 million over ten years, an unheard of amount in England. Against this it emerged that BSB wanted an increased number of live games, at least one per week, but was prepared to concentrate its football schedule on midweek matches to allow ITV and BBC to preserve their traditional weekend output.

BSB's revised offer was formally presented to the Football League Management Committee on 30 March by Trevor Phillips. No objections were raised. Phillips was asked to continue negotiations but was again requested to seek more money. After a flurry of meetings that went on throughout April, BSB increased its bid to £9 million per season. The full BSB proposal was unveiled to the 92 clubs at a special presentation at the Royal Lancaster Hotel in London on 12 May 1988. With show-business hype the new world of satellite television was sold to the assembled chairmen with video displays, laser lights and emotive speeches from Trevor Phillips for the League and Peter Bell for BSB. It was impressive stuff and although there were a number of questions, there was no mistaking the elation that filled the air. Months before, Irving Scholar had told us of his bitterness at the way football was treated in 1985. He was desperate for some competition and said that when the day arrived he would not be unhappy if there was 'blood on the floor', spilt by the remorseful and chastised executives of ITV and BBC. It was a contented Irving Scholar who left the hotel.

The BSB offer was now public and generated huge amounts of media coverage, most of it generally favourable. ITV and BBC had still not made any firm offer themselves, but John Bromley, when he heard that the BSB presentation would take place, hurriedly called a press conference to begin after the extravaganza at the Royal Lancaster to give the ITV reaction. Shuffling uneasily and unable to give any indication of how ITV would counter the BSB offer, Bromley's performance was a mixture of bluff, bravado and evasions, interspersed with disdainful dismissals of BSB's long-term prospects. He rejected out of hand the idea of any accommodation with the satellite company. On being informed of the negative reaction, Trevor Phillips put the case for complementary scheduling. 'As far as we are concerned', he said, 'the BSB offer does not affect the current negotiations with the BBC and ITV. The contract runs out at the end of this season and we are ready to sign a new one with them as soon as terms are agreed'.

The first rumblings of discontent came at a meeting of the big five clubs and Trevor Phillips at Old Trafford in May. Their worry was that BSB's finances were not totally secure and that anyway its audience would be so small that the clubs' income from sponsorship would take a nose-dive, especially since ITV and BBC were refusing to co-operate in the complementary scheduling scheme. Littlewoods, the sponsors of the League Cup, were also rumoured to have expressed reservations. According to David Dein there were 'inherent flaws in an association with BSB. They were not fully capitalised, there was no guarantee that they would sell dishes and they wouldn't give a satisfactory financial guarantee'. The ideal of a spread of football across all channels was receding fast. Perhaps the unease also centred on the fact that this was only the first shot in a war that had been predicted for some time between terrestrial and satellite television, and suddenly the issues had become far bigger than they had ever been. It was nothing less than the start of the struggle for control of British television. What few had foreseen, but would have realised had they looked at their continental neighbours, was that the first battle would be fought over the rights to screen football.

In spite of these misgivings, Trevor Phillips was mandated to take negotiations with BSB to the point of an agreed contract to be put to the vote by the 92 clubs. Meanwhile the pressure on the cartel was beginning to take its toll. The BBC, strapped for cash and having to defend itself from the advocates of broadcasting reform, could not compete financially with either ITV or the new satellite services, so the corporation began to move towards a position of reconciliation. ITV, however, could not afford to lose the first round of such a public fight against the satellites. The issue was too big to be left to the sports departments so John Bromley was quietly moved to the side-lines while the big guns were rolled out. They were led by Greg Dyke, an Australian who had played a prominent role in the revolution in Australian broadcasting brought about by Kerry Packer in the 1970s, which was fought over the rights to screen cricket. Dyke was now head of programmes at London Weekend Television but was also chairman of the Network Committee, which had overall responsibility for programming acquired on behalf of the entire ITV network, and occupied the same position on the Sports Sub-Committee. Dyke had been brought in specifically to beat off the challenge of the satellites, in his own words to 'strangle the satellite threat at birth', and prepare London Weekend for the expected Government measures to deregulate the television industry. It was vitally important, therefore, that Dyke got off to a winning start. Some time in early June David Dein rang Greg Dyke and a meeting was arranged. Dyke reasoned that television could achieve its required football audience from the top five or ten clubs. By offering them alone an amount close to the BSB bid, he could accomplish two initial objectives. First, financially, it was an offer the clubs could hardly refuse, and second, it would drive a wedge in the solidarity the 92 clubs were showing towards the BSB proposal. When Dyke outlined his ideas, Dein called Irving Scholar.

Greg Dyke and John Bromley met with Dein, Scholar, Martin Edwards, John Smith, Peter Robinson and Jim Greenwood of Everton at a restaurant in Knightsbridge on 16 June. They were joined later by Philip Carter. The representatives of ITV spent a good amount of time rubbishing BSB and its plans and exhorting the football people to stay with ITV. The BSB road, according to Dyke and Bromley, would limit the big clubs' power by extending television coverage to the whole League rather than the elite. Irving Scholar complained about the cartel. John Bromley denied that it existed but was brushed aside by Dyke who was only too ready to admit what was an obvious reality. Scholar pressed home his advantage by telling the television men to make an offer. Dyke and Bromley excused themselves from the table and talked earnestly for ten minutes. When they returned Dyke told the five clubs that ITV would offer them, but not the whole League, an exclusive deal, worth £1 million a year to each of them. A further £2 million was available to another five clubs which the 'big five' would help ITV to select. Dyke's thinking now centred on two points. First, he was convinced that there was bound to be a superleague at some point and ITV was interested in becoming its sponsor. In fact, a memo from Dyke later came to light which referred to the 'ITV Superleague'. Second, by wooing the top clubs alone he could increase their income without having to top the BSB bid in cash terms.

A few days later a second meeting took place, at which the big five were joined by Aston Villa and Newcastle United, whose chairman, Gordon McKeag, had been elected to the Management Committee in preference to Bobby Charlton at the June AGM. The seven soon became the 'big ten' as West Ham, Sheffield Wednesday and Nottingham Forest were invited to become parties to the talks. When Trevor Phillips briefed the Management Committee on the state of negotiations with BSB at Lancaster Gate on 20 June, three members of the Committee including the president, Philip Carter, were secretly talking to Greg Dyke about a deal for the big ten clubs alone, yet none of them made their conflict of interest known to the full Management Committee. The offer Dyke had made went against the very principle of collective action that underpinned the basis of the League's existence – that any arrangement which would affect the whole of football should be decided by the whole of football. With regard to television this principle meant that any deal should be negotiated by the League as a whole and no individual club could or should alter the process.

Although ITV had made its approach, John Bromley still attended a meeting with Jonathan Martin and the League on 21 June as if nothing had changed. Greg Dyke had effectively broken the cartel agreement at the lunch with the big five clubs, yet here was Bromley still maintaining the fiction of joint negotiations. The next day Trevor Phillips, whose delicate series of negotiations had brought the League to the strongest position it had ever enjoyed with regard to television, received word at his Wembley office of the secret ITV offer. Phillips found the situation almost unbelievable. For the first time English football had the opportunity to control its own destiny yet here was a small group of clubs who were prepared to put it all in jeopardy through what he saw as narrow self-interest.

Events now began to move quickly. On 23 June the BBC finally disowned the cartel in a letter to the League. Four days later ITV publicly announced its offer. The ten clubs now involved were based on the biggest teams in each of the catchment areas of the regional ITV companies and these were the only teams ITV wanted to screen. Under this arrangement, ITV was now willing to pay £10 million per season for a four-year deal, all the money going to the big ten. Greg Dyke said: 'We are prepared to pay big money for the clubs people want to see'. The same day, after repeated questioning, Philip Carter and David Dein finally admitted their involvement to the Management Committee, to the fury of the other members, particularly Ron Noades, chairman of Crystal Palace, who saw the negotiations with ITV as a complete betrayal. Another member of the Committee, David Bulstrode, chairman of Queens Park Rangers, saw the actions of Carter, Dein and McKeag as dishonourable: 'It was ITV's right to negotiate separately but I guess if I had gone to the first meeting of the clubs involved I would have felt it my duty to report back to the Management Committee'.

The fact that the ITV offer was being made to ten clubs only also infuriated the rest of the League. If the ten signed with ITV the value of their own product would be undermined. When Liverpool and Everton publicly supported the ITV bid it provoked an outcry that soon led to a bitter split within the ranks of the League. With nothing in the ITV deal for them, the majority of League clubs wanted the BSB offer to be accepted, while the big ten seemed mesmerised by the money being offered to them by ITV. It emerged in early July that the original five clubs approached by ITV would now receive £600,000 each per season plus £150,000 for every televised home game. The remaining five would receive £500,000, plus £50,000 per match. If Dyke's aim was to divide and conquer, he could not have been more successful.

The month of July saw Trevor Phillips criss-crossing the country visiting more hotels than an Egon Ronay inspector in an attempt to preserve the unity of the League. Then the BBC, which did not have to compete with the satellite service for advertising revenue, decided to throw in its lot with BSB and began to work on a complementary schedule and a plan for sharing costs. The same day a meeting was held between Greg Dyke and the big ten, at which the clubs agreed to proceed unilaterally to an agreement with ITV, no matter what the rest of the League decided. In this scenario, the big ten would either have to take the League to court to challenge the rules which state that the Management Committee and the full 92 clubs must sanction contracts any club makes with television or go it alone in a new version of the superleague.

The next Management Committee meeting in Plymouth got underway in a farcical manner as the president, Philip Carter, along with David Dein and Gordon McKeag, were excluded from the discussions by the remaining members of the Committee, who were incensed at the dual role played by the three. Five hours of discussion followed with no apparent outcome, whereupon the meeting was adjourned. During the hiatus players' union leader Gordon Taylor was contacted at his home in Lancashire and asked if he would drive the 400 miles to Plymouth as soon as possible and use whatever influence he had to resolve what now looked like a terminal split. 'What hadn't been foreseen', Taylor remarked, 'was that when we broke up the television cartel, any loser in that cartel would turn round and try to break up the League.' The meeting at Plymouth broke up with a compromise suggestion put together by Trevor Phillips and Gordon Taylor to the effect that the BSB money could be split differently to give the top clubs an even larger proportion than that agreed in 1985.

Trevor Phillips was now in the awkward position of having to carry out his mandate by continuing negotiations with BSB, who did not take the ITV tactics lying down. In fact the satellite company increased the money it was prepared to pay to £11 million a season. Meanwhile, Robert Maxwell, now chairman of Derby County, took out an injunction against the top five clubs to stop them from concluding a deal with ITV. Reactions from both fans and media to events were hostile to the big clubs' actions in what was, after all, the League's centenary season. Carter, Dein and McKeag were severely criticised for representing the League on the Management Committee negotiating with BSB and at the same time involving themselves in direct talks with ITV. David Bulstrode, who had arrived at Queens Park Rangers amid accusations that, as a property developer, he was only interested in football for the redevelopment potential of certain London stadia, became a vociferous defender of the integrity of the League. On one of the few occasions he went public with his thoughts, he was moved to say: 'The whole thing has been motivated by greed and self-preservation. People feel let down, that those they regarded as their colleagues have gone behind their backs. The call of Judas has been heard. Pieces of silver have been rattled'. It is fair to say that Bulstrode's stand in the television war considerably enhanced his standing within the game, and when he suddenly died of a heart attack some months later, the eulogies were effusive in their praise for his efforts during this grim period.

The barrage of criticism, coupled with the less than clear legal position after the injunctions were granted slowly began to force the top clubs towards some kind of compromise, although the hard-line opposition to BSB continued. Urgent talks took place with Greg Dyke to find an accommodation short of a split which might backfire in the courts. Meanwhile, armed with the new distribution arrangement of BSB monies, Gordon Taylor attempted to talk the big ten round at a meeting at Old Trafford on 12 July. After an eight-hour marathon Philip Carter emerged to claim that there was no intention on the part of the ten to split from the League, although the possibility of a reduced premier division remained. The same day Greg Dyke upped the ITV offer to £11 million a season and agreed to include the remaining 82 clubs. The extra money would go to clubs in the lower divisions.

The leap-frogging in the money bids continued apace as BSB increased its offer to £12 million a season for ten seasons plus pay-per-view and advertising revenue contributions. The proposal cut no ice with the original five, however. They had already decided that they must remain with ITV. It was a short-term (though admittedly lucrative) position to adopt given ITV's poor record in its presentation of the game. By now it was clear that the big ten would refuse to allow their games to go to BSB no matter what the rest of the League wanted, or indeed how it voted. Given this the remaining clubs would have little to sell and so cracks began to appear in the opposition to ITV. John Poynton, chairman of Coventry City, who had emerged as the unofficial spokesman for the 82 clubs, indicated that if ITV dealt with the League's official negotiators rather than the chairmen of a few clubs, the 82 might be prepared to support the ITV bid.

The scene was now set for a meeting of the League on 15 July at the Cumberland Hotel in London. This occasion saw the first official approach by Greg Dyke to the League, when he met Lee Walker for breakfast. The big ten were politely asked not to attend. As the chairmen met in groups at breakfast and in the lobby to discuss earnestly the latest developments and plan strategy, David Dein and Martin Edwards appeared as if from nowhere, looked round briefly to observe their fellow chairmen then, as Ken Bates began to bear down on them, stepped smartly through the lobby, into the lift and closed the doors before a public confrontation ensued. It emerged that the two had been invited to put the ITV case. Before the meeting the mood was one of defiance and support for BSB with almost total opposition to ITV, although the meeting had been called ostensibly to examine the merits of both deals. Ron Noades, chairman of Crystal Palace and a Second Division representative on the Management Committee, said of the Old Trafford Carter declaration: 'There was nobody in Manchester who had the authority to negotiate any television deal at all. I am totally against any group of clubs negotiating individually with television and then carrying on negotiations for others as well'. The meeting ended with a vote of support for the BSB-BBC deal, with a final decision to be taken at the extraordinary general meeting scheduled for 8 August.

Greg Dyke and the big ten used the interim period to woo, persuade and coerce the rest of the First Division to accept the ITV offer. BSB would not get any viewers they said. Sponsorship would dry up, football would become marginalised on a minority channel, with a few sops going to the BBC. The pressure was most intense on clubs like Wimbledon and Millwall who had fought hard as small outfits to get into the First Division. In Millwall's case, the club had waited for over 100 years for the right to face the Liverpools and Arsenals and now they saw it disappearing before their very eyes. At a meeting at Villa Park on 19 July the First Division clubs voted to reject the BSB offer and accept the ITV deal – a complete turnaround from the way they had voted four days earlier. As the bitterness continued, a motion of no confidence in Carter and Dein was put forward. It was clear that the smaller clubs felt they had been forced into the ITV deal, but that Carter and Dein would have to answer for their actions. The motion was to be presented by David Evans, chairman of Luton Town, who had been thrown out of the Littlewoods Cup at the behest of the Management Committee because of the club's ban on away supporters. Ron Noades expressed the feeling of many small clubs: 'All my life I have watched football take the short-term option and grab whatever money is on the table instead of taking the long-term view of what is best for football – and that is exactly what is happening again now'.

Although the Second, Third and Fourth Divisions tried to rally support for the BSB bid, the writing was clearly on the wall once the First Division had agreed to plump for ITV. Crisis meetings took place at BSB where a new strategy was devised. On the one hand a short public relations campaign was implemented to the effect that BSB was fighting back and would soon come up with an improved offer. It was even suggested that one of BSB's main shareholders, Richard Branson, boss of the Virgin group, was taking a personal hand in preparing the new bid. On the other hand the satellite company secretly decided to pursue a separate deal with the FA and the BBC for FA Cup and international matches. On 2 August the satellite company pulled out of the now crumbling deal with the League, having already signed its contract with the FA.

The withdrawal of BSB left the League in the embarrassing position of being back with only one bidder for its product. Six days later, after more wrangling over the distribution of money which was only resolved when Gordon Taylor agreed to take a cut in the percentage automatically paid to the players' union, the ITV deal, £11 million a year over four years, was accepted and League football was now to be screened exclusively on ITV. In many ways the popular FA Cup package represented a better prospect than League matches despite the smaller number of games. In his headlong rush to deal with the top clubs Greg Dyke had overlooked the fact that the clubs had no rights over the televising of FA Cup matches, which were handled by the FA. The acquisition of these FA-controlled games gave BSB and BBC some consolation for the loss of League action. Perhaps even more important the FA, exasperated by the performance of the League, agreed to allow BSB to show some foreign football, the mainstay of which would be Scottish, something it had resisted for years. This concession could prove to be a decision that will one day come back to haunt the League.

The behaviour of Philip Carter and David Dein has been subject to much analysis in the period since the events took place but the main issues are that they, as members of the Management Committee, used their positions to promote ITV and subvert BSB without informing anyone of their interest until after they had committed themselves, and that the support they gave to the ITV bid was based on what was good for their own clubs rather than what was good for the League as a whole. When David Dein first approached Greg Dyke and the response was positive, in normal circumstances it would have been expected that he would act in concert with the rest of the football establishment. But these were not normal times. The League had become a dangerously split and factionalised organisation, as had the Management Committee, and its ability to take sensible decisions for the good of the whole game was seriously in doubt. This situation had developed since the squabbles leading to the reorganisation of 1986, which had left so much bitterness that little could be accomplished within the League without intrigues and cries of betrayal. It had been fuelled by the television blackout and the threats of a superleague, by wrangling over restructuring and voting procedures and by a split along divisional lines which meant that policy was now decided in divisional meetings, which held no official status within the League.

As he considered his position Dein realised that taking anything to a Management Committee that was already beginning to fall apart would be fatal. He remembered the difficulties over the move to London. He remembered the time he had tried to reach a compromise between the Management Committee and Robert Maxwell when the latter tried to buy Watford, and had been rebuffed. He could see the dreadful state of the organisation of the League's centenary season. There was finally an incident in 1987 when Blackburn Rovers played host to Chelsea in a play-off game. Dein proposed that the match be relayed to London on closed circuit television in order to deter the notoriously violent Chelsea supporters from travelling. Dein recounted what happened when he put the idea to Blackburn's chairman Bill Fox, who was also a member of the Management Committee. 'Bill Fox asked me, "What's in it for Blackburn? We are going to lose the Chelsea support. What about the programmes I would lose? What about my meat pies?" I said, meat pies! What about the town of Blackburn? What about the benefit of the game? Why don't we wake up in the morning and smell the coffee? Are we worried about another thousand pounds because of the meat pies and programmes you're going to sell?' In the event, the match went ahead without closed circuit television.

In such a situation Dein can perhaps be forgiven for wanting to play his cards close to his chest. There was somewhat less of an excuse for Philip Carter, who was after all president of the Football League. Irving Scholar, Martin Edwards and John Smith, who were not members of the Committee, could sit on the side-lines while Carter and Dein took the flak. No wonder serving on the Committee was such 'purgatory' for David Dein.

In their public statements both Dein and Carter sought to establish that the way they had conducted themselves during the negotiations had been honourable as well as profitable. In defence of the two beleaguered Committee members Irving Scholar pointed to the immediate exposure ITV could offer and to the fact that BSB was, as yet, an unproven service. Scholar received support from an unusual quarter some months later when American entrepreneur Ted Turner, the doyen of satellite broadcasters, forecast doom for the satellite industry in the UK. 'The first terrible mistake over there', he said, 'is the simultaneous launch of two projects [Sky and BSB] with incompatible receiving systems. It is crazy, absolutely insane, and I believe that both parties are going to be haemorrhaging red ink for a very long time.' The arguments obviously cut no ice with the League chairmen, however, as both Carter and Dein were thrown off the Management Committee at the next available opportunity in December 1988. The vote was succinctly explained by Jack Dunnett, now reinstated as president, when he said, 'You can't wear two hats'. As he walked from the meeting which dismissed him and was about to be interviewed by a television news crew, a passing bird deposited its mess on David Dein's expensive suit. Eyeing it, Dein was heard to remark: 'That's not birdshit! That's the Second Division chairmen for you'.

The way in which the negotiations were handled dealt a dreadful blow to the game's stature in its centenary year. In all the public statements any obligations the chairmen might have had to supporters were never mentioned. Nor was any debate ever instituted on the standards of television coverage which had fallen so far behind those on the continent or the way in which television could serve the game. The chief consideration had been money. ITV still had access to any game it liked for highlights purposes but once again no highlights programme was guaranteed, indeed the half-time interval during live matches was extended so that ITV could show all the previous day's First Division goals, which were dealt with in barely five minutes. The very public money-grabbing also prompted the Government to remark that with such an increase in prosperity, the argument the League was putting forward against the proposed national membership scheme, namely, that the cost was too high, was nonsense. It has never been acknowledged by those in football that their public rows during the television war severely damaged their credibility in the great debate that would soon come to the fore over the membership scheme.

With the ITV deal signed Greg Dyke moved on to other things, but before he left he issued instructions to the producers at ITV to come up with a new, exciting format. Thus 'The Match', ITV's new concept for televised football, was born, with more cameras and more resources generally devoted to the operation. Despite this, ITV's advertisers were less than enamoured with the new deal, claiming that the viewing figures did not justify the ballyhoo. Bob Hunter of BSB said, 'ITV appear to have scored an expensive own goal'. Ratings for the early programmes seemed to bear out these views, although the figures began to pick up as the season progressed, with over 10 million households watching at least part of the Liverpool–Arsenal Championship decider on the last day of the season in 1989 and Greg Dyke claiming that ratings were 'up 20 per cent' on 1988. One bonus for armchair fans was the time devoted to the FA Cup by the BBC, which now screened highlights of rounds one and two for the first time and in later rounds put out three programmes over each FA Cup weekend. The ITV deal may have eventually encompassed the whole League financially but as the first season of 'The Match' reached its conclusion it was clear that when it came actually to choosing which games to screen, the television network was sticking almost entirely to the big ten. Eight First Division clubs were not featured at all and Norwich, who led the table for long periods, were shown only twice, in away matches against Millwall and Arsenal. The producer of 'The Match', Jeff Foulser, said that there was a 'gentlemen's agreement to put the big clubs on television'. In a letter to John Poynton, chairman of Coventry, who had been very critical of the selection policy, Dyke wrote: 'The evidence of viewing figures for this season shows quite clearly that the viewing public wishes to see the more glamorous clubs. Having paid £11 million for the contract my job is to maximise the audience and that is what I intend to do'.

At the end of the 1988–89 season, there were calls for a new distribution of ITV money. Ron Noades said when advocating the idea: 'Television has no right to decide the balance of power on the pitch by virtue of the payment it makes. ITV do not have the right to dictate where football's resources go'. Greg Dyke outlined the possible consequences of such a move: 'If the League were unable to deliver either the television rights of the clubs we wish to cover, or sufficient of their matches, then clearly the contract would be null and void'. The matter came up in the wake of the disaster at Hillsborough, which seemed a little insensitive to say the least, and prompted David Lacey to write in the *Guardian*: 'It [a meeting of First and Second Division clubs at which the redistribution was discussed] sounded like one of those Big Power conferences which took place towards the end of the last war when a few lines drawn casually across a map of central Europe would settle the fates of millions while the armies were still in combat. Almost every other day, it seems, a bright new scheme is hatched in the fertile mind of Ron Noades, the League Management Committee's Chiang Kai-shek . . . Some clubs still do not seem to have cottoned on to the fact that the most powerful man in English football is Greg Dyke . . . who has become both paymaster and ringmaster'. No one from football seemed to think it was worth the effort to criticise the television companies for refusing to screen the European Champions' Cup final live. In 1989 ITV took one of the best performances in the history of the Cup and reduced it to 33 minutes of edited highlights. Every other European country took the game live and treated it as a major event. This was the third year running that the main British television networks had not shown the game live and the full impact of the spectacular display by Milan was missed.

Although the money the English League now earns from television is substantially greater than before, with First Division clubs receiving a minimum of £200,000 compared to £65,000 under the old deal, it must be said that the way the negotiations were conducted reflected no credit on the vast majority of football chairmen. And the same increase wrung out of ITV could have been achieved with BSB, which had offered a deal to the whole League rather than to the elite alone. Against this the view that BSB may not succeed and that ITV offered money and security is equally acceptable. Those forecasting difficult times for satellite television were proved right to some extent during 1989 as sales of Sky dishes proved slow and BSB announced that it had not completely secured manufacturing arrangements for its distinctive dish known as the squarial and would postpone the start of its transmissions. And it is certainly the case that if the chairmen of the original five had acted within the rules and urged ITV to deal through League channels, it is unlikely that both deals could have been judged on their merits in a calmer, less public atmosphere.

The ultimate result of it all is that the game is still in thrall to traditional television, with no input into scheduling and presentation and no guarantee whatsoever of highlights programmes. There is none of the increased awareness and independence that exists in France, Germany, Italy, Spain or Scotland, where competition has been used to broaden rather than lessen the spread of televised football using a variety of formats. Instead of using the radical BSB offer to force ITV and BBC into a compromise, the game was seduced by short-term cash benefits. Instead of assuming control over their product the game's leaders have once again handed over everything to ITV. Instead of getting into satellite television from the start, becoming the flagship of its sports channel, the League is once again left out in the cold. It was as if a window of opportunity had at last appeared which could have enabled English football to move to a situation such as that enjoyed by the NFL. But being unable to agree amongst themselves, the clubs let the opportunity slip by and have put all their eggs in one basket.

The sorry performance of the English administration had surfaced again just as it did when Chelsea were refused permission to enter the first Champions' Cup over 30 years before. The lack of objectivity inherent in the unwieldy structure of the League had finally made it impossible to put the collective interest of the organisation before that of its own clubs. As for leadership and vision, these qualities were notable only by their absence.

David Dein's parting shot revealed some of the bitterness. 'What other employer', he said, 'fires a man who has just brought him £44 million?'. The episode had confirmed to him and to Irving Scholar that they should not be compromised again. By putting their own clubs first they thought they were doing all they could for the game by providing a national showcase for the best in English football. Subsequent developments showed that this belief was naïve at best and thus the issue of superleagues in the UK and the rest of Europe remain central to the two men's thinking. They now more than ever believe that Arsenal and Spurs have more in common with AC Milan and Bordeaux than with Coventry and Wimbledon.

8
IN A LEAGUE OF THEIR OWN

If a house be divided against itself, that house cannot stand

MARK
Chapter 3 Verse 25

In early August 1984 a suffering Irving Scholar hobbled into the Saatchi and Saatchi office on Charlotte Street in London's West End, his discomfort stemming from ligament trouble sustained when he failed to get out of the way of an ill-timed journalist's boot while playing football for a Spurs XI against a team from the gentlemen of the press. It would not be the last time that Scholar fell foul of the fourth estate, although it is debatable whether the physical injury was anything like as painful as the biting words fashioned by the pen which would be his lot in the days and months to come.

Scholar had been invited to be the chief speaker at the annual lunch which launches the *Rothmans Football Yearbook* and had gone to Saatchi's for a first-hand account of the advertising strategy used by the agency in the Spurs marketing campaign. The Tottenham chairman had only recently returned from Monaco to live in England and in the year since the take-over had been something of an absentee landlord, keeping in touch with the club from his tax haven while Douglas Alexiou and Paul Bobroff controlled day-to-day affairs. So although he had approved Saatchi's campaign from the principality his direct knowledge of the thinking behind it was limited. Thus the discussions turned to one of Scholar's signings of the previous season, Mrs Ridlington, a grandmother from East London. Mrs Ridlington was one of several life-long Spurs fans featured in the television and radio campaign that Saatchi's had designed to boost gates by encouraging supporters to believe they were all an essential part of the club.

The conversation, however, soon turned from the parochialism of advertising Spurs to the method by which similar principles could be applied to the whole of football. What Saatchi's outlined at that meeting was to have a profound effect on Scholar's thinking and would eventually exert a powerful influence on all aspects of the English game, leading to a major schism within the Football League and the real possibility of the demise of the oldest League competition in the world.

The vision outlined to Scholar rested on the concept of the 'event-like nature' of football games, unashamedly borrowed from the NFL in America. The main thrust of the Saatchi argument was that the currency of the game had been devalued by over-exposure, that English football had destroyed its scarcity value by playing too many matches in too many competitions, many of them spurious. Unlike American Football, which was both a live event and a television spectacular, League football in England was fast becoming a non-event. In this scheme of things, Liverpool versus Manchester United is an event of national importance whereas Liverpool versus Charlton Athletic is not. Further down the League, Peterborough versus Cambridge United, a derby match, is an event of local significance but Peterborough versus Tranmere Rovers is not. Recognition of this could facilitate viable restructuring of the League on the pyramid principle. At its base would be regional matches in Divisions 3 and 4, which could lead to an increase in the overall size of the League. Above this level would be National Division 2 and a First or Premier Division of between ten and 18 clubs. At all levels the reduced number of games with promotion and relegation play-offs occupying a central role would mean that every game became important, an event. At the apex of the pyramid would be the national team and a recognition that the performance of the England team affects spectator interest throughout football. As he staggered along Charlotte Street to look for a taxi, Irving Scholar had far more on his mind than the contents of a speech.

Restructuring of the Football League was something that had been on the agenda for some time. For at least five years the top five English clubs had been making known their feelings that the small clubs of the lower divisions were holding them back, particularly in such matters as the sharing of television revenues and match receipts or the 75 per cent majority needed for changes in League rules. The big clubs thought that the influence the small clubs could command was out of all proportion to their importance in the game. Before long these feelings had developed into some specific proposals, namely, a reduction in the three-quarters majority needed for rule changes to two-thirds; changes to the structure of the Management Committee which had been based on regional representation since 1975 and which, by 1985, contained four First Division representatives out of ten and only one from the big five; and rearrangement of the League's finances in a number of crucial areas, notably television and sponsorship income and the 4 per cent tax levied by the League on gate receipts which was redistributed to subsidise the smaller clubs. The man at the heart of these moves was Philip Carter, the chairman of Everton.

Carter had been involved in restructuring talks since at least 1981 when he hosted a meeting of six First Division chairmen at Goodison Park to discuss ideas. The philosophy was clear: sponsors, advertisers and television were only interested in football because of the participation of the big clubs, yet the share-out of income from these sources did not reflect this reality. The meeting resulted in a decision to sound out the rest of the First Division and the Second Division clubs on the prospect of radical changes. There could be no mistaking the intention. The big clubs were prepared to break away from the League to form a superleague if changes were not forthcoming. They did not have it all their own way, however. There was considerable opposition from the media and from within the game, led by Ron Noades, chairman of Crystal Palace and Gordon Taylor, secretary of the players' union, who said that in the event of any superleague his members would push for total freedom of contract, which would mean the end of any transfer payment when a player reached the end of his contract.

The debate came to a head in 1983, at the same time as live football was being conceded to television. The big clubs were still threatening to go their own way if the rest of the League did not agree to their demands, and the arguments coincided with the publication of a report by Sir Norman Chester on the restructuring of football, the second such report Sir Norman had delivered to the League – the first had been shelved in 1968. In fact there was rumoured to be a special shelf in a dingy cupboard at Lytham St Annes, the Sir Norman Chester Shelf, where reports calling for anything at all progressive were dumped, consigned to oblivion in the dust of 100 years of procrastination. Among the 18 points of its conclusion the second Chester report recommended that the First Division be reduced to 20 clubs with regionally based lower divisions; it promoted the reduction of the majority needed for rule changes to two-thirds and suggested that home clubs should retain all match receipts. Of these, the only measure actually implemented was the one concerning gate receipts, which was approved by the annual general meeting in 1983. This change, of course, helped the big clubs to become richer and accentuated a growing divide between large and small clubs. If the example of the NFL had been strictly followed, this would not have happened. American Football is structured to achieve competitive balance and gate receipts are split 60–40 in favour of the home team. Indeed, 90 per cent of NFL income is shared. NFL spokesman Dick Maxwell explained the philosophy: 'Equality has been the key to the growth of the League'.

Philip Carter stood against the incumbent Jack Dunnett in the elections for president in 1984 on a platform calling for the restructuring of the Management Committee, but the popular Dunnett, chairman of Second Division Notts County, won by 35 votes to 17. The defeat presaged a more bitter fight, however, which would only be resolved, in the wake of the disastrous television negotiations of 1985, when Carter was elevated to the presidency. In 1983, though, the rebels, under intense media pressure, pulled back from the idea of a breakaway, more because such a move was full of practical difficulties that no one had properly addressed than because there was any renewed commitment to the League. It was commonly assumed that the big five were bought off by the television agreement of 1983 and the arrival of League sponsorship in the shape of a three-year agreement with the Japanese company Canon.

The television blackout and the appalling events involving supporters in 1985 caused Irving Scholar to reflect deeply on what he had been told by Saatchi and Saatchi. Here at last was a plan which encompassed the practicalities necessary to implement the superleague, even though the Saatchi concept was actually based on an increase in the size of the League and not a breakaway. However, Scholar felt that there would be a complete lack of support within the League for this kind of restructuring and believed the big clubs were being pushed towards a superleague. Scholar quickly brought in the rest of the big five and Saatchis were asked to produce a detailed report. In fact the agency produced two discussion documents, the first of which outlined three possible scenarios of restructuring, two involving the existing Football League but with the emphasis placed on the remaining option, a breakaway superleague of ten clubs playing each other four times a season along the lines of the Scottish Premier Division. This League would be a self-perpetuating oligarchy based on a franchise system of history, status, facilities and size of crowds.

After a meeting at Old Trafford at the end of September the five went public. The story was broken by Jeff Powell in the *Daily Mail* on 1 October 1985 under the headline 'SuperLeague rebellion!'. Powell wrote: 'It is the hardening conviction of leading chairmen that only drastic action can rescue the long-term future of the major professional game from the economic crisis following the Brussels and Bradford disasters'. The Saatchi plans for a ten-club league had by now been revised to include a number of possible options, the most popular figures for the size of any superleague being 12 and 18. Although only the big five were directly involved at this stage they correctly surmised that if they gave a lead, other clubs would scramble over each other to become involved. But even the big five could not have imagined the numbers eventually reaching 44!

The impetus for the 1985 push towards a superleague had been sparked by a nose-dive in the finances of all clubs. While most were virtually insolvent and two, Wolverhampton Wanderers and Swansea City, were in imminent danger of going out of business altogether, even the large clubs were suffering from a combination of the European ban, the lack of television exposure and income and the consequence of these events, a dramatic fall in spectators. For Irving Scholar, the duties of running a public company meant that shareholders' interests, rather than those of supporters, were paramount and gates at Spurs games were down by 24 per cent in the first part of the 1985–86 season. Scholar, the only chairman who was willing to be publicly interviewed about his commitment to a breakaway, said: 'Had the Chester recommendations been adopted, football would not . . . be facing its most testing time this century . . . If we continue without modification designed to promote the best in entertainment, standards and facilities, then the future and the outlook for our sport will continue to decline'. Sir Norman Chester himself told the press, 'A breakaway would be good for the game'.

The next few days were full of press speculation about clubs rushing headlong to join the superleaguers. Little space, however, was devoted to the possible fate of those First Division clubs not included in the superleague's plans, such as Birmingham City, Queens Park Rangers and Leicester City, all of whom had, at various points in the recent past, thrilled lovers of the game through the skills of home-grown players such as Trevor Francis, Clive Allen and Gary Lineker.

The response from Lytham St Annes was characterised by almost total consternation. In the days of Alan Hardaker a vigorous counter-offensive could have been expected, but Hardaker's successor, Graham Kelly, was more quiet administrator than provocative spokesman, so for the moment the League followed the path of least resistance, and Kelly put his faith in the League's creaking machinery to somehow come up with a compromise. At a Management Committee meeting on 15 October it was decided to try to head off the breakaway by offering First Division clubs the prospect of more power when it came to votes and a larger slice of League income. After the meeting Jack Dunnett and Peter Robinson appeared before the press seemingly united on the changes that needed to be made. Rumblings of disagreement were not far from the surface, however. Ian Jones, chairman of Doncaster Rovers, said after the same meeting: 'It's a question of whether the top clubs can survive their difficulties caused by television and other matters in the way we have had to for many years'. An indication of the difficulties ahead emerged when an anonymous spokesman for the big five commented, 'The Management Committee are nowhere near the answer. All they've come up with is the Chester Report, three years too late. Things have moved on. I can't think of any way they can come up with what we want, which is total control of our own affairs'.

One of the first notes of disapproval came a few days after the first announcement of the breakaway from Danny Blanchflower, the inspiration behind the great Spurs side of the 1960s. Writing in the *Sunday Express* Blanchflower addressed the question of how the members of any superleague would be decided. 'On previous occasions when this was discussed', he remarked, referring to an earlier incarnation of the superleague concept in the 1970s, 'Wolves were in the top six, Derby County were nearing the Championship, Leeds at the peak of their success, Aston Villa in the Third Division and Manchester United in Division 2.' Blanchflower went on to castigate the League for its stance in the television negotiations, then put the case for the supporter: 'And what about the fans, the guys that count? What can they believe when they read about all this ducking and weaving by big clubs and television and football officials? How could people like that produce a superleague?' Blanchflower was making a serious point. Despite opinions that this development was wanted by the fans, no one had bothered to find out what their true feelings actually were, indeed the formation of the Football Supporters' Association as an independent body in response to the 1985 disasters was generally shunned by both clubs and the League. It was becoming increasingly clear that the rhetoric of chairmen claiming that breakaway or restructuring would be good for the game was masking the real reasons, money and power.

Events moved on to a meeting of the First and Second Division chairmen at the Mount Royal Hotel in London on 12 November. There had been, in the intervening month, a recognition by many smaller clubs that change would have to be conceded. It was pointed out, for instance, that a club like Brentford, which had not appeared once on television during the previous contract, received exactly the same income, £25,000, as Manchester United, who had been screened 18 times. The purpose of the Mount Royal meeting was to see whether change could be accommodated within the League and whether the threat of a breakaway could be avoided. The day before the meeting it was announced that gates at English League matches were down by half a million on the previous season, with First Division attendances down by a staggering 347,603, fully 60 per cent of the total decline. During the same period, crowds in the Fourth Division, which according to everybody provided games no one wanted to see, actually increased by 15,000. The overall deficit represented a loss of £2 million in revenue.

Before the Mount Royal meeting the First Division superleaguers put their demands forward and voted to break away if their proposals were not accepted by the rest of the League. In essence, the Second Division would have to give up some of its power and influence for the League to stay together. The Second Division, however, led by the redoubtable Ron Noades, was not prepared to simply roll over and came back with some compromise proposals. Instead of a reduced First Division and an increased Second the status quo should remain. Sponsorship money should be split 55–45 instead of the 70–30 advocated by the elite. Votes should remain at one per club instead of each First Division club having two votes, as the big five wanted. The First Division, led by Philip Carter, Martin Edwards and Irving Scholar, rejected the proposals totally and the meeting broke down, deadlocked on all points but one. The Third and Fourth Divisions would be chopped from a new superleague within the League. At a meeting at Saatchi's that month Scholar asked the assembled advertising executives if they knew how many teams he now had in his superleague. 'Twelve?' 'Fourteen?' 'Eighteen?' suggested the Saatchi people. 'No,' beamed the Spurs chairman, 'we have forty-four'.

The day after the Mount Royal disaster Gordon Taylor issued a statement in support of the traditional League structure. 'I strongly believe', he said, 'that the leading players in the game will not sell their less well-paid colleagues down the river. Nothing can be done which affects the conditions and work of our members without our approval and that will certainly not be forthcoming for the proposals that have been put forward'.

There was a certain irony in Taylor's intervention. For years the players' union had been at loggerheads with the League over such issues as the maximum wage and freedom of contract, yet here, in the absence of any real leadership from Lytham St Annes, was the sight of the union coming to the League's rescue. Taylor also became the first establishment figure to put the case for the fans when he pointed out: 'The game's biggest sponsor is not the pools, television or any other commercial company, but the football public, who contributed £49 million to income last season'. Nevertheless Taylor was in favour of some changes to the League. 'If we don't get some sensible restructuring now, I fear the worst.'

Taylor took his message to anyone and everyone who would listen: his members, chairmen and directors, League administrators and the media. In the days after the 1 October declaration the superleague seemed a distinct possibility but the longer the big five took to act the more time there was for opponents like Taylor and Ron Noades to attempt to change minds. Taylor was in fact in a powerful position because any breakaway needed the support of the players, something the big five chairmen had taken for granted, if it had occurred to them at all. It was Taylor's adamant stance on behalf of his members that weakened the resolve of the less purposeful superleaguers. In an emotive interview, in which he also referred to the 'dream factor', that is, the ambition of tiny clubs like Wimbledon to play with the elite in the First Division, he said, 'I believe that clubs like Preston . . . with all their tradition, are not being treated properly. Well, the players won't spit on their roots like some people are prepared to do'. On the superleague itself Taylor said, 'Any talk of a superleague of 12 clubs based on finance and gates, a League that would be self-contained . . . is not only morally wrong but, I think, doomed to failure'. The issue for many of the top clubs now, however, was not really a breakaway, but rather how much power they could wield within the League in order to maximise their income. Taylor, like many, was in favour of some change but not too much. What many saw as a weakness – the traditions of English football – 'is also our strength', he concluded.

Despite the reality that the issue was now one of who controlled the League, the superleaguers kept up the public pressure on the rest of the clubs. On 22 November it was reported that six leading Scottish clubs, including Rangers and Celtic, were ready to leave the Scottish League and join a British League with the rebel English clubs because of a new television deal, approved by a majority of Scottish League clubs, with which they profoundly disagreed. This story ran in conjunction with another referring to a proposed 'British Cup', to be instituted in 1986, announced after meetings attended on the English side by Philip Carter, Martin Edwards and Irving Scholar. After a meeting at Villa Park on 28 November the First Division spokesman, Philip Carter, made soothing noises, claiming that those who had threatened to break away were actually trying to save the League. He told the waiting press that agreement could be reached with the recalcitrant Second Division. He even tried to woo the associate members of the Third and Fourth Divisions to go along with the elite: 'The message we want to get across at this stage is one of reassurance, especially to the public and the smaller clubs. There is no way we want to see any of the Third and Fourth Division clubs going out of business or any of their players being put on the dole . . . nothing will be to the detriment of the smaller clubs'. While Carter was making this reconciliatory speech, a well-placed leak to the media let it be known that a 'secret' vote had been taken which affirmed the decision to break away if the First Division failed to get agreement from the Second for the changes they proposed.

On the same day as the Villa Park meeting, Carter's old employers, Littlewoods, cut some of the ground from under his feet when they announced sponsorship of the League Cup, at the time known as the Milk Cup, which was to become the richest prize in British team sport. As entry to the competition was restricted to League clubs only, those breaking away would be denied the right to participate. The Littlewoods Cup would be far more lucrative for clubs than the FA Cup and would provide a much-needed financial incentive for them to stay within the auspices of the League. At last the League was fighting back.

The League discovered the extent of Gordon Taylor's influence and found powerful new allies on 2 December when the players met in Manchester. The packed meeting voted to remain solid and gave Taylor the authority to call a strike if necessary to prevent a breakaway. On the positive side the players also voted through a plan prepared by Taylor to be put to League chairmen which included the provision that no single division should be given voting control over the destiny of the Football League. Taylor would attend the plethora of divisional meetings set for the coming days and weeks, continually pushing for his plan to be accepted, and emerged as the only person neutral enough to be able to command the confidence of all parties. Taylor's diplomacy culminated in the so-called

Heathrow Agreement, thrashed out after six hours of talks at the Post House Hotel near London's airport on 18 December. The meeting lined up Philip Carter, Martin Edwards and Irving Scholar for the breakaway clubs and the First Division against Ron Noades, Lawrie McMenemy of Sunderland and Bill Fox of Blackburn Rovers for the Second Division. The associate members put up three representatives: from Aldershot (Reg Driver), Brentford (Martin Lange) and Doncaster Rovers (Ian Jones) while Gordon Taylor played peacemaker between the factions. All these meetings were conducted entirely independently of the League and its structures. No members of the Management Committee, for instance, attended the Heathrow meeting. Whatever the original intention, decisions were now being taken concerning the League's future without any elected League representative being present.

The agreement, which was subject to a vote of all 92 clubs at an extraordinary general meeting, set out fundamental changes to the structure of the League. The First Division was to be cut to 20 clubs while the Second Division was to be increased to 24. The changes would be phased in over two years through the device of end-of-season play-offs which would supplement the existing system of promotion and relegation. The thorny old issue of the three-quarters majority needed to change League rules was finally resolved as all parties agreed to the First Division demand for its reduction to two-thirds along with the plan for each First Division club to have two votes at future general meetings. Finances were to be changed so that the First Division took a larger percentage of sponsorship and television income and a cut in the 4 per cent League levy of 1 per cent was proposed. Additionally, the Management Committee would be restructured along divisional lines with the First Division guaranteed four representatives to the Second Division's three, with one from the associate members. In return for these concessions on the part of the lower divisions the First Division agreed the principle that no single division could decide League policy. There would also be automatic relegation for the club finishing last in the Fourth Division which was to be replaced by the team finishing first in the premier part-time competition, the Gola League (which later became the GM Vauxhall Conference). Also, the play-offs could be extended to all divisions. Taylor evoked some of the atmosphere of the meeting afterwards in his comments to the press. 'It's quite an historic occasion to get so many factions together and reach agreement. We have had a helluva job and there were times today when it looked difficult. Lots of points were thrashed out and we got there. I now hope all talk of a breakaway and split is averted'.

The EGM was arranged for 4 March 1986 and the Management Committee set to work to present a formula that could be voted upon based on the Heathrow Agreement. In the meantime Philip Carter consolidated his new power by assuming control of the television negotiations, reaching a settlement with ITV and BBC just before Christmas 1985. On 7 January Canon announced that the company would not be renewing its sponsorship of the League at the end of the season. The following day it emerged that Carter was having difficulty selling the Heathrow Agreement to a number of First Division clubs who felt that too much had been conceded to the Second Division. Some unhappy club directors, including David Dein of Arsenal and Doug Ellis of Aston Villa, wanted more radical change but agreed to postpone their demands, which included the appointment of an overall League supremo from outside the game, for two years. The Second Division approved the proposals at a meeting at Lancaster Gate on 9 January.

When the Management Committee's formula was made known it managed to alienate just about everyone. Two key points in the Heathrow Agreement had been omitted altogether. These were the change in the voting system and, not surprisingly, the restructuring of the Management Committee. Martin Edwards gave the response of the big clubs. 'I think the League proposals will be thrown out and the majority of clubs will want to wait until our own proposals are put forward at a later meeting.'

The First Division met to consider the Committee's proposals at Villa Park on 17 February and rejected them by 22 votes to none. Once again Philip Carter spelled out the reality of the outcome if the big clubs did not win the war. 'We hate bringing up the idea of a superleague or a breakaway, but if things stay the same there is no way the major clubs will allow themselves to be dragged down into obscurity.' After severe criticism of the Heathrow Agreement at a meeting of the associate members two days later, at which it was pointed out that Third and Fourth Division clubs would lose 50 per cent of their income from sponsorship, television and the levy under the proposed new financial share-out, the 4 March EGM was postponed. A new date was fixed for 28 April. The First Division agreed that if their own ten-point plan, a new version of the Heathrow Agreement, was not agreed they would leave the League. Carter, making reference to the earlier Saatchi documents, spoke mysteriously of 'feasibility studies' of the superleague having been instigated. The Sword of Damocles, which everyone thought had been removed back in December, hung threateningly once again over the oldest League in the world, wielded by those who claimed to be acting in its best interests. The administration of the game had publicly degenerated into a shambles.

In the run-up to the EGM just about everybody who was any-body came forth with their opinions on the situation in all sections of the media. Ted Croker, secretary of the FA, lent his weight to those advocating change. 'I don't think there is any way that it is possible to support 92 clubs with full-time players. It's just not on any more.' Croker went on to say that any changes had to be made by the clubs themselves but there was no doubting where he stood. There had been press speculation that Croker would be asked to administer the new superleague but another reason for his support might have rested in the need for any new League to be under the control of the FA in order to be legitimate under FIFA rules. Also, the development would significantly strengthen the power of the FA in relation to a weakened Football League.

Around the same time a survey of fans' opinions was published by a team from Surrey University under Professor David Canter which found large-scale disillusionment stemming from three basic causes. These were the threat of hooliganism, poor facilities and a lack of value for money. Professor Canter explained: 'Football must recognise that it is in decline because it is no longer in the entertainment industry. Clubs are part of the leisure industry and like the cinema and the theatre they must rise to the challenge of the comfortable seat in the living-room'. Against these views, Terry Neill, who had managed both Spurs and Arsenal and should there-fore have been in a position to know the prevailing attitudes at the two clubs, said: 'They [Spurs and Arsenal] have reached the stage where they want to look out for their own selfish interests. It's purely a selfish thing. Top clubs are entitled to their share of the cake, but it's the secrecy, the way it's being done, without regard for their lesser brethren. I know it dismays the public. Fragmentation will lead down the road to ruin'. The case for the lower division players, threatened with the spectre of widespread unemployment should the changes result in part-time football in the nether regions of the League, was put by Steve Wignall of Brentford, who remarked: 'If part-time football came to the lower divisions I think that overall standards would eventually drop'.

By the day of the EGM confusion still reigned. The Cumberland Hotel was completely taken over as the various factions held separate meetings in advance of the main event, with Gordon Taylor yet again playing the role of mediator which had apparently been abdicated by League administrators. For all Alan Hardaker's faults, such a situation would have been inconceivable when he was around. Taylor ferried between meetings trying to obtain agreement to a compromise plan put forward by television pundit and former player Jimmy Hill, then a director of Charlton Athletic, who were about to be promoted from the Second Division to the First. The bottom line of the conflict between the First and Second Divisions concerned the new voting formula of two votes for each First Division club. Hill proposed that the elite should have one and a half votes instead of two. When the meeting began it emerged that Philip Carter was in the unique position of holding all 22 First Division votes. The ten-point package, with Hill's amendment, was accepted by 43–10.

The Management Committee resigned en bloc, as they were obliged to do under the deal, soon to be replaced by the new guard, the 'proactive League' that Philip Carter outlined 12 months later as he approached the television negotiations of 1987–88. Only one member of the old Committee survived – Jack Dunnett. Dunnett stood again for president. Once again his opponent was Philip Carter. No incumbent president had ever been voted out of office in the 100-year history of the League and Philip Carter was the outsider who, despite the enormous power he now wielded, had never served on the Management Committee. But Dunnett's club, Notts County, had by now been relegated to the Third Division and the First Division was determined that one of its own should assume the position of president. Even an experienced politician like Dunnett was unable to resist the tide and Carter won by 37½–26½. The coup was complete.

The events of 1985–86, coinciding as they did with the bitter television dispute, the ban from Europe and the growing intervention of a Government committed to 'tackling' football hooliganism, dealt football's image a severe blow. The concept of a superleague has a history stretching back for decades – indeed its ideal was one of the motivating factors behind the formation of the original League by 12 clubs in 1888. But the emphasis on money and the almost total lack of concern for the supporters gave a squalid air to the proceedings in 1985–86. When Irving Scholar had enthusiastically listened to the persuasive arguments of the Saatchi executives, the ideal had been that much needed restructuring should take place to benefit all levels of the game and be designed to raise standards of play. The objective was to produce a successful national team and a competitive premier division whose members offered supporters an attractive product in the best possible surroundings, the whole system underpinned by regional events at the lower levels. This philosophy quickly degenerated into a movement for change based on the desire for more power and more money. That the man who had led the process was now president of the Football League should have been a source of concern for the rest of the 92 clubs if the issue was raised again, as indeed it was, in the television negotiations of 1987–88.

What was it that the much-vaunted revolution had achieved? There was still a 92-club League even though the First Division now received more money. Although the majority needed for rule changes had been reduced the First Division still needed 11 votes from the lower divisions to reach the two-thirds majority now necessary to implement change. The 92-way share-out of the money derived from the pools remained unchanged. The changes in the Management Committee were no guarantee of a peaceful period, indeed the opposite proved the case as the League was hit with even more upheavals and controversies. Although the First Division was undoubtedly more powerful, and unquestionably richer, basic problems had not even been touched by the split.

Hooliganism and the proposed Government membership scheme, for instance, or the future of television contracts which had now been shown to be of supreme importance to the standing of the game and the specific reason a superleague could exist in the first place. The one innovation, the play-offs, proved to be the only bonus for the supporters, who took to them immediately, but they had nothing to do with the superleague principle. The single most visible result was the transfer of power to different individuals, in particular Philip Carter, although the new regime lasted only two years until Carter and David Dein were removed from the Management Committee. Carter was replaced as president by a triumphant Jack Dunnett, who returned despite the fact that he was now a director of a Third Division club.

When the television negotiations of 1988 took place bitterness surfaced once again as the First Division demanded all the television income. This flew in the face of the Heathrow Agreement which gave them 50 per cent of the revenues from the small screen. Predictably, those involved were led by Philip Carter, Martin Edwards and Irving Scholar, this time with David Dein as their ally on the Management Committee. The press immediately latched on to the possibility of a superleague as the League split once more. However, the superleague was never a realistic possibility in 1988, despite the fact that Greg Dyke had advocated the idea and went so far as to indicate ITV's willingness to sponsor it. This time the big clubs simply threatened to sign their own television deal, irrespective of the wishes of the majority, even if they could not muster the required support under the procedure they had voted for in 1986. Any penalties imposed would be fought in the courts.

Another factor was also at work in 1988 militating against a breakaway by the top English clubs. The British Cup and the British League never materialised as the rebel Scottish clubs settled their differences with their colleagues over the television contract and fears were expressed over potential crowd problems if games between English and Scottish teams took place. The Scottish game had gone from strength to strength, however, prompting David Holmes to tell us that Rangers would never join a British League – he saw the club's future in Europe, a position reiterated by David Murray when he took over Rangers. Wallace Mercer, the chairman of Hearts, made similar pronouncements on behalf of other Scottish clubs: 'When we get total freedom of movement in 1992 I see no reason why Hearts couldn't play PSV Eindhoven one week and Bordeaux the next, with Rangers playing Real Madrid. I see there being three or four European divisions with promotion and relegation, all underpinned by television demand'. In addition to the noises coming from Scotland, news was reaching England that a true superleague was being promoted which would cover the whole of Europe and be a rival to the only real superleague in the world, the NFL in America. The man who was leading the moves for change was Silvio Berlusconi.

The idea of a European League predates Berlusconi's involvement in football by a generation. The notion grew up alongside the post-war vision of a united Europe, and as some nations of the continent moved towards the European Economic Community, so there were those in football who had the same vision for the great game. Naturally enough, the vision took root first in France. The former French international and editor of the daily sports newspaper L'Equipe, Gabriel Hanot, posed the question 'Which is the best team in Europe?' The article appeared the day after Wolverhampton Wanderers had beaten a Honved side containing Ferenc Puskas 3–2 in a floodlit friendly in December 1954. Hanot put his plans for a tournament to decide the issue to a number of clubs who backed him enthusiastically. The concept even found some favour in England where friendlies such as the Wolves–Honved game were drawing huge crowds, especially after the advent of floodlit matches, which in England were necessarily played against continental opposition as the League and FA, with their usual far-sightedness, banned the use of floodlights in domestic contests. As the idea gathered momentum it ran into opposition from the national Leagues of Europe who naturally saw their power threatened. Eventually FIFA, under pressure from the clubs involved, gave the new tournament its backing provided it was modified to preserve the integrity of national Leagues. The compromise turned out to be the European Champions' Cup which, along with the Inter-Cities Fairs Cup (later to become the UEFA Cup), was so successful that it was followed by the instigation of the Cup-Winners' Cup in 1960, all of which increased the number of clubs who could play in European competitions. The fledgling European governing body, UEFA, was given the role of administering the new competitions.

This compromise, which the French saw eventually evolving into a true European League, had two opposite effects. On the one hand European competitions were so successful that it was inconceivable that they would be changed. On the other, seeing the best merely whetted the appetite for more. There is no doubt that the great European teams of the 1950s and '60s, such as Real Madrid, Benfica and Barcelona, caused many to believe that this should be the staple diet, not the icing on the cake. The European League would simply not go away. Prince Rainier of Monaco carried the idea forward at a series of meetings in the 1960s when there was a question-mark over Monaco's appearance in the Champions' Cup as representatives of France. It surfaced again in the early 1970s, unusually with English participation. A formal conference on the European superleague, attended by UEFA's general secretary, was held in London under the auspices of the *Daily Express,* whose football correspondent David Miller had put the issue to UEFA with backing from Ajax Amsterdam, Glasgow Rangers and Arsenal. By then, however, UEFA was powerful enough to head off what it saw as a challenge to its authority and nothing came of the scheme.

But by the 1980s the issue had become one of television and money. Silvio Berlusconi recognised the appeal of a European League and could not accept the possibility of going out of a European competition in the first round when his investment demanded a lengthy and successful campaign in Europe each season. He said: 'In the Champions' Cup you run the risk of many hazards: rain, refereeing, bad luck and the risk of first round elimination. It's not modern thinking'. Moreover, Berlusconi had international ambitions for the whole of his empire and regular exposure on the European stage was central to his plans. Determined at least to test the waters he began talks with a number of leading clubs, including Real Madrid and PSV Eindhoven, the Dutch side entirely owned by the Philips organisation. Rebuffed by UEFA, Berlusconi turned to his advertising agency, none other than Saatchi and Saatchi, to come up with more detailed plans which might win

UEFA backing. Realising that taking clubs out of national Leagues was probably a non-starter the agency recommended a European League grafted on to existing national competitions, although the Champions' Cup and the other competitions remained a problem. The response from UEFA was a firm rejection. The new secretary general, Gerhard Aigner, said: 'A European League is for the moment an illusion and today it is totally unrealistic to consider a change in the format of the Champions' Cup'. Aigner's statement is interesting. While it appears to slam the door on any European superleague he carefully uses phrases like 'for the moment' and qualifying words like 'today', leaving the way open for negotiations which might lead in the future to some new format, one which could perhaps apply the pyramid principle to the whole of Europe.

Something of Berlusconi's ambition can be seen in comments he made just before the 1989 Champions' Cup final. 'If we win the European Cup', he said, 'I will propose to my colleague Pellegrini [the president of Internazionale, who won the Italian League in 1988–89] two friendly games, then a supergame between a selection from our two clubs and the rest of Italy.' When asked who would coach the composite team, he answered at once, 'Neither Sacchi nor Trapattoni [Inter's coach], but happily, Pellegrini and I. It would be the best way for us to realise our old dream of one day taking the role of manager'. There is no doubt which television network would screen the matches. Where Berlusconi leads, others follow. Paolo Mantovani, the shipping magnate and president of Sampdoria, who reached the Cup-Winners' Cup final in 1989, explained how it was done. 'I wanted a place at the table of European clubs, and not as a waiter. For such a future, you have to pay.'

The big five clubs in England showed in 1983, in 1985 and in 1988 that they were quite prepared to jettison their colleagues if it suited them. The fact that an English superleague was not a serious issue in 1988, notwithstanding the Greg Dyke memo, owes more to a desire to be part of any European development, should it arise, than dissatisfaction with the current position. The problem they have not yet addressed is that for all their machinations, the big five in England are really the poor relations of Europe in economic terms. The turnover of Barcelona, for instance, which is currently over £18 million per season, dwarfs the £7.5 million coming in at Manchester United. None of the big English clubs could even claim to be the biggest in Britain: that title now belongs to Glasgow Rangers, which also sees its future in a European League. As Alan Montgomery said in April 1989: 'It has to come. We must make it happen. The future of Rangers is in Europe. I shall be liaising with key European clubs to put a plan to UEFA for a European superleague'. With no sign of the European ban ending and Government controls on hooliganism getting closer all the time, it seems as if the big five are suffering from severe delusions of grandeur. After all, if their own arguments at home were applied to a European League they would be the minnows. On financial criteria, on facilities, perhaps even on playing ability after years outside European competition; in any plans for a new European competition, they would be the last to be invited to join. Their continental colleagues are quite literally in a different league.

9
IN THE NATIONAL INTEREST

Unhappy is the land that is in need of heroes
BERTOLT BRECHT

The entire move took just 18 seconds to complete yet its outcome touched the sporting hearts of two nations as years of history were overturned. When the ball arrived in space on the edge of the penalty box, a mere three passes after it had left the goal-keeper's hands, two figures began the short race to gain possession. Striker and sweeper strained for the extra half-yard that would make the difference. Falling on one knee, the man in the orange shirt connected a split second before the tackle came in and the ball rolled beyond the reach of the goal-keeper into the corner of the net. It was the 89th minute, and Marco van Basten's decisive strike saw to it that there was no way back for the Germans, defeated at last by a Dutch team which had been given little chance when the tournament began and was virtually written off after an early defeat by the Soviet Union. Yet it was the Dutch who would now contest the final of the 1988 European Championships while the lone figure of the German manager, who had spent the entire 90 minutes standing in majestic isolation on the touch-line, was left to reflect on defeat, his memory perhaps returning to another place, to another time, when things had turned out so differently.

Fourteen years earlier Franz Beckenbauer, the greatest footballer Germany has ever produced and the man who perfected the position of sweeper, had faced the Dutch in the World Cup final in Munich. Opposing him that day was another of the great players of world football, Johan Cruyff. The Dutch side had thrilled lovers of the game throughout the competition with breathtaking performances that were dubbed 'total football', but the discipline and togetherness of the Germans, marshalled as ever by Beckenbauer, saw them come from behind to win 2–1. That day symbolised the dramatic influence the two individuals had exerted on the football of Germany, Holland and beyond. It was a pattern established through the force of their personalities and the systems under which they operated, which would remain long after their great days as players were behind them. Beckenbauer, the upright and steadfast Bavarian, playing for the nation, probing relentlessly for the opposition's vulnerabilities and not averse to a little rule-bending or referee-baiting to achieve the desired result. Cruyff, the crafty artist and juggler, constantly at odds with club and country over money, placing his individual rights above those of the collective at every opportunity, yet possessed of a skill which has been matched by few in the history of the game. Beckenbauer spoke many years later of their philosophy. 'If you've decided tactics and they don't work, you try to change them in some way. You might argue with the referee or the opposition or do something to the crowd. Anything that might change the situation. It's part of the game. Johan Cruyff was a master at this. When he started it was on purpose. Then sometimes the game changed.' German–Dutch rivalry, which had far more to do with recent history than with the sporting arena, was heightened by the intensity and drama of the contest that took place in Munich in 1974, so much so that by the time of the 1988 encounter, the Dutch were still seeking revenge.

The morning after the defeat of the West Germans in 1988, the Dutch players were understandably in buoyant mood. Not only had they beaten the Germans 2–1, they had achieved the victory on German territory, in Hamburg. Hans van Breukelen, the former Nottingham Forest goal-keeper and the man who had begun the move which led to the winning goal, announced to his team-mates that they had already won their final. Van Basten, however, did not share his opinion. Saturday's game in Munich was still to come and to the AC Milan forward that was now the one that mattered. Since he had become an outstanding member of the Ajax team in the mid-1980s van Basten, like his contemporaries, had always been compared to the great Dutch masters of the 1970s: Cruyff, Neeskens, Rep, Krol and van Hanegem. Yet for all their prodigious talent, that Dutch team had failed to win a major trophy, being beaten in successive World Cup finals in 1974 and 1978.

That Saturday in Munich offered van Basten the chance, not just to emulate his predecessors and exorcise their ghosts once and for all, but also to establish a new Dutch footballing dynasty.

It is now history how the Dutch turned the tables and defeated the Soviet Union in the final, courtesy of a header from their dreadlocked captain, Ruud Gullit, and a stunning volley from van Basten, one of the great goals of international football. The welcome that greeted the players' return to Amsterdam showed how crucial the victory had been for Dutch national pride. The man who had coached both the 1974 and 1988 teams, Rinus Michels, encapsulated the feelings of his countrymen. 'I have been asked yet again to compare our team and our success here with 1974. No way! We have no reason to talk any more about 1974. We beat West Germany in Hamburg in the semi-final so now 1974 is history.'

For the West German public, elimination from a major competition, even at the semi-final stage, was something of a new experience, although Beckenbauer had tried to take the pressure off both himself and the team before the tournament started, saying: 'We are missing the experience of playing at this level [the Germans, as hosts, did not have to qualify for the competition]. I am working for the long term, the World Cup of 1990. The European Championship is only a step along the way. If we reach the semi-final we shall fulfil our objective'. The Germans had built up an almost invincible reputation over the years, most of it achieved while Beckenbauer was player and captain, but the World Cup of 1982, in which the West Germans finished runners-up to Italy, showed how much was now expected of German teams. Winning or losing narrowly were no longer enough and the performances in 1982 drew widespread criticism of the manager, Jupp Derwall, who had been given the job after spending many years as Helmut Schoen's assistant. The criticism was not muted because Derwall's team had reached the final. Beckenbauer put it this way: 'There is a lot of pressure in Germany. To win the game is normal but you have to play well and score lots of goals, then people are satisfied'.

When Derwall's side failed to make any impression on the 1984 European Championships in France, Hermann Neuberger, overlord of the German game, decided that a change was needed. He turned to the man who had been the inspiration of his country in three World Cups and who was now quietly contemplating a retirement filled with golf, skiing, advertising work, writing a newspaper column and playing some exhibition matches. Neuberger offered Franz Beckenbauer the post of national manager when they met at the Georges V Hotel in Paris after the European Championships. Beckenbauer, who, like Michel Platini in France, possessed none of the formal qualifications usually required to become a coach in Germany, had been made offers by Neuberger in the past but had always refused. This time he accepted and was given the title of 'Teamchief' to allay any criticisms from coaches who had struggled long and hard to achieve their positions. 'It was an emotional decision', he declared. 'I can't explain why I took it at that precise moment.' Like that of Platini, however, the status of Beckenbauer in Germany was such that any voices raised in opposition to the appointment were quickly stilled.

The new manager immediately made public his analysis of the team's weaknesses when he lamented the lack of either a playmaker or a natural leader in German football. 'The Bundesliga has fallen from the best League in the world to international average', he declared. In a savage attack on the current crop of German players, he branded them 'fat-cat pros with £100,000 contracts, Cartier gold chains, sunglasses in their tailored silk shirt pockets and Porsches in the stadium car parks. What I expect from my players is that they have a longing to play, that they will tear themselves to pieces to gain selection. Anybody who isn't ready to do this can go home. I don't want them. On the other hand, if anybody is ready to give his best, he can make mistakes, that won't bother me. We must have the courage to take risks. This is what we have lost'.

The man whose management style consists of standing alone on the touch-line throughout each international match secured his position by taking the self-confessed below-par German team to the 1986 World Cup in Mexico and, against expectations, making it all the way to the final, where once again the side came from behind before eventually losing the match 3–2 to Maradona's Argentina. The Germans might have fared even better had they managed to retain the services of their wayward midfielder Bernd

Schuster, who had been at odds with the requirements of national team managers since the early days of Derwall and obviously did not come into the category of player Beckenbauer insisted he wanted. However, the new manager clearly recognised that even if Schuster was not willing to 'tear himself to pieces' to gain a place (the player had more than once refused to play for the national team), his talent was such that he had to be given every chance of returning to the fold. Schuster, then playing for Barcelona, was asked by Beckenbauer to play in Mexico a full year before the tournament began. 'Take your time, think about it and let me know', the new manager told him. When Schuster had not replied 11 months later Beckenbauer finally forced the issue but Schuster refused to play. Despite this set-back, Beckenbauer was still able to say, 'Bernd Schuster, I like him, I like him as a player but he's a strange person. I don't understand him at all'.

One year after Beckenbauer's appointment to the managership of the national team, his great rival from the 1970s, Johan Cruyff, became manager at Ajax Amsterdam, the club for which he had played with such success over the years. Like Beckenbauer, Cruyff possessed no formal qualifications for the job but was given special exemption from normal requirements by the Dutch FA (the KNVB). Cruyff's success as a manager – he led Ajax to the final of the Cup-Winners' Cup in 1987 where the team beat Locomotiv Leipzig 1–0 – coupled with an all-too-familiar dispute with the Ajax directors over money, brought interest from Barcelona. By the summer of 1988, as his countrymen were on their way to that memorable European Championship final, Cruyff had arrived in the Catalan capital the returning hero as press and public recalled his previous spell at the Nou Camp when he was at the peak of his playing career, one of the more successful periods in Barcelona's history.

Both men symbolised the emerging order in European football during the 1960s and 1970s, thoroughly modern players of bza new, prosperous era, when the rewards for winning were becoming as important as winning itself. Both played for clubs which were unknown when they arrived but were giants of the world game when they left. Both had graduated through junior club teams and were products of their respective countries' systems, which, though they differed in many respects from one another, had two important factors in common. They consistently produced successful national teams and they were able to accommodate their greatest-ever performers once their playing days had come to an end.

When Franz Beckenbauer joined Bayern Munich as a talented youngster in the early 1960s, the club did not even occupy the premier position in the Bavarian capital – that place was claimed by TSV Munich 1860 – indeed Bayern was unheard of outside its home state. At the time, the country's football, the development of which had been held back due to the economic situation in post-war Germany, was regionalised and semi-professional. Eintracht Frankfurt had reached the Champions' Cup final in 1960 but apart from this one exception the German domestic game had not kept up with the rest of Europe, particularly Spain and Italy. Even a small country like Portugal was producing teams like Benfica which eclipsed the best the Germans could muster. On the international front, a World Cup win against the odds in 1954, when the team came from 2–0 down to beat the Hungarians of Puskas (the side which had twice comprehensively demolished England some months previously), had whetted the public's appetite for the national team's success, but the feat could not be repeated as Brazil rose to prominence with World Cup wins in 1958 and 1962.

By 1963 it was obvious to most Germans that something would have to be done to bring the domestic game up to the quality of the other European nations and at the same time improve the national side's chances of success. The formula that was decided upon created something of a superleague, the Bundesliga, in a major restructuring of the game from a regional to a national base. At the same time full-scale professionalism was introduced. The purpose of the changes was to build a structure that would simultaneously enable German clubs to compete with the best in Europe by playing consistently against high-class opposition and produce from the stronger, richer clubs which would join the 16-team Bundesliga players who could come together to form the nucleus of a strong national side. The number of fixtures, the finances of clubs, even the playing style and the timing of the season were all to be secondary to the needs of the national team.

The Bundesliga was a huge success and was expanded to 18 teams after two years. Attendances at games rose as the standard of play improved. Beckenbauer's club, the essentially amateur Bayern, was quick to grasp the financial potential of both the Bundesliga and the city of Munich and, under commercial manager Robert Schwan, who brought business planning to the previously unresponsive administration, and president Wilhelm Neudecker, who had the vision to transform the multi-sports and social club into a football-led colossus, began to move into a position from which it could challenge the dominance of its grand neighbour, TSV. This was an ambitious plan considering that in 1965 TSV reached the final of the Cup-Winners' Cup, the first German team to make it to a European final since Frankfurt appeared in Glasgow in 1960. But with Beckenbauer leading the way, Bayern gained promotion to the Bundesliga in 1965 and in its first season in the new League finished third to TSV, had the consolation of winning the Cup and saw Beckenbauer elected Germany's Footballer of the Year.

Suddenly German football was no longer the odd-man-out of Europe. The formation of the Bundesliga had transformed playing standards and laid the foundations for German teams to become among the most formidable in the world. Bayern Munich beat Glasgow Rangers to win the Cup-Winners' Cup in 1967 and took its first domestic championship in 1969. As TSV's fortunes slipped, Bayern flourished, and by the beginning of the 1970s had established itself not only as the biggest club in Munich, but arguably the biggest in the whole of Germany.

In the years when Beckenbauer was at his peak as a player, Bayern's record became one of the outstanding achievements in football, culminating in three successive European Champions' Cup wins in the mid-1970s. A move to the new Olympic stadium in 1972 gave the club the impetus for expansion as income grew from attendances now reaching 75,000 for big games. As TSV dropped out of the Bundesliga altogether after a disastrous decline, Bayern emerged as an institution in Munich, with the wealth to match its new status. Moreover, the new financial climate of German football permeated the Bundesliga, with clubs like Hamburg, Cologne and Borussia Moenchengladbach becoming challengers on the European stage. The first objective of the Bundesliga had been achieved.

That the second objective, success for the national team, also occurred during the Beckenbauer years was no coincidence. The performances of Germany's national team outdid even those of the country's club sides. The team, managed by Helmut Schoen, who had been schooled in the job for a number of years under the previous manager, Sepp Herberger, and led on the field by Franz Beckenbauer, reached the World Cup final in England in 1966 then the semi-final in Mexico, in 1970. If the defeat by Alf Ramsey's England in 1966 announced the arrival of the Germans as a major force in world football, it was the quarter-final game against their former conquerors in Leon, Mexico, in 1970 that showed the progress German football had made. The team came back from 2–0 down to win 3–2, ending the England team's reign as world champions. Beckenbauer was asked by Schoen to play in midfield during this period and performed the task as required but the measure of his influence, and his willingness to wield it, can be seen in his move in the national team from midfield to sweeper before the 1972 European Championships. Beckenbauer invited Schoen to stay at his house and used the visit to convince the manager that he should be playing at the back with the whole field in front of him: 'I told him, "Mr Schoen, now it's time for me to play in the position I like the most".' After initial reluctance Schoen let Beckenbauer have his way and the era of German supremacy was born. The two reached their zenith with the win against Holland in the 1974 World Cup final but the true measure of the success of the German structure can be seen in the consistency of the national team since 1966. The Germans have not only qualified for every World Cup but have achieved a record in the competition which is second to none. Although they lost two more World Cup finals, in 1982 and 1986, they won the European Championship on two occasions, in 1972 and 1980, and were runners-up in 1976. By the time Beckenbauer left German football for the United States in 1977, the national team was the most successful in the world and his club was established as one of the most successful in Europe. Beckenbauer himself played for Germany a record 103 times, 50 times as captain, and was European Footballer of the Year twice.

In the same year that Beckenbauer made his first appearance for Bayern Munich, 1964, Ajax Amsterdam introduced a talented young player of their own into the first team. Johan Cruyff would prove to be as important to the world game as his German contemporary. Within 12 months of his debut Cruyff became a fixture in an Ajax side being built by coach Rinus Michels, a former player with both the club and the national team. Whereas Germany possessed a long tradition of competitive football that was disrupted by the war and needed to be brought up to date, the Dutch game had been virtually unknown outside the Netherlands before Feyenoord of Rotterdam reached the semi-final of the Champions' Cup in 1963. Although it was a big city club, Ajax was anonymous beyond the Dutch border. The club had won the domestic Championship in 1957 and 1960 and lifted the Cup in 1961 but had made little headway in European competitions, going out in the first match in two out of three attempts. When Cruyff left the club for Barcelona ten years after his debut, Ajax had won six Championships, four Cups and, like Bayern, had won the Champions' Cup on three successive occasions. Moreover, the reputation of the club, and that of Dutch football generally, had been transformed from that of also-rans to trail-blazers at the very pinnacle of the world game.

The creaking machinery of the Dutch administration would have been unable to cope with European success in the 1960s. Officially the game was amateur or semi-professional but since a rebel professional league had been briefly set up in the 1950s the wealthier clubs had been making payments to players, even tempting foreign stars to play in the Dutch League. Cruyff's football developed in this freewheeling atmosphere and was mirrored in the quality of his performances. His need to win, however, always asserted itself, even in those early days. He was sent off in his second international for striking the referee and subsequently banned from playing for the national team for six months, one example among many of his frequent brushes with officials and administrators. Where Beckenbauer's career was in the main remarkably smooth and serene, Cruyff's was dogged with arguments on and off the field, often about money, which gave the Dutchman something of a mercenary image in his own country. Essentially, these conflicts boiled down to Cruyff's desire to get his own way, in everything from team matters to the way the clubs he played for were run. The sublime quality of his play, however, dispelled any negative feelings about the man on the part of spectators in much the same way that in Britain George Best could be forgiven anything as long as he kept turning in those match-winning performances.

Ajax with Cruyff began to impose itself on Europe, reaching the Champions' Cup Final in 1969 where the club suffered a 4–1 defeat at the hands of AC Milan. In fact Ajax were not the first Dutch team to win a European trophy – that honour went to Feyenoord, who lifted the Champions' Cup in 1970. But the next three years belonged to Cruyff and the Amsterdammers who won the Champions' Cup three times in succession. After the first European win in 1971, Michels left for Barcelona and Cruyff's contract with Ajax ran out. He turned to his father-in-law, Cor Coster, to negotiate a new agreement.

Coster was a wealthy Amsterdam jeweller who, when he became Cruyff's business manager, threatened to sell his new client to Ajax's hated rivals Feyenoord, via a Belgian club if necessary, unless the Ajax Board agreed to his financial demands. Coster had seen the huge sums of money that Dutch football was beginning to generate and, quite naturally, was determined to see that some of it went to the newest member of his family. When Coster announced that Barcelona were interested in signing Cruyff, the Ajax directors gave in and agreed to the manager's terms. This victory gave Coster the impetus to increase his involvement in football and led to him becoming one of the most influential figures in the Dutch game. Three years later he finally did negotiate Cruyff's move to Barcelona, the richest club in the world. The talks with the Catalans assumed soap-opera proportions as Coster appeared enthusiastic over the proposed move one day and cool the next. According to Coster, the protracted affair was all for Mrs Coster's sake: the poor woman could hardly bear the thought of her daughter and grandchildren living so far away. Others pointed to the large amounts of money eventually extracted from Barcelona, to a world record transfer fee of over £900,000 and to Cruyff's personal share of the deal, which stood at £450,000, as a more pertinent reason. On signing, Cruyff said: 'For the next five years I am not a man, I am not a footballer, I am an industry'. At Barcelona Cruyff went from strength to strength. After 13 long years without a title, the club, rejuvenated by Michels and his protégé, won the League. Cruyff scored twice on his debut and went on to win the European Footballer of the Year award.

Back in Holland, the success enjoyed by the country's club sides was not immediately translated into similar achievements by the national team. Failure to qualify for the final stages of either the World Cup in 1970 or the European Championship in 1972 forced the administration, under pressure from an impatient public, to re-evaluate the set-up of the national team. The League had been streamlined in 1970, leaving a 50-team structure; some clubs, like Den Haag and AZ Alkmaar, came into existence as a result of mergers between weaker teams, others dropped out of the professional set-up altogether. While the reorganisation had certainly improved playing standards – top Dutch clubs were fast becoming recognised as the best in Europe – the performances of the national team had not benefited from the new system. This situation was to change in dramatic style.

Matters came to a head in the qualifying stages of the 1972 European Championships. As the team approached a tough game in East Germany, manager Fadrhonc selected a squad containing eight players from Feyenoord and PSV Eindhoven, two clubs drawn together in a domestic Cup tie due to be played the weekend before the game against the East Germans. The national manager's appeals for the Cup tie to be postponed fell on deaf ears at the KNVB. The match went ahead, going to extra time and penalties and was followed by the withdrawal from the national team of several key players through injury. A 1–0 defeat in Leipzig four days later effectively ended the Dutch team's chances of progressing further in the competition. The outcry that followed forced the KNVB to admit its mistake and begin plans for the domestic game to follow the German example and become secondary to the needs of the national team.

Holland scraped into the 1974 World Cup finals in West Germany on goal difference. Some players whose commitment to the cause of the national team had hitherto been less than absolute rediscovered their desire to wear the orange shirt and a number of exiles returned. Rinus Michels, fresh from his Championship-winning season in Barcelona, was brought in as supervisor to the national side as Fadrhonc departed at the 11th hour. Previewing the Dutch chances in 1974, the magazine *World Soccer* praised many of the country's individual players like Cruyff and Neeskens but dismissed their chances of lifting the trophy: 'It would be foolishness to expect Holland to go all the way. They are not in the same league as Italy, West Germany, Brazil . . . or even Yugoslavia or Poland at their best'. This conventional wisdom was turned on its head as the competition was set alight by the performances of the mobile Dutch team led by Johan Cruyff, in which each member of the side played the all-purpose game of total football. By the time of the final against the hosts the Dutch were, if anything, favourites. This team though, for all its talents, was beaten by the more resilient Germans. There were many who said that the Dutch threw the game away by trying to toy with their opponents when leading 1–0. Whatever the case, it cannot be denied that the Dutch team displayed a level of invention and technique that thrilled followers of the game all over the world.

The commitment of the KNVB to the success of the national team ensured that the 1974 tournament would be no flash in the pan. Despite the success of Dutch club sides in Europe, the small size of the country – its population was just 15 million – meant that even the richest of Holland's clubs could not compete financially with the giants from Spain and Italy and many of the best Dutch players earned their living abroad. The commitment to the national team on the part of these players was secured, after much wrangling, by huge payments from the KNVB. In the 1974 tournament the Dutch players took 70 per cent of the total KNVB revenue, more than the winners, West Germany. Negotiations with players over money were to become a regular feature of Dutch teams' participation in major championships in succeeding years and the 1988 European Championships ended with the KNVB making an overall loss of £70,000, despite an income in excess of £1 million.

In Barcelona, Cruyff was joined by his former Ajax team-mate, Neeskens, in another expensive Coster deal. Having qualified for the Champions' Cup, the Catalans were confident of winning the trophy that had not only always eluded them, but had established the reputation of their bitter rivals, Real Madrid. However, semi-final defeat by Leeds United dashed their hopes and cost Michels his job. Under new German coach Weisweiler, who had built Borussia Moenchengladbach into a force in his homeland, Barcelona was not the happiest of clubs. Cruyff was upset at being denied his usual free role on the pitch – Weisweiler insisted he play to a rigid system – and led a players' revolt which engulfed the whole club and its ruling junta. As the in-fighting continued, it became clear that either Weisweiler or Cruyff would have to go. To the Barca fans, it was Cruyff who had brought them the Championship win and Cruyff who could make sure the glory days continued. After a skilful public relations campaign, which some said was masterminded by Coster, Cruyff won the support of the directors and Weisweiler resigned, clearing the way for Rinus Michels to be reinstated as coach. It is unlikely that any other player in the world could have so publicly taken on his manager and won and the incident must rank as one of the more remarkable in Barcelona's stormy history.

The story of European and international football in the early 1970s is dominated by teams from Germany and Holland and by the supreme skills and personalities of Beckenbauer and Cruyff. Both countries had committed themselves to full scale restructuring of their domestic Leagues which had resulted in triumph at club and international levels. The forcefulness with which Cruyff and Beckenbauer exerted their influence cannot be overstated. Beckenbauer was Schoen's general on the field but it was Beckenbauer who managed to convince Schoen of the need to play him as sweeper, a decision which elevated the German team's play to a standard that led eventually to the winning of the World Cup, while Cruyff continued to play exactly as he liked in every team for which he turned out. Nonetheless, both countries' new systems were more than able to accommodate these gifted if difficult individuals and were able to continue successfully after both had left the international stage. Holland reached the final of the 1978 World Cup in Argentina without Cruyff, who refused to go because of fears that he would be kidnapped, while Germany managed the same feat without Beckenbauer in Spain in 1982.

Cruyff was set to retire from the game altogether in 1978 but a series of financial problems culminating in tax investigations in Holland and Spain forced him to reappraise his plans. Coster, whose football empire now included over 100 players, arranged a deal to take Cruyff to the USA to play in the burgeoning North American Soccer League (NASL) with the Los Angeles Aztecs. The NASL was then at its peak, Pele and Beckenbauer had brought huge success to the New York Cosmos whose crowds numbered up to 70,000 and Cruyff was expected to do the same in Los Angeles. For a time it seemed as if the game would finally take off in the one country that had continually spurned it but the writing was already on the wall. The lack of a substantial television deal, which is a prerequisite for success for any spectator sport in the US market; too many well-paid overseas stars with too few home-grown talents; the lack of any grass-roots game; the ambitious expansion which was undertaken by the NASL before the game was ready for it: all were possible reasons for the ultimate failure of the League. While all must have played a part, it is illuminating to see what was said of the great Franz Beckenbauer when he first began playing for the Cosmos. The vice-president of Warner Communications, the owners of the New York club, watched in horror as the expensive superstar strolled around at the back playing his normal game. 'Tell him', he roared, 'to get his ass up front. We didn't pay a million for him to hang around in defence.'

Years later, in a television interview with journalist Hugh McIlvanney, Beckenbauer referred to his time in America as the happiest of his footballing life. 'In America', he said, 'football is sport. In Germany it is more.' In Beckenbauer's opinion, football was killed in the USA by the gridiron game. 'ABC were broadcasting the games', he ventured. 'Then, at the same time as the NFL renewed its contract, they dropped it.'

Beckenbauer and Cruyff were enormously successful in America but both ended their playing days with swansongs in their own domestic Leagues. Cruyff won two more Championships with Ajax and one with Feyenoord, who offered him a percentage of gate receipts after the Ajax Board rejected his demands for increased money. The legacy they left, however, shows clearly how the domestic set-ups of both countries were able to come to terms with such gifted individuals and to utilise their talents after they had finished their playing careers.

Bayern Munich, without ever recapturing the glory that came its way in the 1970s, has remained a force in Europe. The club is now the wealthiest in Germany and can take up to £600,000 in gate receipts for a big match. Playing in the city-owned Olympic stadium the club can afford to devote resources to the development of players, from the large youth section to the first team with its expensive stars. The structure of the Bayern club follows the pyramid pattern with the Bundesliga side at its apex and the youth programme at its base. Another playing stalwart, Uli Hoeness, was appointed business manager in 1979 since when the club's turnover has doubled to stand at £8 million in 1988. When a prestigious summer tournament was instituted at Wembley in 1988, the Bayern team was immediately invited, as it was when the English League was looking for opposition to play champions Everton in a centenary match earlier in the year. During the Wembley tournament Uli Hoeness related something of the club's philosophy. 'Our members receive a newspaper every two weeks and reduced prices for admission. In addition they can vote every two years for the offices of president, vice-president and treasurer. We have lost players abroad and we can't match the wealth of clubs in Spain and Italy because of tax differences but the television deals might help us. There is a potential so large that nobody knows where it will end.' Hoeness is one of a number of German ex-internationals, including Gunter Netzer and Felix Magath, who have made the transition to general or business management. Encouraged by the environment in which they played, all looked to wider horizons than is usual for players in most countries. 'I always opened my eyes wherever I went in the world', was the way Hoeness put it.

In Holland, the success story has continued despite a slight hiccup in the early 1980s. Ajax are planning to build a completely new stadium and PSV Eindhoven, the club entirely supported by Philips, took the Champions' Cup in 1988 to set alongside the national team's triumph in Germany. The rise of the club from Eindhoven shows how the Dutch set-up has managed to accommodate total sponsorship. Philips and the club were totally integrated in 1986 since when PSV have become roving ambassadors for the company. A new stand was opened in 1988, the first part of a planned redevelopment designed to increase capacity to 40,000 in preparation, according to commercial manager Kees Ploegsma, for the formation of a European superleague. Ploegsma said: 'In every country you will see a split by four or five top clubs. It will happen though I cannot say in which year'. It is the ambition of the club to become one of the giants of Europe, on a par with Barcelona or AC Milan. In 1988 its turnover was up to £3.1 million, and is expected to rise to £6.3 million in 1991. The football club proved an unexpected asset to Philips when the company's money in Brazil was frozen by the government. Philips, through the intermediary of NMB, a Dutch bank, negotiated the release of £2.5 million of its Brazilian assets to the almost bankrupt Brazilian football club Vasco da Gama in return for the transfer of striker Romario Farias to PSV. The money was reimbursed to Philips in Holland from the coffers of the Eindhoven club, which has now become a profit-making subsidiary of the multi-national company. Other Dutch clubs are also heavily sponsored, though none is as closely allied to a corporation as PSV is to Philips. Most sponsorship deals in the Dutch league are handled by the company Interfootball, owned by none other than Cor Coster, who controls the commercial interests of a large number of players and clubs and is now moving into the even more lucrative area of television programming, buying and selling the rights to several important matches in 1988–89 including the Holland–USSR friendly international.

While the patriotic Beckenbauer was made chief of the national team, the more mercenary Cruyff has so far stuck to club management with Ajax and Barcelona. Cruyff himself said of his departure from Ajax, 'When we regularly let the best players like Frank

Rijkaard or Marco van Basten go [abroad], how can we build something solid that will last? It is impossible. I am not disposed to rebuilding a competitive team at the highest level each season'. Given this view of his homeland, which takes little account of the achievements of 1988, it is doubtful whether the KNVB would have had the courage to offer Cruyff the national manager's job after his retirement but in many ways club management seems to suit Cruyff better. In time the lure to compete once again against Beckenbauer and Platini may prove irresistible to both Cruyff and the KNVB. For the moment, at Barcelona, he is guaranteed the highest income possible from the club's enormous financial resources and can work with young players, which has proved to be a Cruyff management forte. In direct contrast to the way he liked to play the game himself, Cruyff has imposed a strict system of play on Barcelona, expecting each player to fit into the role assigned by the manager. 'The players are all men of character,' he said, 'but they know they must conform to collective discipline and put into practice the lessons I have determined should be applied.' Looking for an extension of total football in the Catalan capital, Cruyff remarked: 'Every player involved in an action must take part in it to 100 per cent of his capability without seeking to know whether he is an attacker or a defender'. In his first season at Barcelona, Cruyff won the Cup-Winners' Cup, but while this may be classed as a huge achievement for most clubs, the Catalans will be satisfied with nothing less than the League title and the Champions' Cup.

Beckenbauer, the disciplined and methodical performer who was always ready to sacrifice his natural game to the demands of Schoen's tactical plans, now exercises a degree of democracy in the German camp, continually prompting his senior players to say what they think. 'Football is not one opinion, it is thousands of opinions', he said. 'Often I cannot explain my selection or the choice of tactics. I cannot give reasons; what I do is through intuition. I have never learned the job of manager, I sense what is necessary.' A more marked reversal of roles would be difficult to imagine. What is interesting is that during the period of the duo's greatness as players the game in England was unable to come to terms with gifted individuals, such as Peter Osgood,

Frank Worthington and Alan Hudson, who were spurned by successive England managers. The side of 1966, with the notable exception of Jack Charlton, has faded into the memory, its experience almost wholly lost to a game bedevilled by humiliation and failure. And the one true world-class England player of the 1970s, Kevin Keegan, languishes on a Spanish beach, his knowledge and proven powers of leadership unwanted in his homeland. Keegan stands little chance of emulating Cruyff and Beckenbauer in management yet his credentials are not dissimilar. He was, like them, European Footballer of the Year on two occasions and succeeded in the game at the highest level. Will we ever see the day in England when Bryan Robson will succeed his namesake?

Meanwhile Jack Charlton, who had managed English clubs with some success and was once a contender for the England job, was soon to show that his grasp of tactical plans and formations was well-suited to the demands of international management. Finding the system of coaching and responsibilities at English clubs oppressive, Charlton had to go outside England for the chance to coach a national team, eventually landing the manager's job in neighbouring Eire.

10
ENGLAND EXPECTS

We live and learn but not the wiser grow

JOHN POMFRET

By 1.15 pm on a steamy afternoon in June 1970, near the southern fringes of the Sierra Madre, Jack Charlton had seen enough. He strolled out of the stadium into the midday sun and made for the nearest bodega where he sought solace in an ice-cold bottle of Mexican beer. It could not have been the score or the performance of his countrymen that prompted the England defender to leave his cool position in the shade for the comfort of the bar. But Charlton could not shake off an uneasy feeling. Somewhere inside he felt that events on the pitch in Leon were set to change dramatically, that something sensational was about to happen. As he emerged from the stadium his brother Bobby was making the long walk to the bench, having played an immaculate game for 60 minutes in a match that would shape England's destiny for a generation. His substitution, and that of Martin Peters, by manager Sir Alf Ramsey would be debated for years as the resilient West Germans, led as ever by the Schoen-Beckenbauer alliance, came from 2–0 down to beat England 3–2 in extra time and end the nation's ambition to retain the World Cup. What Jack Charlton could not possibly have realised was that he was witnessing the beginning of the inexorable decline of the English national team, a decline that would see more than a few equally disastrous incidents in the years to come, and that he himself would knock the final nail in the coffin of his homeland's football aspirations on a memorable afternoon in Stuttgart 18 years later.

The three losses suffered by a labouring England team at the 1988 European Championships in West Germany exposed the manager,

Bobby Robson, to a series of vitriolic attacks in the British press which were carried on into the 1988–89 season as England continued to turn in poor performances: in particular, a disappointing 0–0 home draw against Sweden in the first qualifying game for the 1990 World Cup in Italy. Since the defeat by West Germany in 1970 the England team had gone through a number of traumatic periods – failure to qualify for two successive World Cups in 1974 and 1978 and lacklustre performances on the two occasions when the team did finally make it to the finals in 1982 and 1986 are some examples – but the sheer ineptitude of the displays in West Germany in 1988 saw England reach the nadir of its unfortunate recent history. By contrast, during the same period, English club sides began to make remarkable inroads into the European club competitions and by the time of the ban on English clubs in 1985 the country's teams possessed the best record of any country in Europe. The subsequent period of enforced isolation has undoubtedly contributed to a widening gap between English players and their continental counterparts but the truth is that England's abysmal record at national level began well before the ban and paralleled almost exactly the rise to prominence of the nation's club sides.

The basic reason for this success was that, unlike the national side, clubs played to a system, and like the roots of most good things in English football the system's origins lay in the bootroom at Liverpool. In 1973, after Liverpool were outplayed by Red Star Belgrade in the second round of the Champions' Cup, manager Bill Shankly and his coaching staff decided that success would only come if they turned their natural way of playing into a system, the English system. The long ball was certainly a part of it, but it was allied to skill, team-work and what the French call 'la rage de convaincre' – the will to win. It was a system that the continentals couldn't and wouldn't think of emulating but it laid the foundations for the domination of European football by English clubs for a decade.

After showing initial hostility, the Football League began to embrace the European concept in the 1950s. From the first win in a European competition by Spurs, who took the Cup-Winners' Cup in 1963 by beating Atletico Madrid 5–1, English clubs have enjoyed more success than any other nation, gaining 22 European trophies up to 1985. The spread of clubs winning competitions is also greater than that of any other country, comprising Liverpool (six trophies), Spurs (three), Leeds, Nottingham Forest (two apiece), West Ham, Manchester City, Chelsea, Everton, Newcastle, Arsenal, Ipswich, Manchester United and Aston Villa (one apiece). After initial dominance by Real Madrid in the 1950s and the Dutch-German teams of the early 1970s, English sides gained a monopoly on the Champions' Cup, winning the most important European trophy six times in succession from 1977. These successes were deceptive, however, and pointed to the important benefits that accrued when English, Scots, Welsh and Irish (not to mention Danes, Dutch and Argentinian) players were fused together.

Many English club sides are conglomerates, comprised of players from all four home countries and further afield, and this tradition has not diminished in recent years. Indeed, the Liverpool team that won the League and Cup double in Kenny Dalglish's first season as manager, 1985–86, often took the field with no English players at all. This state of affairs often leads commentators to point out the need for a Great Britain team, bringing together the best from Scotland, Wales and Northern Ireland as well as England. Franz Beckenbauer remarked that 'If they joined together to form a Great Britain team, I think it would be very hard for the rest of the world to beat them'. Such a plan, while having much to recommend it, is unrealistic given the jealously-guarded autonomy of the four separate Football Associations of Britain. It may be that any impetus for change in this direction will have to come from outside. There is some indication that this could happen as there have been moves within the world governing body of the sport, FIFA, particularly from third world representatives, to challenge Great Britain's historical privilege of having four separate associations affiliated to the organisation. For the moment, however, such a development seems extremely unlikely, although the English FA, through its secretary Ted Croker, expressed an interest in 1988 for a Great Britain team to be revived for the Olympic Games, in which the whole country has not participated since the abolition of the 'amateur' status of Olympic football.

The lack of Scottish, Irish and Welsh players did not prevent England from winning the World Cup in 1966, nor from dominating the world game in an earlier era. However, while other countries were streamlining their domestic structures and coming to terms with a new environment which recognised the growing importance of international competition to the viability of national leagues, the game in England remained weighed down by a century of tradition from which it has always appeared incapable of struggling free. It never fails to astonish other footballing nations that the ultra-competitive English League still demands that players often have to play on the Saturday before important international games, whereas most European countries cancel their entire First Division programmes, even before a friendly. Something of the prevailing attitude can be seen as far back as 1973, when a 1–1 draw with Poland wrecked England's chances of qualifying for the World Cup in West Germany. The result was greeted with dismay by the media and there can be no doubt that the match was regarded as something of a national catastrophe. Alan Hardaker, then the dictatorial secretary oɪ the Football League, said that the English public was far more concerned with what happened at Old Trafford or at other League grounds on a Saturday afternoon than it was with the progress of the England team. Before the game he remarked, 'It is a football match, not a war. Let's keep our sense of perspective – if we do lose, the game is not going to die. It will be a terrible thing for six weeks and then everyone will forget about it'.

Hardaker's view reveals a divergence in English football administration which is unheard of elsewhere. Part of the problem has always been that the two bodies in charge of the English game, the Football Association and the Football League, have maintained a strict demarcation line between their individual operations. The FA is responsible for the whole game, its organisation and discipline at all levels, from grass roots to professional football. The organisation also runs the FA Cup and the affairs of the national team and provides the country's representation to international football bodies such as UEFA and FIFA. The League is a kind of trade federation, responsible for the administration of the League Championship and its associated competitions, such as the Littlewoods Cup. Whereas the structure of the FA is based essentially on the amateur game – its officials are appointed from the county associations that are affiliated to it and only seven of the FA Council's 92 members represent professional football – the structure of the League is built on the interests of the 92 professional clubs who take part in its competitions. League decisions are generally taken by the Management Committee, which is composed entirely of club directors. This has sometimes led to areas of tension between the two bodies, particularly where the national team is concerned.

Matters affecting the England team, including the appointment of its manager, are in the hands of the men of the FA Council, led at present by chairman Bert Millichip, who at the age of 74 is still a spring chicken compared to some of his co-members on the council, and Dick Wragg, 78, chairman of the International Committee. The lack of a compulsory retirement age means that the higher echelons of the FA are a sinecure for those who are not as young as they were and has resulted in the front row of the council chamber being labelled 'death row'. Other than an ineffective Joint Liaison Committee, no system of FA and League co-operation exists, which means that the kind of League restructuring that has taken place in other countries is almost impossible to contemplate in England, where the FA has been loath to interfere in the League system. The effect of all this is that the game remains dominated by the interests of clubs, rather than those of the national side.

In virtually every other country there is no argument about whether the national team comes before the clubs. It is taken for granted. Michel Hidalgo explained the French way, which is typical of European systems: 'The federation is the supreme football authority', he said. 'The clubs are under the control of the federation. It is essential that they work hand in hand. Professional football cannot be above the president of the federation.'

The abuse hurled at Bobby Robson after the 1988 experience served only to deflect the public from the real reasons why things were going wrong. After all, Robson was the choice of just about everybody when he was appointed to the job after the 1982 World Cup and it is difficult to see where there are any other English managers who could do much better. Robson himself is absolutely certain he is the right man for the job, because the FA's criterion for the position was success as a First Division manager. He said: 'I served my apprenticeship as a Football League manager. To have as good a track record as I had when I took the job, they [other contenders] would have to have been in charge of a Football League team in the First Division for 14 years. And in the last ten years I managed Ipswich Town; the club was hardly out of the top five and in my last two years I finished second on both occasions. So anybody coming to the job would actually have to be successful to that point. I think a lot of people have forgotten what I did in club management'.

Of course neither the FA nor the media has ever looked to see if there are any suitable candidates for the England job who are not English. Such a course of action would be tantamount to treason to many, but this is exactly what other European countries have done to such great effect. Ernst Happel, the Austrian who took Holland to the 1978 World Cup final, or Stefan Kovacs, the Romanian who revitalised the French national team in the mid-1970s, are two notable examples. The ease with which people move from country to country in Europe has always seemed vaguely suspect to the English, who have never allowed a foreign coach to get within shouting distance of an English First Division side, let alone the national team. The criticism of Robson was also nothing new. Alf Ramsey had suffered it, as had his successors Don Revie and Ron Greenwood, each to varying degrees but all as an accompaniment to failure.

When the winners of recent World Cups and European Championships are examined, one common feature emerges which is entirely lacking in the English game. Each victorious nation has deemed its international performances to be more important than its domestic competitions. In nearly all cases, including those of impoverished Latin America, the result of this thinking has strengthened both players and domestic competitions in the longer term. In England, the priority has always been the interest of the clubs, and after the upheavals of 1985 and 1988, when the balance of power swung towards a few top clubs, this emphasis has if anything become more marked. We have seen how the detailed restructuring in Germany and Holland led to vast improvements in the national teams of both countries but other examples can be found. Italy, for instance, which eliminated England from the 1978 World Cup and won the trophy in 1982, operates an 18-team First Division (recently increased from 16) with significantly fewer fixtures and meaningless competitions than is the case in England. Even Spain, whose fragmented structure and history make it exceedingly difficult to harness existing natural talent to national ends, manages to keep international weeks free of League games. The country reached the European Championship final in 1984, while England failed even to qualify for the final stages of the competition. In France the national team won the 1984 European Championship from the base of an 18-club First Division while Argentina put the winning of the World Cup in 1978 before everything. The subsequent transfer of many Argentinian players to Europe, combined with the emergence of the Maradona talent in the wake of the inspirational win in 1978, undoubtedly contributed to the ability of the country to regain the Cup in Mexico in 1986. In Brazil, where ultimate success has eluded the national team since the triumph of 1970, full scale restructuring of domestic competitions has already begun. In all these cases the national team has been placed at the top of a pyramid structure in which the individual domestic games are geared to provide international sides with the best chance of success.

The decline and failure of England is rarely looked at in this world context. It always seems to be the fault of an individual manager or a group of players. Although criticism can and should be levelled at those who do not perform to the limit of their capabilities, it escapes the attention of most critics that there exists no messiah in the wings who could be dragged to the centre of the stage to work the magic of success, nor is there a cavalry of young players waiting over the hill for the sound of the clarion call. On the contrary, as the immediate future is contemplated the outlook is bleak.

After Ramsey's team had been beaten by West Germany in 1970 there was a feeling that the defeat had been a matter of bad luck (the loss of Gordon Banks and the dreadful performance of his replacement, Peter Bonetti), or poor tactical awareness (asking too much physical work of players in the heat and altitude of

Franz Beckenbauer.

LEFT: Kevin Keegan.

BELOW: Jack Charlton.

OPPOSITE:
Johan Cruyff.

RIGHT: Sir Alf Ramsey.

BELOW:
Bobby Robson.

OPPOSITE:
Glenn Hoddle.

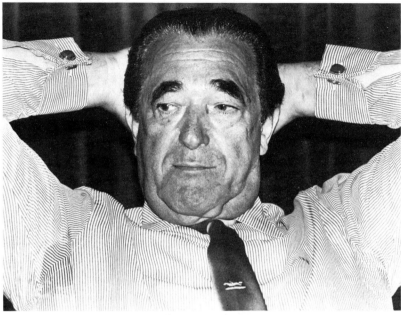

Robert Maxwell.

Graham Kelly.

OPPOSITE: Peter Mead.

Sir Stanley Rous.

Joao Havelange.

Mexico, or the substitutions of the manager when England were leading 2–1). After all, England's narrow 1–0 defeat by Brazil in Guadalajara had been one of the highlights of the entire tournament and there was certainly no shame attached to the team's eventual elimination. The side failed to recover, however, and two years later its failings were exposed dramatically at Wembley when once again the West Germans knocked England out of a major competition, this time the European Championships, in a 3–1 win inspired by Gunter Netzer and Franz Beckenbauer. Thus the defeat by Poland in 1973 did not come as a great surprise although this did not limit the traumatic effect. Alf Ramsey had never enjoyed the best of relations with the press and most football journalists turned on him with a vengeance after the Poland match. It may well be true that by the 1970s Ramsey had lost touch and was the wrong man for the job but the decision of the FA to sack him and, as there was no line of succession, simply to go for the most successful club manager of the time, Don Revie of Leeds United, exposed the lack of continuity for all to see. The irony of Ramsey's dismissal is that he remains the only England manager ever to be fired by the FA, though he is also the only manager ever to win an international competition with the English national team.

When Ramsey was originally offered the job of team manager he accepted provided that he could do it his way. His view of the councillors of the FA was made clear at the outset when on his first summer tour he publicly thanked them for their 'sense in keeping out of our way'. This was a remark that was never forgotten. As long as he kept winning, the resentment was held in check but as soon as results began to go against him his nemesis arrived in the form of Sir Harold Thompson, who had become vice-chairman of the FA in 1967. Ramsey, outwardly polite even when he could not tolerate people, was obviously offended by Thompson's public school habit of referring to him by his surname. When, in April 1974, after the defeat by Poland and elimination from the European Championships, the executive committee of the FA voted unanimously to sack him, the horrified reactions of his fellow professionals were summed up by an anonymous comment given to Brian James of *The Sunday Times* by a First Division manager. 'This is bloody awful. I played for England before Alf. It was a shambles. The way the team was picked was a joke. The greatest thing Alf did for England? Not winning the World Cup but putting the amateurs in their place, turning England into a team as professional as any club. That's his real achievement . . . that's why they've got together and slung him out. The clock's gone back ten years this week.'

Don Revie was palpably the worst choice the FA could have made. As manager of Leeds, not only had he pulled out his international players from successive England squads through dubious injuries, to the chagrin of Alf Ramsey, but his Leeds team, despite some superb performances, often displayed a cynical attitude towards the spirit of the game which would translate uneasily to the international arena. Revie's 'godfather' approach, his obsessive fear of the opposition (especially when it came to important games) and his lack of a consistent tactical plan made him unsuitable for a role which demanded inspiration rather than perspiration, long-term vision rather than short-term expediency. Failure to qualify for either the European Championships of 1976 or the World Cup in 1978 brought the national side to a new low.

The FA could not understand what was going on. While Dick Wragg, chairman of the International Committee, was defending Revie to the media – 'It makes me angry to hear criticism of a man who is working himself into the ground and trying to get things right for the England team' – Revie was busy arranging alternative employment in the United Arab Emirates. He signed an exclusive contract to explain it all to the readers of the *Daily Mail*. 'The job', he said, 'is no longer worth all the aggravation'.

After Revie, the FA turned to Ron Greenwood, who was given the job ahead of the mercurial Brian Clough, not for footballing or managerial reasons, but because Greenwood could be relied upon to bring stability after the upheavals of the Revie era. This time the decision of the International Committee went, not to the manager with the best track record (Clough or Bob Paisley of Liverpool) but to a man whose integrity would help avoid a repetition of the worst excesses of the Revie regime.

Unfortunately, most of the changes that Don Revie had brought to England's international set-up had more to do with the commercial side than with the team, earning him the sobriquet 'Don

Readies'. A deal with Admiral sportswear for a new England kit brought direct sponsorship to the national side for the first time and, although his players appreciated the financial rewards he was able to win on their behalf from a previously parsimonious FA, their loyalty was severely tested by his over-paternalistic regime, in which players were expected to take part in games of bingo and carpet golf. On the playing side, Revie's style brought few plaudits. Excessive fear of the opposition's strengths led to complicated dossiers being compiled which many players failed to understand. But Revie also carried on a trend begun by Ramsey, placing too much emphasis on the physical side of the game with the effect that a number of very talented English footballers failed to realise their international potential. Later, Kevin Keegan put the failures of the Revie era down to the lack of quality in the English game. 'The manager was not to blame for England's disappointing results in the mid-1970s', he said. 'He was just unfortunate to take over when he did because all the players he could choose were moderate.' Revie himself came to believe this was the case and on reflection felt that he should have selected a 'real bastard of a team'. It is a curious feature of the careers of successive England managers that while their teams failed so miserably some of the country's finest players made only sporadic appearances. This squandering of a generation's supreme artists is the greatest indictment that can be brought against not only the managers of the national team, but those responsible for the system that allowed such a crisis to develop and continue.

Peter Osgood was one of the League's most creative players and consistent goal-scorers of Ramsey's period in charge of the national team. Tommy Docherty, his manager at Chelsea, said Osgood was in a class of his own. 'I gave him ten games to prove himself, he did it in ten minutes. After Finney and Besty, he would come next in my list of the greatest ever.' Osgood also proved himself at the highest level, scoring regularly in Chelsea's appearances in the Cup-Winners' Cup in 1970–71. He scored the goal that earned the club a replay in the final against Real Madrid and got the winner two days later to help Chelsea lift a European trophy for the only time in the club's history. Yet, remarkably, Osgood only appeared for England on four occasions. Two of these were as substitute in the Mexico World Cup and one came in 1973 at the tail end of Ramsey's reign. During his most effective period, the European campaign of 1971–72, when he also scored 19 First Division goals, Osgood was never picked. If Osgood were an isolated case of a face not fitting it would be understandable. But a series of extremely talented individuals were similarly ignored or used fleetingly then discarded. Ramsey was known to prefer runners and workers to players with flair, but it was also true that forceful characters like Osgood did not sit easily with a succession of England managers. Gradually, the gift of skill or the holding of opinions, assets most valuably prized in every other footballing country, were becoming suspect attributes as far as the England team was concerned.

The list continues throughout the 1970s. Tony Currie, Alan Hudson, Charlie George, Stan Bowles, Frank Worthington and Rodney Marsh are all players who fit into this category. Although he made his name outside the First Division with Queens Park Rangers, Rodney Marsh spent five successful seasons enthralling the Manchester City faithful, yet he was capped only nine times. Currie, perhaps the most skilful midfield player of his time in England, played for the national team just 17 times in seven years from 1972. The stylish Hudson won only two caps in 1975 and was not chosen at all during his great period at Chelsea. Charlie George won one cap in 1976 when he was with Derby County, fully five years after he made such an impact at Arsenal. Even that one appearance was cut short when he was replaced by Gordon Hill. Stan Bowles, like Frank Worthington, was distrusted by Don Revie for some supposed lack of defensive capabilities and played for England only three times in 1974 and twice three years later. Worthington, whose performances during the interlude of Joe Mercer's short stewardship between Ramsey and Revie won him much praise, was used twice by Revie, once as substitute in a 0–0 draw with Portugal. Worthington's grand total of eight caps is surely nothing less than scandalous at a time when England was crying out for skill and goal-scoring ability. The same is true of all the players in this, by no means complete, list. The trend was all the more galling because the nation's football was hardly graced by an abundance of talent at this time. In the modern period the number of creative players in the English League has diminished, but of those who have managed to ally their skill to the demands of the English First Division marathon, most have suffered criticism for some supposed 'lack of work-rate'. And the player who in recent times has most polarised this debate over skill is Glenn Hoddle.

Hoddle was first chosen to play for England by Ron Greenwood in 1979. Like Michel Platini, he scored on his debut from a long-range shot but there the comparison ends. Whereas Michel Hidalgo saw the young Frenchman as the cornerstone of a successful future and built a team around the talented play-maker, Hoddle came under intense pressure from the start for not fulfilling the defensive role that English coaches had come to expect from all midfield players. After that first appearance against Bulgaria, Hoddle was dropped by Greenwood for the next three games. The manager said, 'Glenn has to learn that the career of a footballer is built on disappointments'. It was a strange decision by a man who, as a club manager with West Ham United, had encouraged his teams to play fluent, attacking football and had always promoted players with flair. As an international manager, though, Greenwood became infected with the all-consuming fear that militated against players such as Hoddle making a significant international breakthrough. The manager could not even make up his mind who to play in goal, ushering in the ludicrous spectacle of alternate appearances by Peter Shilton and Ray Clemence. While Hoddle was used intermittently, both Greenwood and his successor, Bobby Robson, preferred to put their faith in the more prosaic talents of Bryan Robson, who was always seen as a more 'reliable' player than Hoddle, although Greenwood has called Hoddle's ability 'prodigious' and Bobby Robson has said, 'Hoddle is a fantastic player'.

By the time of the European Championships in Italy in the summer of 1980, Hoddle was still not fully established in the team and made only one appearance, in England's last match, against Spain, by which time the team was effectively out of the competition. Hoddle had to wait nine months and three more games before winning his next cap, when he scored again in a 2–1 defeat by Spain. But he was not retained for the following two matches, neither of which England won. In the 1982 World Cup in Spain, Hoddle played in only two games, because of an injury to Bryan Robson, and one of those was as a substitute. Despite the team's success in both matches, Hoddle was not chosen for the all-important second round games which saw England eliminated after two sterile 0–0 draws.

Hoddle, with 53 caps to his name, does not fit entirely into the pattern set when previous creative players were ignored by English managers. However, he was rarely able to get a decent run in the team to establish himself and was often made the scapegoat when things went wrong. The player had his detractors, one of whom was Alf Ramsey, who criticised his commitment in a newspaper column. The central point about Hoddle, though, also applies to the other players mentioned earlier. While he was sitting on the side-lines there was hardly a plethora of skilful newcomers ready to take his place, and the England record during this period is once again characterised by failure. As *Sunday Times* football correspondent Brian Glanville commented after a defeat against Denmark in 1983, in which Hoddle did not play: 'Robson tells us he wants Hoddle, provided he will play more than 20 minutes in each half. That's 40 minutes, sports fans! Would that Gregory, Wilkins and Lee [the England midfield] had given us 40 decent minutes between them'.

At Tottenham, the team's whole style of play was built around Hoddle's supreme gifts, the Argentinian Osvaldo Ardiles acting as the perfect foil. Hoddle's seasons in European competitions were as productive as might be imagined and he played a prominent role in the 1984 campaign which ended with Spurs winning the UEFA Cup, although he missed the final matches through injury. When he was transferred to Monaco in 1987, Hoddle once again turned in some incredible performances and the club were only eliminated from the Champions' Cup in 1989 after injury had kept him out at a crucial time, just before the quarter-final tie with Galatasaray of Turkey.

When asked in 1989 about '*les meneurs de jeu*' – play-makers – Michel Platini replied: 'You know there are practically no longer any great number tens. Even abroad. In France there is Hoddle. There was Brady. Where are the others?'. Hoddle himself spoke of his experiences in England and his view of the continental game since his move to the principality. 'I had my admirers in England, especially at Tottenham, but I was always being criticised for a lack of defensive work. When I look back to the days when I first went to Spurs at 14, I remember some of the players then and I feel they had their natural game knocked out of them. I'm doing more defensive work here than I ever did at Tottenham, but I'm doing it in the opposition's half of the field. In England the defensive side has improved by 80 per cent, but what has stopped still has been what I call the offensive side, the technical side. They respect the English attitude over here and try to bring it in to some part of their game. But I don't think we really respect them and try to bring the technical side into our game. We really think we still have the best way of playing. We've closed our minds. We play this way. We're England and that's it.'

Hoddle's view is borne out by the almost unbelievable comment made by Charles Hughes, the FA assistant director of coaching, who is reported to have said on a trip to America in 1989: 'We are now certain that practically the whole world has got it wrong and, more particularly, Brazil has got it wrong in the method of playing'. Hughes made this statement after claiming that a study of statistics showed that the majority of goals scored in foot-ball matches came from long balls played out of defence rather than good movements. Of course, if the English game provided Hughes with his statistical sample, then this result is only to be expected. If the same technique were applied to goals scored in just about any other country of the world an entirely different picture would emerge. Another example of Charles Hughes' chauvinistic approach to football is the case of Ossie Ardiles, a World Cup-winner with Argentina and a star of the English game with Spurs for almost ten years. He sought to prolong his involvement with English football but his application for the FA coaching badge was rejected because he is foreign. Ironically, Ardiles was nevertheless able to become manager of Swindon Town because, unlike in most other countries, no coaching badge is required to manage an English League club.

On the subject of the England side, Hoddle confirmed (as has Bobby Robson) that the team was never designed to function in a way that would bring out the best in his game. His main point however was that England rarely operated a settled system of play. 'The first job of any manager is to decide the way he wants his team to play, then to pick the best players to fit his system. If he hasn't made a decision, if it's left to whoever is in form at club level, you'll never get success in international football.' There is no doubt that Hoddle is enjoying the new lease of life continental football has given him. The Monaco team has been built around his style and the club's coach, Arsène Wenger, says of him: 'He is indispensable, we know that. He allows his colleagues to express themselves. All teams need this'. At the end of the 1988–89 season Hoddle signed a new two-year contract with Monaco that made him one of the highest-paid players in the world. This came after a season in which he scored 18 League goals in 32 appearances, of which only two were penalties. Hoddle's performance against Orléans in the French Cup prompted Henri Zambelli, the Orléans defender, to say: 'It's difficult to play against a player who has hands in place of his feet'.

When the recent history of the English national team is examined in detail the profligate waste of talent emerges as a significant difference between the attitude of England and that of other major footballing nations. Another is the system under which successive managers have been forced to operate. After 1966 the football world moved on. Alf Ramsey, like most autocrats, could not change with the times and remained rooted to the system he had instigated that year. Years later he reaffirmed the limitations of his views, the narrowness of his ideas: 'I am always suspicious of "crowd pleasers". I have never encouraged them in my sides because I always believed those stars with a high profile and brimming with outrageous ability were also inconsistent, and the first to let the team down'. The total football of Holland and the sweeper system evolving in most of the rest of Europe completely passed him by, as they did all other England managers and the English game in general. The five-man midfield which emerged as a feature of the 1984 European Championships was used by only one or two managers in the English League in succeeding seasons, notably by David Pleat while he was manager of Spurs. When Joe Mercer was appointed interim England manager after Ramsey's dismissal in 1974 his philosophy was altogether different from that of the more permanent appointees. 'I'll pick the best players', he said. 'If you pick the best players, they'll go out and play.' Mercer's record of three wins, four draws and one defeat does little justice to the excitement his short reign provided, particularly on an undefeated three-match tour of Eastern Europe. By contrast, Don Revie was simply unable to make the transition from club to international management, with all its different emphases and demands. Ron Greenwood, the great stylist, was reduced to picking almost all of his first England team from Liverpool and seemed always to be looking over his shoulder for the spectre of defeat and humiliation which had ultimately been the fate of Alf Ramsey and Don Revie.

Unlike the West Germans, the FA had no policy of continuity and no England manager has ever been schooled in the job as Helmut Schoen was as assistant manager in Germany. Nor could the system have coped with gifted individuals like Beckenbauer or Cruyff. And while other Leagues were streamlining themselves to improve the prospects of their national teams, the English League carried on, seemingly oblivious to the effects that the national team's poor performances were having on the game in general. The success of the clubs was bought, to some extent, at the expense of the England team, which has continually been ravaged by injuries and other withdrawals caused by the excessive number of fixtures English clubs are expected to fulfil. In 1985, the Football League clubs voted to reduce the number of First Division teams from 22 to 20 but even this modest change has come under attack twice, in 1988 and 1989, by clubs anxious to play as many games as possible per season to maximise their income.

The failures of Ramsey, Revie and Greenwood increased the pressure on Robson. His own initial failure to qualify England for the 1984 European Championship meant that his position rested on his ability to get the side to the World Cup in Mexico in 1986. That objective was realised, not without a number of scares en route, but the expectations that qualification generated proved too much for the team and for Robson. After a series of appalling performances, including defeat by Portugal and a 0–0 draw with Morocco, Robson was saved from what looked like certain humiliation by being forced to change his team following an injury to Bryan Robson and the sending-off of Ray Wilkins against the Moroccans. The FIFA technical report on the competition said that the loss of Robson and Wilkins enabled Hoddle 'to make use of his brilliant skill in the middle and assume command. With quick short passes and plenty of direct moves the attacks were now constructed in a more variable way'. The report went on to slam the English preparation: 'Manager Bobby Robson was faced with the same problems against which all his predecessors had to struggle. Every year, the all-powerful Football League puts up such a compact programme that for the national team only a few free dates are at his disposal . . . England's manager is frequently forced to play without some of his key players. Not one football nation can afford to neglect its international team in such a way'. That Bobby Robson's team ended up qualifying for the quarter-finals, where it put up a creditable performance against Maradona's Argentina before unluckily losing 2–1, blinded many to the side's previous deficiencies, which had been righted only by accident and the goals of Gary Lineker.

The FIFA technical report also questioned the development of young players in the English system: 'The England youth team qualified for the World Youth Championship [in 1981 and 1985] but not a single player from these squads was picked for Bobby Robson's World Cup team'. The performance of the England youth team in 1985 had drawn criticism from another FIFA report, which said: 'Seeing the team finish bottom of its group [below Paraguay, China and Mexico] should be a clear warning to all those concerned with English football. There was no outstanding player, all were good average. Above all, the English players' lack of creativity was evident . . . the physical condition of the English players was also not above reproach . . . whether the people responsible for running English clubs will learn a lesson from this is by no means certain'.

Of course, nothing had been learned. Qualification for the 1988 European Championship from a weak group containing Yugoslavia, Northern Ireland and Turkey led many, not only in England, to conclude that the nation had a real chance of its first international success in 22 years. Even Franz Beckenbauer made England favourites before the tournament began, despite the fact that his West German team had demolished England in a friendly only a few months previously. Beckenbauer may well have been using one of his managerial ploys – making it clear to the German public that his team was really not good enough so that any subsequent success became a bonus rather than an expectation – but such pronouncements were taken seriously in England. English success was not to be, however, and the side's weaknesses were about to be exposed as never before as Robson's team, which still had no regular place for Glenn Hoddle, was utterly destroyed in three successive games. In the UEFA technical report that followed the tournament, England's play was again castigated. It said: 'The England defence seemed to be out of its depth tactically, unable to adapt to the style of continental European forwards. They obviously miss the regular exposure to European football in club competitions, with more and more players coming into the First Division in England without ever having played against continental teams, thus making the gap between England and the rest of Europe even bigger'.

The talk in English football circles in 1988 summed up the predicament of Robson and the England team. Club chairmen were far more concerned with the expected bonanza from television than with any constructive ideas to help the national side. Whenever restructuring has been discussed, it has been in the context of channelling more money to a few top clubs and lip service at the most is all that is paid to the England team. Nonetheless, the expectations of both the media and the public of England's chances in West Germany were high.

Meanwhile, the idea of employing a foreign coach had bypassed the British mainland but had found a home in Eire. The tiny country has exported many excellent players to the English League over the years but consistently failed to reach the final stages of any major tournament. In a bid to reverse the situation, the Irish turned to the old England international, Jack Charlton, who had managed a number of clubs in England, none of them for very long. Charlton fulfilled his prime objective when Eire qualified for West Germany. The first game could not have been more dramatic. Pitted against neighbours England, the Irish were given little chance but Charlton's well-drilled team approached the game in Stuttgart full of optimism. Once again the English claims to greatness were cruelly exposed as the Irish beat their old enemy 1–0 by playing to a rigidly predetermined tactical plan worked out by the manager. That all the expectations should be deflated by someone who had worn the white jersey with such pride in his playing days was the ultimate irony. England never recovered, and bowed out of the Championship a thoroughly demoralised outfit, the only time they failed to gain a single point in a major championship. Anatoly Byshovets, coach of Moscow Dynamo and the Soviet Olympic team that won the gold medal in Seoul, succinctly summed up the reason for England's failure by pointing to the growing gap in ability that had emerged during the championships. 'The team was not well enough prepared. Football is becoming quicker and more versatile. It is not enough for a player to do one job, every player has to be able to do everything. Only by having that ability will you achieve good results at the highest level.'

In April 1989, support for the idea of a foreign coach working with the England team came from an unusual quarter. Bert Millichip, chairman of the FA, proposed that Leo Beenhaaker, who had announced he would be leaving Real Madrid at the end of the season, be taken on to the England coaching staff as a possible successor to Bobby Robson. Beenhaaker had expressed an interest in working in England. 'I've always been a great admirer of English football because they play so much with the heart and have such a fine temperament', he said. 'There is such an ambience about the English game. If I could work with these qualities – maybe give a team that touch of influence to play more with the head . . . it's one of my dreams.' But the International Committee of the FA, which is responsible for such matters, did not even consider the idea.

After the ignominious exit from West Germany the press went to town on Robson, but none of his critics bothered to analyse why the catalogue of failure should be so continuous. One voice which was raised against both the system and the England manager was that of an ex-player. Kevin Keegan had been one of England's few success stories in the 1970s, winning championships and cups with Liverpool at home and in Europe. Following his transfer to Hamburg in 1977 he won the European Footballer of the Year award, the first Englishman to do so since Bobby Charlton. Keegan's performance in the Champions' Cup final for Liverpool in 1977 was outstanding and the game is still often referred to as

Keegan's final. Unfortunately for Keegan, his time as a player with the national team coincided with the Revie-Greenwood eras of failure. Despite this Keegan was recognised as perhaps the one true world-class player of his time and his qualities of leadership and commitment were widely admired. Like that of so many others, though, Keegan's experience has been totally lost to the English game. In the wake of the defeats in West Germany, and a poor start to the business of qualifying for the World Cup in Italy, Keegan went public with his thoughts. Pointing to the precedents of Beckenbauer and Platini, he made a pitch for the England manager's job. Identifying the problems of the English game which, according to Keegan, stemmed from the ban from Europe, he remarked: 'It's not a case of Europe missing us. We need Europe. Our young players are losing out on experience which you cannot buy and it's starting to show at international level. The danger is that they [young players such as Paul Gascoigne and Tony Adams] will think English football is the best in the world. It isn't any more'. Of Bobby Robson, Keegan said: 'There is a new wave of managers coming through into the game. Look at Franz Beckenbauer and Johan Cruyff. I was horror-struck when I heard Robson . . . talking about planning for the next ten years after virtually ruining the last ten. Why shouldn't someone like me be given a chance at international level? Come to that, why shouldn't Kenny Dalglish be in with a shout? Being Scottish shouldn't come into it if you really want the best'.

Keegan also attacked the system at the FA which he sees as equally responsible for the country's footballing plight. He was not able to understand, for instance, 'the organising of certain friendlies, like the one against Greece. We should be testing the players against the best, like West Germany and Holland'. The build-up of England teams for big tournaments certainly seems to bear out the Keegan analysis to some extent, being based more on expediency than any recognisable plan. The emergence of third world countries has gone entirely unnoticed by the septuagenarians at the FA. One of the features of recent World Cups has been the performance of African countries (Algeria beating West Germany in 1982 for instance), yet no African team has ever appeared at Wembley, despite historic connections between Britain and the

African continent. At a time when attendances for Wembley internationals are in sharp decline it is odd that the FA does not seek to market the game actively through matches against these countries, many of which would now be capable of giving England a stern test. Such a course might also be politically favourable. Not only would games against third world opposition help to recreate the historic role of Britain, which took the game around the world, and help to stimulate football in the countries themselves, it might also cement friendly relations which could deflect future moves to lessen British representation within FIFA.

It is certainly not the intention of this book to promote the claims of any particular individual, but it is astonishing that no place can be found to utilise the talents of Kevin Keegan. There surely would be few who could plausibly argue that the quality of the national team, or indeed of the League itself, is so high that they can do without the likes of the former Liverpool star. In other countries Keegan may well have been encouraged to learn the manager's job alongside the existing coach, taking over when the time was right in an effort to ensure continuity. Such a policy simply does not exist in England, however, and the track record of the English authorities leaves little hope that it ever will.

As a vital World Cup qualifying game against Albania approached in April 1989 the League refused to cancel the preceding weekend's programme and got itself into more difficulties by allowing a vital First Division game between Liverpool and Arsenal to be scheduled for the benefit of the television cameras just three days before the Albania match. Once again, money for the clubs proved more important than the performance of the England team. When the media questioned the sense of the decision it emerged that the FA had not asked for the game to be shifted. Jack Dunnett said: 'I can't see what all the fuss is about. A day or two extra makes no difference'. Bobby Robson summed the situation up: 'No other country in the world would do something like this'. Eventually the game was postponed because of the Hillsborough tragedy, which merely left the issue unresolved for the future. And this situation occurred fully 18 years after the same mistake had caused the Dutch to reappraise their priorities after defeat in East Germany.

England has rarely managed to reconcile the demands of the League and the national team. This is because it is only possible to achieve that aim by putting the national team first. If the history of League and FA decision-making were filled with unmitigated success, or even modest efficiency, this situation might just be tolerable. But this is not the case. In all crucial respects, from the employment of overseas coaches to the devising of a system to accommodate the best available talent at every level, the football authorities have failed. The man who plotted England's most recent downfall, Jack Charlton, was being hailed as a hero in Dublin, and was even granted the status of 'Honorary Irishman'. After 100 years, no way has been found to ensure that those with the experience of Charlton remain in the fold after their playing days to bring the benefits of their years at the top to a new generation of players. Meanwhile, the oldest League in the world had just finished its centenary season the same way it began it: racked by disarray and chaos; unable to make the most elementary decisions over its future and that of the game it is there to promote.

11
ORGANISED CHAOS

Don't take the whole thing too seriously. Football has a crisis every other week

TED CROKER
FA secretary, to his successor, Graham Kelly

The Saturday joggers and walkers out on the cold December morning could have been forgiven for thinking that something dramatic was about to happen. The peaceful calm of the Hertfordshire countryside was suddenly shattered by the sound of Robert Maxwell's helicopter as it descended from the skies and came to rest on farmland adjoining his destination. By the time the rotors had stopped turning Maxwell, resplendent in the baseball cap that has become the trademark of his footballing persona, was sitting in David Dein's lounge, ready to negotiate.

The meeting had been arranged on the initiative of Dein who, in his capacity as a member of the Management Committee of the Football League, was attempting to defuse another potential rift within the game during the League's centenary year. It was the latest in a series of disasters that had dogged football's administrators in the three months since the official start of the celebrations to mark 100 years of League football in England. Unlike the other mishaps, this could not be dismissed as something of an amusing *faux pas*, the consequences of which, while embarrassing to those in the high offices of the League, were not ultimately serious in themselves. Now the very future of at least four League clubs was directly at stake.

At the start of the 1987–88 season it was clear that Elton John was becoming disillusioned with his involvement in football. Since he had become chairman of the club he supported in his boyhood, Watford had risen from the lower reaches of League football to a place where the team was challenging for the game's major honours, an achievement almost entirely due to the efforts of

Elton John and Graham Taylor, the man he had brought to the club as manager. It was the earning power of Elton John, one of the true international superstars of the entertainment world, and his willingness to devote large parts of it to the football club that had kept Watford in business and had given it the financial base to compete with the best. However, the bubble had burst. Graham Taylor, after 11 years with the club, left to join Aston Villa, and results under the next two managers, Dave Bassett and Steve Harrison, would eventually see Watford relegated to Division 2. Elton John himself had decided to give up live performances for a time after undergoing throat surgery, but in addition his personal life had been subject to the unrelenting scrutiny of the tabloid press and he may have wanted to reduce his high profile, part of which was due to his involvement in football. Whatever the reasons, John announced that he was putting his 95 per cent share of the club up for sale. 'I love the club passionately', he explained, 'but I'm no longer touring so there's no cash coming in. I could carry on as chairman but I don't want to destroy what has been achieved.' Enter centre stage, Robert Maxwell.

Robert Maxwell's active involvement in the game began in January 1982 when ailing Oxford United, which was due to fold if a large injection of cash was not forthcoming, made a desperate plea for help. Maxwell recalled the circumstances. 'I was on holiday in Jamaica that Christmas when I received a call from the then chairman of Oxford United to say that Barclays Bank had closed their accounts and refused to allow the money to pay wages. Unless I put up £120,000 the club would go bankrupt. I told them, "Why don't you go and find somebody else?" To cut a long story short, they came back, there was nobody else, so I took on Oxford United.' Maxwell had stepped in to save the club in an area in which he already had business interests. Fifteen months afterwards he acquired 30 per cent of a neighbouring team, Reading, and proposed merging the two into one club, to be called the Thames Valley Royals. This plan was abandoned after vociferous protests from both clubs' supporters but Maxwell's interest in football did not wane. On the contrary, he attempted to buy Manchester United in 1984. His offer was seriously considered by the Edwards family but, as Maxwell revealed, 'the price of £10 million was changed overnight to £15 million and I told them to get lost'. In the same year Maxwell acquired Derby County, a club which was also on the brink of financial collapse. The acquisition of Derby came after Maxwell received a request from League president Jack Dunnett to save the club, which had large debts to the Inland Revenue and was within hours of going into receivership. At the time, there was not a great deal of concern about saving football clubs and Maxwell was the last resort of a desperate club and League. The take-over of Derby took place with the blessing of the president, Jack Dunnett, and the Management Committee, despite the fact that the arrangement clearly contravened Regulation 80 of the Football League, which states that 'no person shall have an interest in more than one club'. Maxwell already owned Oxford, which passed through family trusts to his son, Kevin, and 30 per cent of Reading. It is clear, however, that his involvement kept these clubs in existence at a time when they may well have disappeared. Consequently, far from suffering, both Derby and Oxford considerably improved their positions under Maxwell's leadership. Derby regained its First Division status and Oxford reached the top flight for the first time in its history and won its first major trophy, the League Cup in 1986. When no buyers emerged for Watford Maxwell, who had plans to consolidate his business in the area, came forward in November 1987 with an offer to buy the club for £2 million.

When the news of Maxwell's interest became public, it provoked a hostile reaction in the media and from the chairmen of other clubs. There was the quite legitimate concern that one man owning or controlling a number of League clubs was bad for the game because results and transfers might be 'arranged' between such clubs to the detriment of others, although no one directly accused Maxwell of having any such intentions. The later transfer of Dean Saunders from Oxford to Derby, however, caused the issue to be raised again. Perhaps more significantly, the argument was made that Maxwell, by owning three First Division clubs, would control 15 per cent of First Division votes, the importance of which was enhanced by the new voting procedures agreed in 1986. It may also have been the case that Maxwell's abrasive style and his involvement in the television debacle of 1985 fostered personal antagonisms that had little to do with the merits of the case. Five days after Maxwell's offer was made public, on 26 November, the League Management Committee (which after the coup of 1986 contained only Jack Dunnett from the previous administration that had supported Maxwell's take-over of Derby while he still had interests in two other clubs) met to discuss the issue and voted unanimously to seek ways of blocking the transfer of Watford to the Maxwell empire unless he divested himself of his other football holdings.

A war of words ensued, with Maxwell questioning the Management Committee's right to interfere, but also giving the impression that he was ready to do business with them. On the one hand, one of Maxwell's newspapers, the *Daily Mirror*, launched into a savage attack on the game's rulers, saying: 'The Mismanagement Committee's remarks seem like those of a group of frightened men, who know they are responsible for the parlous state in which British football finds itself, but are reluctant to have their guilt exposed. They failed to respond to the hooligan menace which has emptied so many grounds. They failed to secure the best possible deal with BBC and ITV, depriving the clubs in the lower divisions of badly-needed money to ensure their survival'. In a more conciliatory gesture, Maxwell proffered an olive branch. 'I have made it a condition of the contract with Elton', he said, 'that if the League's Management Committee do not sanction this with wholehearted approval we will walk away from it. Who knows what will happen to Watford then?' However, the Management Committee clearly did not trust this statement as it went to the High Court to gain a temporary injunction stopping the sale from going through before Regulation 80 could be enforced. The phrase, 'one man, one club', became the slogan of the campaign against Maxwell, while little account was taken of the future of either Watford, Derby, Oxford or Reading. Indeed, the Management Committee offered no comfort to the supporters and players of the four clubs nor any alternative method of keeping them in existence.

After the meeting on 26 November David Dein began to have second thoughts about the position the Management Committee had adopted. The vote, however laudable the intentions that lay behind it, did nothing to solve the problems of the clubs involved.

Moreover, the League's actual power in this area was unclear – Regulation 80 was not watertight and the Committee could not simply issue an edict forbidding the sale. And anyway, the legal ownership of Derby, Oxford and Reading was not clear-cut, being spread between Maxwell's companies and his family. Dein's concern was that 'Maxwell was trying to increase his football empire. Once he had made a bid for Watford that was accepted by Elton John, I felt it needed somebody on the Management Committee to approach him and discuss with him where his future in football really lay, what he really wanted to do and I decided to take the initiative.' With all this in mind Dein telephoned Maxwell and arranged the meeting that took place at his home in Totteridge the following Saturday morning, 5 December. As Everton were playing in London, at Charlton, that day Dein also phoned League president Philip Carter and asked him if he would attend the meeting. Dein thought that if Maxwell came to a meeting of the whole Management Committee it would end in disarray, whereas a quiet get-together might achieve something. Carter readily agreed to the proposal.

When the meeting began at 10.30 am, David Dein explained to an affable Robert Maxwell that he was seen as a predator in football circles. 'Robert,' said the Arsenal vice-chairman, in an attempt to break the ice, 'you're building a football empire. You've got Derby, Oxford, Reading and now you want Watford. You only have 88 clubs to go, you're bound to win the League.' The serious question behind Dein's tongue-in-cheek remark was that no one knew which club or clubs Robert Maxwell really wanted or whether football was just a game of monopoly, a minor diversion for the sake of publicity. Maxwell's reply was to the point. 'No, gentlemen. Above all I want Watford because my business interests are in Watford. I've agreed to buy Elton John's shares and I'm determined the deal will go through.' Philip Carter explained that this was unacceptable, given Maxwell's involvement in the other clubs.

'What do you want me to do?' asked Maxwell.

'Get out of the other clubs', was the response.

'You can't be serious. I'm already in them with the acquiescence of the Management Committee.'

After some hard bargaining the three eventually reached an agreement. Maxwell would buy Watford, sell his shares in Reading immediately to the chairman of the club, Roger Smee, and sell Oxford by the end of the season. Maxwell also agreed to look for a buyer in the longer term for Derby County, as the finances of that club were still in a poor state. The phrase used was 'at a suitable time in the future', although all agreed that this would probably take two or three years. Maxwell further accepted that the business of Watford would be run by his company, BPCC, and that he would not personally influence the affairs of the club or seek to become involved with any other club. In return, the League would drop its legal action to clear the path for the purchase. The helicopter was duly despatched to collect John Holloran, chief executive of BPCC, who was to become chairman of Watford. Holloran was delighted that a compromise had been reached and the four drank a toast to their success in agreeing the deal. At 1.00 pm Carter and Maxwell put their signatures to a document outlining the details and the meeting ended. Maxwell was satisfied because he now had an agreement with the League which gave him the support he had been looking for, while Carter and Dein were similarly pleased with the compromise. The principle of one man, one club had been upheld, although Maxwell had been given time to make the divestments, and the interests of the clubs involved would be safeguarded. Moreover, as David Dein said: 'It was the start of an exercise to prune Robert Maxwell's football empire'.

After the meeting Carter and Dein tried to telephone their fellow members of the Management Committee to explain the deal, but because it was a match day, few were contactable. The agreement was well-publicised in the media over the next two days, however, and most Committee members only found out about it by reading it in the press. It was an inauspicious beginning to the deal with Maxwell, and one not calculated to bring wholehearted support. The repercussions would also eventually lead to the rift in the Management Committee which continued through the television negotiations some months later, ending with the ejection of Carter and Dein from their posts on the Committee and the reinstatement of Jack Dunnett as president.

It soon emerged that not everyone on the Management Committee was happy with the arrangement made at David Dein's house. Ron Noades, chairman of Crystal Palace, had been forced to give up his stake in Wimbledon when he took over at Selhurst Park, and was certainly unhappy that Maxwell should be seen to flout the rules by which he had abided in his own football dealings. Noades soon found allies on the Management Committee. These included Jack Dunnett, whose overthrow by Carter in the elections for the presidency still rankled. Dunnett accused Carter of exceeding his powers and claimed that there could be no agreement with Maxwell unless it was ratified by the full Management Committee. Gradually Carter and Dein found themselves isolated and unable to deliver the promise made to Maxwell that the injunction would be lifted. Ron Noades said: 'I believe there are five members of the Management Committee who are not prepared to withdraw the injunction. The Second and Third Division representatives were not aware of this meeting, neither do we yet know the details of the agreement and we do not agree with what has been approved'. In the wake of the opposition, Philip Carter asked Elton John and Robert Maxwell to postpone the sale until after the Management Committee had had a chance to ratify the agreement. Both men agreed. When the Committee met ten days after the meeting at David Dein's house, the deal was thrown out by a 4–2 majority with two abstentions, only Carter and Dein voting for the agreement. The Committee called on Maxwell to sell all his interests in other clubs before buying Watford, something Maxwell had already stated he would not be prepared to do.

David Dein was mortified. If Maxwell pulled out of the Watford deal he would still be left controlling three clubs, the very situation that the other members of the Committee claimed they wanted to avoid. 'I was ready to pull my hair out', he said. 'Football needs entrepreneurs like Maxwell. He's never taken a penny out of the game, in fact he's put money into every club he's been involved with. I despaired.' For his part, Jack Dunnett put the opposition's view. There was no guarantee that Maxwell would sell Derby or even Oxford and that situation was undesirable. Of Philip Carter's role, he said: 'Mr Carter, in an attempt to create amity, has perhaps gone too far without the authority of the Management Committee. He was entitled to negotiate but he couldn't take decisions without referring them back to the Committee and he should have made this known to the other party. He didn't do that but we were fairly kind to him. We said, "Everybody's entitled to one mistake, please don't do it again"'.

Maxwell took the Management Committee's vote as a personal insult and launched into a furious attack on the integrity of the Committee members. 'The Committee is not only incompetent. It cannot be trusted. It has proved that its word is not worth the paper on which its president has put his signature. Football now faces a crisis. It is not of my making. It is the making of those whose palsied hand has reduced the professional game in this country to penury and which is forcing our best stars abroad. If BPCC walks away from Watford, it is not the chairmen of competing clubs who will suffer. It is the footballers who play for Watford and the many thousands of supporters who have stood by them.' With Watford at the bottom of the First Division and obviously in crisis, Elton John said: 'I am astonished to hear that the Management Committee has opposed the agreement which was signed by its president, Philip Carter, and Mr Maxwell on 5 December in the presence of David Dein . . . I cannot believe this is happening, it is damaging to Watford as well as to Derby and Oxford. The way I feel at the moment I could walk away from football for good'.

In his statement issued after the original Management Committee vote on 26 November, Maxwell had called the Committee the 'Mismanagement Committee' and had castigated Philip Carter's public position. Now, once again, Carter, as president, was forced to announce the latest vote and to defend it under press questioning, which made his position somewhat untenable. He said: 'Mr Dein and I worked in good faith but the Committee have now agreed, in a democratic way, that they wish to go no further'. Maxwell, having assumed that by obtaining presidential agreement the implementation of the deal would be a formality, felt personally let down by Carter. His statement reflected the bitterness he felt. It ended: 'Mr Carter's attempted justifications for interfering in Watford Football Club's decisions are as untrue as they are childish, scandalous and slanderous. Mr Carter's real motivation is that he is scared that his and his friends' cosy little cartel, which has been lording it over our national game with such damaging consequences, could come to an end. What we have is a professional game dominated by incompetent, selfish, bungling amateurs and it is time that those who love the sport woke up to the fact and kicked them out'.

Philip Carter's response to Maxwell's attacks and his now stated intention to press ahead with the deal in any event exacerbated the situation, coming as it did after a complete about-turn by the League president. He said: 'We find it difficult to understand why a man like Mr Maxwell feels it is now necessary to have an open confrontation with the League in an attempt apparently to obtain a degree of control which we think would not necessarily be in the best interests of football. I don't think Mr Maxwell will back down in this particular case. He made his intentions quite clear. I am just disappointed he didn't honour the statement that he would walk away if he didn't have wholehearted support'.

In fact the Management Committee had no power to enforce its decision. Maxwell could have gone ahead and purchased Watford anyway, but having made several public statements to the effect that he would 'walk away' from the deal if he did not get wholehearted support from the League, Maxwell was true to his word and pulled out of it. With the very public wrangling once again doing nothing to improve football's image, Elton John had little choice but to abandon his plans to sell Watford and remain as chairman. He could have been forgiven for thinking that those in charge of the game had completely lost their powers of reasoning.

The bad feeling surrounding the Watford affair, attended as it was by some of the worst publicity even the Football League had encountered, was not isolated to these events alone. The whole season was beginning to degenerate into a farce as the centenary celebrations lurched from simple failure to outright incompetence and continued to alienate the public more and more. It had all started with such high hopes when a centenary committee, headed by Chelsea chairman Ken Bates, was formed to organise the birthday party. Profits from the various functions and events would amount to £2 million, the committee proclaimed, which, according to Bates, would be put towards the cost of establishing a football university and museum. It was a bold idea and certainly one that merited serious attention but it was entirely dependent on the financial success of the centenary year, a year which would, in the event, turn into an unmitigated disaster.

The portents for the centenary year were not good when the League's sponsor, the *Today* newspaper, pulled out before the season had even started. Speaking of complaints going back to the previous March, David Montgomery, the newspaper's editor, said: 'They [the League] failed to get the promised sponsorship of *Today* across on television and they failed to get the sponsor mentioned in other publications as the agreement required them to do'. There were many who thought the sponsorship ill-conceived in the first place as it was always going to be difficult to get other newspapers and media owners to give publicity to a rival, but even so it was not the most auspicious of starts to a birthday celebration. The withdrawal of *Today* was totally unforeseen at League headquarters despite Montgomery's assertions. League spokesman Andy Williamson said: 'It came like a bombshell'. Just as the *Today* situation became critical the centenary committee announced its plans, which were to begin with a banquet at the plush Grosvenor House Hotel on London's Park Lane on 7 August, followed by an historic game between the Football League and the Rest of the World at Wembley the next day, to be called the Centenary Classic. The weekend would be the curtain-raiser to the new season. In addition, the whole affair would have its own sponsor, financial services company Mercantile Credit, which was to pay an estimated £750,000 for the privilege. Trouble began early, however, when not one League representative turned up for the media briefing organised by the sponsors, while the world's greatest player, Argentinian Diego Maradona, refused to commit himself to playing in the showcase match.

Gradually the presence of Maradona began to assume a position of supreme importance. In the first place the press were focusing on the 'will he, won't he' aspects of Maradona's response to the invitation to play and in the second, without the guarantee of Maradona, ticket sales for the game were slow. Eventually Maradona agreed to play, but not before his fee of £100,000 was widely publicised, tainting the celebratory nature of the event for many supporters. In his defence, the Argentinian arrived in London, saying: 'I've wanted to come to England and show people something positive. There was never a time when I wasn't going to come. It's an honour to play in a match like this'. Once Maradona's appearance was certain the League ran some desperate advertisements to drum up enthusiasm. 'See Maradona play at Wembley' they screamed, attesting to the over-importance they themselves placed on his presence.

In the event, the game drew only 61,000 paying customers, many of whom spent the entire afternoon subjecting Diego Maradona to boos and cat-calls. The attendance was 27,000 lower than that for the FA Charity Shield game at the same venue a week previously and, surprisingly, there were even fewer spectators than there were the next day for the annual 'American Bowl' game of the US National Football League, which grossed £3.5 million in gate receipts, television income and merchandising. As Simon Barnes succinctly put it in *The Times*: 'Is this because American Football is getting it particularly right? Or because our own game has been getting it wrong?'.

Yet everything could so easily have been turned into a celebration of a major sporting occasion. There was tremendous interest all over the world – 64 countries took the game on television, 43 screening it live, which made it one of the most televised British football matches of all time. Given such a stage, spectators would have liked to have seen an authentic drama rather than the anti-climax that the liberal use of substitutes engendered. Indeed, the star of the game turned out to be the man to whom the match meant the most. Michel Platini desperately wanted to play. 'Throughout my career', he said, 'I never had the opportunity to play at Wembley. I couldn't miss out on that chance now. That is the only reason that pushed me into playing [Platini had by now retired]. Anywhere else I would have turned down the invitation'. Platini did not disappoint. Spontaneously applauded by both the crowd after being substituted and the press in the post-match conference, his display recalled the commitment of Di Stefano, Puskas and company, whose efforts in the 1963 FA centenary match before a capacity Wembley crowd showed how a centenary should be marked, by a memorable game of football.

Criticism of the appalling organisation of the Centenary Classic game came at the same time that the banquet at the Grosvenor House Hotel was blasted in the press for not only being extremely poorly organised but, perhaps worse, terminally boring, as visitors from a huge number of disparate countries were forced to listen to jokes told by the president-elect of the MCC. A few days later it became clear that the centenary committee had decided to organise a six-a-side tournament for all 92 League clubs which would be contested over the weekend of 16–17 April 1988, just three weeks before the end of the season when many clubs would be reluctant to use their best players because of important championship, promotion and relegation matches at the year's most crucial time. In addition, the League had cancelled that weekend's fixtures to make room for the competition, something the organisation often failed to do when games featuring the national team were imminent. This fact did not go unnoticed by the media, or at the FA.

Five days after the centenary was inaugurated the Football League announced a new sponsorship deal with Barclays Bank, worth £4.5 million over three years. While the acquisition of such a prestigious new sponsor was a remarkable achievement given that most analysts had predicted that replacing *Today* would be extremely difficult, it was unfortunate that the new sponsor came from the financial sector. It rather undermined the centenary sponsorship by Mercantile Credit, a company which saw itself in many ways as a competitor to Barclays. The fact that Mercantile Credit were now in effect sponsoring the Barclays League did not go down too well with the centenary sponsors. David Lacey, writing in the *Guardian*, summed up feelings towards the birthday at the time. 'It must be obvious that the Football League's centenary celebrations have been inspired by the Monty Python team, whose ability to complement the mundane with the absurd so frequently leads to the downright hilarious.'

If the month of August had been bad for the centenary committee, the succeeding months were, if anything, even worse. September promised a fun run to take place at every League ground under the auspices of the clubs to raise money for a number of charities, including the Heysel disaster fund. In the event, hardly anybody turned up for the poorly-publicised event and some clubs did not even bother to participate. The proposed six-a-side tournament was hastily replaced by a plan for a Wembley Festival of Football featuring qualifying teams from each division, which was based on a system no one could understand and took into account results during only part of the season. The League even managed to lose money on a concert by singer Elkie Brooks at the Albert Hall. In December, the Scottish FA refused to allow Scottish champions Glasgow Rangers to play English champions Everton for fear of crowd violence. In Rangers' place, the League invited German champions Bayern Munich to play Everton at Goodison Park. The game, played while the Watford controversy was in full cry, was a debacle. Ticket prices were increased by a massive 35 per cent in an area of known deprivation and unemployment and only 13,000 bothered to attend. Terry Crabb, a spokesman for Mercantile Credit, who was clearly alarmed at the shambolic situation the centenary celebrations had become and whose company had paid huge amounts of money to be associated with the proceedings, said: 'We are reviewing our position with the League. We urgently need to discuss what can be done to improve things'.

Meanwhile, over at the Football Association's headquarters at Lancaster Gate, the FA was attempting to emulate the League's commercial success by seeking a sponsor for the FA Cup. This was the illogical culmination of a policy initiated by Ted Croker with the sportswear company Admiral in 1976, during Don Revie's tenure as England team manager. Of course the FA requires income, but a glance across the Atlantic to the NFL would have shown the FA the way to go. There, in the hotbed of commercialism, there are no sponsored competitions and no advertisements on perimeter boards or players' shirts. The NFL has retained the purity of the live event by using television, which has turned the Superbowl, indeed the whole game, into an international spectacular providing revenue beyond the dreams of the founders and giving it the supreme status of 'America's Game'. The Superbowl is repeatedly the most popular programme on US television. By accepting a sponsor for the FA Cup, the FA would be destroying the very thing that it wishes to promote – the integrity of the competition – and therefore value would be removed from what is a national institution. Patrick Barclay wrote of the proposal in the *Independent* newspaper, 'The FA already has a sponsor. It is called the British people. If the Cup's name were sold, they would have every justification for withdrawing their support'. The fact that the rumoured sponsor was a brewer added insult to injury and after intense opposition from both the media and the public, the FA quietly shelved the project. To be fair, the FA was still hampered by the 'listed' status of the Cup final, which meant that it could not be sold exclusively to one channel. This made it far more difficult for the Association to maximise television income, and it is indeed the case that the FA Cup final remains one of the few non-sponsored events of any significance in British sport.

In the aftermath of the Hillsborough disaster, new FA chief executive Graham Kelly raised the issue again, this time saying that in addition to direct sponsorship the FA were seeking an interest-free loan of £15 million to help refurbish the country's stadia. Kelly's plan, however, has less to recommend it than his predecessor's, although Ted Croker himself said: 'The situation has changed drastically from 18 months ago. You have to support the principle of a sale now'.

It is also the case that the FA would not need the income that sponsorship can bring if it had negotiated better arrangements with Wembley. The company that owns the old stadium takes 32 per cent of gate receipts, £400,000 for a big game. It also takes 25 per cent of television money and advertising revenue and 17 per cent of the catering profits. Even car park revenue is split and Wembley takes all income from programme sales at the FA Cup final. In the past, the FA has donated money to the stadium for repairs and refurbishment. Today, Wembley is a public company, with profits of £7.1 million in 1988, and it is diversifying into other areas of the entertainment and leisure industry. While much-needed changes have begun to take place in recent times, there can be no getting away from the fact that the stadium is not the optimum choice for the role of national sporting theatre in the 1990s. Ron Noades claimed that with the money the FA has given to Wembley, and the revenues the organisation has lost in its arrangement with the owners, 'football's administrators could have bought their own stadium'.

As April 1988 approached, it became clear that interest in the Festival of Football was limited to say the least. Eventually the BBC agreed to show highlights of the games on television but this hardly kindled the enthusiasm of football supporters, who by now were thoroughly fed up with the League's ineptitude. Over two days of a forgettable tournament at Wembley the attendance was a mere 32,000 and the event lost nearly half a million pounds. The last rites of the centenary celebrations were played out before 22,000 hardy souls at Villa Park on 9 October 1988 when Arsenal played Manchester United for the Centenary Trophy. That a contest between these two giants of the English game could draw such a small crowd would have been unthinkable in normal circumstances and showed how low the celebrations had sunk in the public's esteem. All talk of universities and museums had long since ceased as the centenary committee desperately tried to salvage something from the wreckage. In the final reckoning, the expected profit of £2 million turned into a net loss of almost a quarter of a million pounds.

It is now clear that the League, not for the first time, got the whole thing wrong. The organisation simply did not understand its audience and made fundamental business and marketing misjudgments. It broke the cardinal rule by not giving people what they wanted. Instead of using proven marketing techniques to discover what supporters actually desired, the centenary committee organised a series of totally unconnected events with no thematic appeal. If proof were ever needed to show how out of touch those at the top had become, the 1987–88 season provided it in more than usual abundance. This was a period in which the English game faced severe problems; with television, with the proposed introduction by the Government of a national membership scheme and with the perennial problem of crowd violence. Although Millwall, Preston and a few other clubs had managed to contribute something through community programmes and although Liverpool had played its part on the pitch with some storming performances that took the club to yet another Championship win, these were isolated examples. Bob Paisley, the former Liverpool manager and the most successful man ever to be in charge of an English football team, decried standards in the First Division, calling it the worst he had seen for years.

In its centenary, the League finally had the opportunity to introduce schemes which could have brought the game and its fans closer together and which may have obviated the need for Government action on other fronts. Some kind of centenary club, for instance, linked to a 'Fans of Football' scheme, could have aligned football to its supporters and created a sense of identity, of belonging, something sadly lacking in the English game where the drawbridge between fans and administrators has been raised for decades. Here was an opportunity for a specific marketing policy, a chance to rejuvenate, revitalise and reposition the League for the 1990s. Instead, as the Watford shambles and the centenary fiasco showed, the season which should have been a birthday turned into a wake.

Two years later and nothing had changed. A report by business consultants Arthur Young in 1989 slammed the way the League went about its business. They recommended that the League scrap the existing rules and articles of association and start again. Management Committee meetings displayed a 'lack of clarity on what had been agreed'. Anti-hooliganism measures were discussed 'only very briefly' and they 'were confused over previous decisions and wasted time discussing current positions instead of looking ahead'. The report went on: 'We would expect the Management Committee to take every opportunity to be seen to be taking a clear lead'. But as David Dein had discerned, things had gone just too far. If anyone wanted a clear lead from football, they would certainly not get it from Lytham St Annes.

12
THE FINAL WHISTLE

Sport is like a war without the killing

TED TURNER
President of CNN

Seven days after the Centenary Classic game against the Rest of the World the new season in England began accompanied by a mood of optimism at most clubs. There was even serious talk of English teams being allowed back into European competitions following what was surely going to be a successful year for the country's football. There would be the various centenary events and a general improvement in crowd behaviour inside grounds looked set to continue. Nowhere was the optimism more visible than in the genteel seaside resort of Scarborough. The Yorkshire town, famous for its annual festival of cricket which has been the centrepiece of summer festivities since the days of games between 'gentlemen' and 'players', had never before hosted League football. However, the local club, Scarborough FC, had won the GM Vauxhall Conference the previous season to become the first non-League team to be granted automatic promotion to the Fourth Division of the League since the rule change of 1986, and there was a distinct air of expectation as the new season approached. Preparations to bring the club's ground up to League standard had been completed at a not inconsiderable cost and the town looked to be an interesting addition to the nation's football venues. Nothing, however, could have prepared the inhabitants for the way in which their entry into the reality of the English League would erupt into the ugly scenes with which residents of more traditional football towns are only too familiar.

The first match Scarborough played in the League was to be remembered for events other than football as fans of Wolverhampton Wanderers went on the rampage. Sporadic outbursts of violence in the town before the match were followed by rioting inside the ground. The game was held up for ten minutes; 50 people were arrested as the Wolves supporters who were massed behind one of the goals indulged in a running battle with a bemused local police force and £25,000 worth of damage was caused to the Yorkshire club's modest stadium. As this was Scarborough's debut in the League, television cameras were naturally present and they captured the scenes for all to see on that night's news programmes. To most people it was a sickening reminder of the problems that still faced the English game despite the claims of improved crowd behaviour that the football authorities had been making in their efforts to persuade UEFA that the country's clubs were fit to re-enter Europe. A week later the Football Association met for four hours to consider where the blame lay and what punishment to mete out to any guilty parties. The FA's verdict stunned just about everybody outside the game and led to a strengthening of feeling on the part of the Government and independent observers that the authorities were still incapable of dealing with the hooligan problem; that after years of the prevarication that eventually led to 39 deaths at the Heysel stadium in Brussels, the FA still continued to live in a closed world into which the brutal realities facing those who watched football matches were never allowed to penetrate.

The Wolves club was fined £5,000 for the misbehaviour of its fans in Scarborough. The punishment showed that the FA considered Wolves to have been culpable in some way for what had happened, yet the fine was so small that it could hardly have acted as a deterrent to other clubs by forcing them to keep a tighter control on their fans. Wolves supporters were banned from travelling to away games for six matches, although it is difficult to see how the FA expected to enforce any such ban. Perhaps worse was the fact that the FA refused to make Wolves pay any compensation for the damage caused to the stadium. The head of the FA enquiry, Les Mackay, seemed totally unaware of the furore the verdict would cause when he said, 'It is an attempt to get rid of the small element of people who attach themselves to football and we think the penalty will be sufficient to stamp out trouble for Wolves'.

The violence at Scarborough, coming as it did on the first day of the centenary season, symbolised the tawdry image that football had acquired in more than 20 years of violent behaviour by crowds, a period during which those in authority in the game wrung their hands, pleaded impotence in dealing with what they called 'society's problem' and poverty whenever constructive measures which involved a financial commitment were put forward. After the deaths in Brussels and the ostracism which followed, it appeared that even the FA and League had determined to solve the problem once and for all. The verdict in the Scarborough case was all the more baffling given this new climate. But it demonstrated once again the consistent failure of the game's overlords to make stadia safe places for people to visit. Moreover, it was not only hooliganism that contributed to the danger members of the public faced when attending games. The Bradford fire, the collapse of a wall at Birmingham under spectator pressure and even Heysel itself showed that the antiquated grounds at which many football matches are played are unable to cope with any departures from orderly behaviour or efficient administration.

Most English League grounds were constructed before the 1930s and were integrated into the existing infrastructure of working-class life, which was in the main situated in Victorian residential streets. By the 1960s these streets had become areas of urban deprivation. There was little room around grounds to improve parking facilities to reflect the rise in car ownership and the increase in away support that ease of transport and the affluence of the 1950s and '60s brought to the game. So the sight of hundreds of supporters winding through cities from railway station to stadium became commonplace. In addition to difficulty of access, most stadia retained their Edwardian accommodation, with little improvement in facilities for the ordinary fan. At Bradford the coincidence of an old wooden stand and an inefficient method of clearing away rubbish, even after repeated warnings of the danger it posed, left more than 50 dead. At Birmingham and Heysel violent movements by large numbers of spectators created pressures that ancient walls were simply not designed to resist, again resulting in death. If these are the most obvious examples, there are many, many more, all of which indicate that the twin problems of hooliganism and patently outdated stadia are inextricably linked and the possibilities of major disorder or even disaster are only kept at bay as long as something like normality is maintained. As soon as a breakdown occurs, systems of crowd control and safety procedures which are already working to the limit of their capacities, prove utterly useless. The real tragedy of Hillsborough was that it was a disaster waiting to happen.

Violence at football matches in Britain is nothing new. It has existed in one form or another since the game began. However, the 1960s saw a new development as away support increased, which involved not just violence, but organised violence. At this stage the trouble was not confined to football. Media coverage of violence among young, working-class males began in earnest in the late 1950s and was focused on the 'teddy boys', who were renowned for slashing cinema seats during the screening of rock and roll films. In the 1960s the emphasis shifted to a series of pitched battles between rival youth cults in seaside resorts on public holidays. Gradually, it was realised that the perfect forum to express antagonisms was the football ground, with its acres of terracing and lack of any effective police presence.

The first instances of organised violence associated with football came in the 1960s with the systematic wrecking of trains laid on to take supporters to away matches. Before violent incidents became common there was little segregation within football grounds as those away supporters that did attend mingled with home fans in a generally friendly atmosphere. As the violence and intimidation moved inside the grounds, young home fans began to congregate at one end which became an exclusive place into which any away supporter would venture at his or her peril. A concerted effort by administrators, police and courts at this time might have removed the problem before it reached unmanageable proportions. Instead, clubs were more concerned about the revenue brought in by the masses that still flocked to games and pretended that the problem either did not exist, or if it did, it was confined to such a small minority that it was really insignificant. Equally, the disciplinary measures which the League and FA might have forced on clubs whose fans misbehaved were not forthcoming. As media attention on football violence increased, it seemed as if those agencies responsible for maintaining public order had recognised that, given the more violent nature of English society generally, it might be advisable to attempt to contain the problem to football.

In the 1970s trouble intensified as the hooligan problem came to be seen as endemic. However, some clubs were more prone to violence than others. From destroying trains the brawling supporters took to destroying each other, then Leeds and Newcastle fans rioted on the pitch to stop important games when results were going against them. The authorities' reaction to the growing number of incidents failed to prevent the situation from getting worse. The punishment for the Leeds incident in 1971 was that the club was forced to play four matches away from home, little more than a slap on the wrist when it is considered that the manager of Leeds, Don Revie, the same Don Revie who was later appointed England manager by the gentlemen of the FA, revealed that he considered the pitch invasion justified in some way because the fans were incensed at the injustice of a refereeing decision which cost Leeds a goal in what was a vital Championship match. When Newcastle fans invaded the pitch to stop the FA Cup game that their team was at the time losing 3–1 to Nottingham Forest in 1974 the response of the FA was to order the game to be played again. Newcastle won the replay 2–0.

As these events unfolded the hooligans were becoming ever more organised. Sophisticated gangs began to appear, called 'firms' or 'crews', which met in pubs in the days preceding games to lay plans to ambush supporters of other clubs and to cause general mayhem, often right away from grounds in places like motorway service areas. Some of them went so far as to print calling cards, which they left at the sides of their unfortunate victims.

As violence and disruption began to get even more vicious the FA refused to hand out draconian fines and there were no instances of long-term ground closures or threats to force recalcitrant clubs to disband. In addition to Leeds and Newcastle, Manchester United, West Ham, Chelsea, Portsmouth, Liverpool and Everton all acquired reputations for unruly and violent supporters, but the fans who won the worst reputation of all belonged to the London club Millwall.

Millwall Football Club is situated in a traditionally depressed area in the south-east of the capital. The club's ground, The

Den, is surrounded by the tough streets of dockland London. Its supporters had always been raucous and crowd trouble had closed the ground five times between 1920 and 1978. By the 1980s, Millwall hooligans were among the most feared in the country. On 13 March 1985 the team played a fifth round FA Cup tie at Luton. The game, televised by the BBC, is remembered for the vicious riot perpetrated by Millwall supporters after the match was finished. Forty-seven were injured, there were 31 arrests and £70,000 worth of damage was inflicted on Luton's Kenilworth Road ground. On the way home, the Millwall supporters attacked buildings in the town and wrecked a train. A horrified nation had just about had enough and the Government, not for the first time, announced its concern and its intention to act.

Millwall chairman Alan Thorne, a wealthy property developer, began to believe that the hooligan problem was insoluble; the club was now wholly identified with the violence of its supporters. His disillusionment was not mitigated even when, at the end of the season, the team won promotion to Division 2. In the close season the club honoured a commitment it had given to the Greater London Council and the Sports Council by appointing a community sports development officer. The new post was a contribution to a community sports scheme set up by the GLC as part of its policy of making facilities and expertise available to disadvantaged sections of the community. Thus the 'Millwall in the Community' project was born. Millwall was one of only two professional clubs in London to fully implement the scheme (the other was Brentford), although approaches were made to every club in the capital. Coming to such a place was no easy option as the man chosen for the job, Gary Stempel, explained. 'Everyone was suspicious. I really only had support from two people at the club. Many others, including the players, just could not understand why I was there.' In 1986, in an atmosphere soured by recent events, lack of finances and the collapse of morale, Stempel began football coaching sessions during school holidays at a local park, assisted by several first team players. They were an altogether unexpected success. 'I was stunned', said Stempel. 'Here were groups of kids, from seven to 17, living in some of the toughest neighbourhoods in London, who were used to fighting kids from the next estate, listening respectfully the moment a Millwall player opened his mouth.'

At the same time that Stempel was beginning his first coaching sessions, Alan Thorne left, selling some land adjacent to The Den in exchange for money he was owed by the club. The consortium that took over comprised Reg Burr as chairman and two local men with strong Millwall connections, Jeff Burnige and Brian Mitchell. They were later joined by Peter Mead, who was a director of a leading London advertising agency, Abbott Mead Vickers. Mead and Burr immediately injected much-needed funds to see the club through an initial settling-in period while the new Board decided what to do to get to grips with the problem that was now in danger of putting Millwall out of business altogether. The club was in a parlous state on the field as well. In the space of about six months Millwall had transferred its best player, John Fashanu, to Wimbledon, who subsequently gained promotion to the First Division; lost a high-profile manager, George Graham, to Arsenal; and only eight of the first team had signed contracts for the new season. However, the club's £4.9 million debt was reduced by the land deal with Alan Thorne, and a new manager was found when John Docherty, assistant to Frank McLintock at Brentford, was brought in before the start of the new season.

The planning got underway as reports began to come back to the club of the success of the summer coaching sessions. In essence, the new Board had three possible options. It could enforce a ban on away supporters, as Luton had done after the riot by Millwall fans. This might stop trouble in and around The Den but it would do nothing to halt violence at away matches. Also, Luton's decision was extremely unpopular and, some felt, gave the team an unfair advantage. It could go for a membership scheme, perhaps along the lines of one instituted by Spurs, although there was no evidence that a membership scheme curtailed hooliganism. Indeed, both of these options presented supporters with a challenge to beat the system, one that they would probably be only too pleased to take on. In the absence of any sort of lead from the football authorities the Board decided to put its faith in strengthening ties with the local community at all levels, in the hope of getting people far more involved with the club. As Jeff Burnige put it, 'We may have lost this generation, but we've decided to see if we can save the next by working with them from a young age. We had to put our hearts and minds into the scheme. It was an ideological commitment'.

Support for the new directors came from what seemed at first sight an unusual quarter. Municipal involvement in football is conspicuous by its absence in Britain. Unlike their counterparts in many countries on the continent, local authorities have rarely attempted to utilise their local clubs on behalf of the community and municipalities have seldom become involved in the building of large scale sporting venues. For their part, football clubs are organised and run as limited companies whose aim, like all others, is to make a profit for shareholders. As the mayor of Accrington said when the town's football club went out of business in 1962, 'People do not recognise just how important a League club is to a town's status and prestige until it's too late. I can only hope that people in other towns where the League club is struggling financially heed the warning and realise before it is too late just how vital a League club is to the community'. In London in 1986, such was the enthusiasm for Millwall's efforts that Lewisham Council, controlled by the so-called hard left of the Labour Party, embarked on a partnership with the club to try to shake off the blight of violence for good. A four-year agreement was concluded under which the Council sponsored the club to the tune of £70,000 per season in return for an increase in Millwall's contribution to its community programme.

As a result of the agreement, Stempel's brief was extended. Players accompanied him on school visits to address pupils on such topics as racism and violence, and coaching was widened to cover more sections of the population, including disabled children, and grew to encompass other sports for both sexes. The leader of Lewisham Council, David Sullivan, joined the Board in the capacity of non-voting director as the partnership assumed proportions previously unheard of in Britain. The Council and the club introduced schemes to enable tickets to be distributed among the less well-off in the neighbourhood, to make sure that players were available for local events and to use The Den for a range of community activities including a social club for pensioners and sports such as archery and women's football. A free match-day crêche was started to encourage family attendance. The Council's recreation manager, David White, commenting on how close the ties between the two parties were becoming said: 'A genuine relationship has been formed, over and above the official terms of the agreement'. The benefits of the programme to Millwall's image would be enormous. Peter Mead explained the strategy: 'The great thing about Millwall', he said, 'was that if you were able to do anything it would create so much attention because of the very high level of awareness for all the wrong reasons. So even the little things you did would be such an unbelievable juxtaposition against the original image that it would be newsworthy – "Those terrible people having the sensitivity to put a crêche in . . .".'

Mead was a supporter of the community programme who said on his arrival: 'By talking to the fans, by involving them, by letting them know what is happening at the club, we believe we are changing the image of the Millwall supporter from being a cross between Rambo and Godzilla. If we demonstrate to our fans that we respect them, that we are prepared to look after them and give them an environment to be proud of, then ultimately they might actually respond to that and become the custodians of that environment and change their attitude along the way'.

Later, Mead spoke about his experience. 'I felt', he said, 'that if football was going to survive it must be seen to be part of the local community. It's actually a very potent force in the community, something the Council can be proud of. When I came the fans loved the team but hated all Board members because we had sold their birthright over and over again and we didn't care about them at all. As a consequence of that the only thing the fans had to be proud of were themselves. And out of that the only thing they could be proud of was to have the hardest reputation in the League. There was a terrible feeling of paranoia, everybody was against them. The challenge was irresistible, emotionally and intellectually.'

In the summer of 1987 loans made by Burr and Mead, which were later converted into stock, were used to bring new players to the club and to improve the condition of The Den. New seats were installed, the ground was repainted, floodlights were brought up to date, the pitch was relaid and refurbishment was carried out to bars, terraces and turnstiles. Mead emphasised the importance of spending money on the comfort of the spectators. 'When the fans came back (the following season), they not only had a new team but a nicer environment. The game is a classic illustration of decay. When I first started to go to football 40 years ago we lived in a one-bedroomed flat with a tin bath in front of the fire and the lavatory in the yard outside, so the sort of primitive conditions we experienced at football were not very different from our everyday experience. But football clubs never caught up with the evolution of bathrooms and council flats and everybody having a television set. Football ignored all that.'

Another new face at the club that summer was John Stalker, the ex-chief constable of Greater Manchester who had become nationally known following his investigation into an alleged 'shoot to kill' policy by Government forces and police in Northern Ireland. Stalker was brought in as a consultant to advise Millwall on policing and security. In common with most clubs, Millwall had been subject to increased police involvement in matters affecting spectators as well as larger police numbers in attendance at games. By 1987 extra security had reduced the number of incidents surrounding football matches but at the price of a deteriorating atmosphere and methods of increased surveillance and control that the majority of innocent supporters found oppressive. The Millwall Board were concerned at some of the policing methods and Stalker was employed as someone with a big enough reputation to be able to liaise with the police, someone they would take seriously.

The first real trouble involving Millwall fans since the community programme had been underway came in another FA Cup match, this time at Arsenal in January 1988, when outbreaks of violence on the terraces led to 41 arrests and 73 ejections. Two pubs near Arsenal's Highbury stadium suffered damage caused by fighting and a number of police were injured. However, much of the trouble had begun when Millwall fans were crammed into an area too small to cope with the numbers and as those trying to get out were pushed back by police, they spilled on to the pitch, which was the only means of escape. The lack of perimeter fencing at Highbury prevented a possible disaster but the media saw the scenes as another Millwall riot. Hysterical newspaper reaction called for Millwall to be closed down but both clubs were exonerated by an FA enquiry, which claimed that newspaper articles before the game had whipped up the fans. The enquiry declared that the scenes had been caused by 'circumstances over which neither club could have been expected to have control'. In the wake of the media coverage the club spoke to every reporter who had covered the game and pointed out factual inaccuracies. Peter Mead invited every sports editor to lunch over a three-month period. It was the first time anyone from football had done such a thing and Mead used the occasions to ask editors, not for special favours, but to give Millwall a fair crack of the whip. During the furore over the events at Arsenal, the Millwall Board, which categorically refused to condemn the fans' behaviour, received substantial support from the community it had been working so hard to win over, including offers of help from local head teachers, impressed with the efforts the club had made. It was this support which convinced the Millwall directors that they were indeed on the right lines, that the community programme was actually beginning to pay off. Jeff Burnige said, 'It [the Arsenal trouble] was not a set-back. It was a triumph. In any other time that would have been a near mortal blow but people rallied round and refuted the press reports. In the end it cemented the relationship between ourselves and our supporters'.

As the end of the 1987–88 season approached the Millwall team was in a position from which it could gain promotion to the First Division for the first time in the club's history. After a win at Bournemouth, which was broadcast back to The Den on closed-circuit television, chairman Reg Burr summed up the new-found feelings of the club: 'It would be quite wonderful for us to win promotion this season. Our people identify with us – they know us, they acknowledge you in the street and the whole atmosphere is a family atmosphere at Millwall . . . We don't want people to pat us on the head and tell us how nice we are; all we want people to do is to come and see for themselves. Come on down to The Den and see the atmosphere in which we play. See there is no racial chanting, foul language or violence'. Such a statement from a Millwall director would have been unthinkable a year earlier, and showed how much had been achieved. At the season's end the club finished as champions of the Second Division.

During the close season the Millwall Board took note of John Stalker's warning that trouble might return with the increase in crowds First Division football would bring. They decided to strengthen arrangements with the Council and evolve the community plan still further. Belying its 'loony left' image, the Council urged the club forward in its vision of trouble-free football. Gary Stempel remarked: 'Lewisham appreciates that the club has a lot to offer the local community, in the same way that a library, swimming pool or sports hall have a lot to offer. To the credit of the club, it has also appreciated that over the last three years . . . and its commitment to the scheme has been fantastic'. Meanwhile, a family enclosure was built for life in the First Division where theatre presentations are staged for children and musicians are hired to play and entertain before important matches. Jeff Burnige summed up the philosophy, saying, 'If all you do is go further and further down the road of repressive measures, although they do have a role to play in limiting the scope of the problem in the short term, you have to be working towards the long-term resolution of the causes of any problem at the same time. We have to try and influence people back to more caring and compassionate attitudes to each other, through involvement in sport'.

Apart from the one isolated incident at Highbury, the facts of which are disputed, Millwall's reputation has been transformed in the years since the community programme was instituted. From having the worst supporters in the land, the club can now lay claim to some of the best, and the ugly outbursts of intimidation and violence have by and large been eradicated. The suspicion with which the appointment of a community officer was originally greeted is nothing uncommon in football and the creation of such a post was only embraced at Millwall because the club had to do something or die. But the benefits were quickly recognised by the Board, who, to their credit, committed themselves wholeheartedly to the concept. Millwall has not merely contained the problem, it has begun at last the process by which it may one day be eradicated entirely, if others take note of the experience. Gary Stempel put it this way: 'I don't think it's particularly important that it's Millwall. I think clubs from Torquay United to Liverpool should be doing it . . . it's a crying shame that big teams like Spurs and Liverpool, who have so much to offer in terms of star players, which we don't have down here, can't go and do something like it'.

Early in the new season, Peter Mead stated: 'Of all the things I have achieved in my life, this involvement with Millwall is what my late father would have been most proud of . . . We know we have to live down our past but I'm proud of our fans, this season and last'. None of the Millwall directors are foolish enough to believe that the problem has been solved altogether. Jeff Burnige said, 'Our efforts can only really be evaluated in the long term. It had reached the point where to be a Millwall supporter was to align yourself with psychopathic behaviour but we have uncovered a huge reservoir of desire to see the club's reputation rehabilitated'. Something of Millwall's determination can be seen in the club's reaction to a coin-throwing incident at The Den when West Ham became the first side to beat Millwall on their own ground in the First Division. Although exonerated from blame by the FA, the club nevertheless extended the players' tunnel so that a repetition would be impossible. Peter Mead explained the reasoning. 'I don't care what the FA said. I did not want any player to feel threatened at Millwall Football Club.'

In May 1989 Millwall and Preston North End were voted joint winners of the inaugural Football Trust Community Award. Preston, with its artificial playing surface, had become a focus of year-round activities involving all sectors of the community, from senior citizens to handicapped children. Millwall responded to its award by announcing a scheme for the rehabilitation of young offenders and plans to build a new stadium 600 yards from The Den. Apart from Arsenal, which was awarded a special commendation for its work with women's football, none of the major clubs were cited. It is the small clubs that have made the running, including Halifax Town, the Yorkshire club whose majority shareholder is Calderdale Metropolitan District Council. The Council stepped in to save the club in 1987 and has instituted its own community programme. Deputy leader of the Council David Helliwell said of the arrangement: 'This is a cultural change of the first order. We are about revolution in football'.

In the years since the Luton riot, the football authorities, unlike the Millwall club, have made little headway in the battle against hooliganism. Indeed, Luton's response to the trouble, the introduction of a 100 per cent membership scheme and a complete ban on away supporters, led to the club being thrown out of the Littlewoods Cup by the Management Committee of the Football League. It may well be that Luton's scheme was not in accordance with what other clubs saw as the spirit of the game, but at least Luton was attempting to do something and precious little alternative advice was emanating from Lancaster Gate or Lytham St Annes, where suspicion of the political ambitions of the club's chairman, David Evans, was more evident than positive measures to combat crowd trouble. Luton deserve credit for sticking to their guns. Match-day arrests have dropped to practically zero, the hustle and bustle of shoppers animates the town centre once again and families go to Kenilworth Road. The disadvantage is that during the most successful period in the club's history, attendances in 1986–87 were 27 per cent down on those of the previous season. The chief superintendent of the Luton police, Glyn Spalding, said: 'We wouldn't have had the same results without the away ban'. Nonetheless, for the other 91 clubs the price of peace was prohibitively high.

The lack of action by the authorities in England was illustrated graphically by two important and, to some extent, parallel developments. The first came in Scotland, where the history of crowd disorder goes back to the last century. The Scots had developed a reputation in the rest of Britain for violence long before their English counterparts got in on the act. In modern times, violence at domestic encounters was supplemented by the export of trouble to England, particularly by Glasgow Rangers supporters who flocked to friendly games south of the border in the 1960s and by fans of the Scottish national team, who regularly took over Wembley. Indeed, Scottish supporters were also in the forefront of the second development, the export of hooliganism beyond the shores of Britain to continental Europe, a process which included the 'Battle of Barcelona' in 1972, initially a good-natured celebration of Rangers' win in the Cup-Winners' Cup final against Dynamo Moscow which turned ugly when the police objected to supporters spilling on to the pitch. Rangers were subsequently banned from Europe for two years, later reduced on appeal to one year.

The watershed arrived in Scotland in 1980 when a full scale riot broke out after the Scottish Cup final between Celtic and Rangers. The events, seen on television throughout Scotland and in many other countries, finally forced the Scottish authorities to act. In a tough series of measures devised by the Scottish Office with the wholehearted assistance of the Scottish FA and League, enshrined in the Criminal Justice Act (Scotland) 1981, a complete ban on alcohol and restrictions on the availability of tickets were enforced. A code of conduct was drawn up so the fans knew precisely what they could and couldn't do at a game while policing and security were strengthened. Following the implementation of these measures, the Scots managed to improve behaviour at grounds considerably. The reforms also ushered in a new, friendlier atmosphere and the real benefits of combating violence can be seen in the fact that attendances at Scottish League matches have increased every season since the Cup final riot. Wallace Mercer, chairman of Hearts, pointed to the lessons the English could learn from the Scottish experience when he said: 'I wouldn't want to run a club that was a blight on the community and I certainly don't want to see Governments running football. Once the [English] FA takes the bull by the horns and creates a collective willingness among the English fans to behave, they will find that the mood carries itself forward'.

If Rangers was the first British team to suffer from the actions of its supporters in continental Europe, the idea was soon taken up by hooligans in England, who gladly stepped into the void left when the Scottish game put its house in order. Before that, in 1974, Spurs fans caused destruction in Rotterdam when the team played Feyenoord in the UEFA Cup final. Two hundred were injured while 100 Spurs fans were arrested and thrown out of the country. A year later at the Champions' Cup final in Paris fans of Leeds fought with German supporters and threw seats and bottles at the police. This time £100,000 of damage was caused. UEFA's response to these outbreaks was to punish the clubs. Spurs were fined and Leeds banned. While the FA admitted shame at the night's events, it offered no solutions, nor any measures to stop the same thing happening again. Liverpool fans were in trouble in three successive years of European competition to 1980 and the situation was obviously getting out of control. Still the authorities did nothing to alleviate the problem.

Once the act of hooliganism had been committed abroad and television had shown the supporters returning home as if coming back from some glorious battle, it was only a matter of time before the malaise that was fast destroying English club football was transferred to the national team. The first major trouble involving England came in Turin, during a game against Belgium in the 1980 European Championships. There had been incidents before, notably in Luxembourg in 1977 when England fans caused extensive damage to the stadium and local bars. The FA apologised, paid £10,000 in compensation, but did nothing to prevent such incidents happening again. The Turin trouble, though, was of an altogether different order. On the day before the match 33 Britons were arrested after brawling had broken out in the city's bars and cafés. When the Belgians took the lead in the game itself, Italian fans began to taunt the English, who responded to this assault on their pride by attacking the Italians en masse. The Turin police, unused to such behaviour in a football stadium, took time to react. When they eventually intervened they set about the English fans indiscriminately with batons but the fans had the audacity to fight back. This caused the police to reply with CS gas, which they fired into the crowd. The smoke spread across the stadium and affected the players who had to retreat to the centre of the pitch. The repercussions of the incident included an apology given to the Italians by Prime Minister Margaret Thatcher.

The violence of Turin left 78 English in need of hospital treatment and one Italian with serious knife wounds. UEFA fined the FA £8,000, an inconsequential amount considering the damage caused to both the city of Turin and the image of the game. The FA itself, however, could not produce a single measure to ensure that the situation was not repeated in the future. When the inevitable happened and violence erupted again at England's away games, the Government began to threaten direct action if the football authorities did not put their house in order. The

FA's response to this was to blame the problem on society and to ask the Government to intervene. After renewed trouble at England games in Switzerland and Denmark, FA secretary Ted Croker said: 'I don't think the Government are treating this matter seriously enough. It should be the concern of the Home Office, the Foreign Office and possibly the Prime Minister herself. We have to ask the Prime Minister to look at this as a national problem, not a football problem. This is a matter of law and order and this Government came in largely on a law and order ticket . . . We had trouble in Switzerland . . . and we wanted to do all we could to stop any repetition in Denmark. So we asked for the names of all the people arrested in Basle and we weren't given them. We tried repeatedly through various ministries to get the information and they all refused . . . and it is quite likely that some of the people arrested in Switzerland were on the trip to Denmark, causing trouble again'. The extent of the problems in Switzerland prompted Swiss chief of police Dr Markus Mohler to remark: 'The Swiss police are accustomed to dealing sensibly with political and student demonstrators. We have special units to combat terrorists at our airports and elsewhere but the behaviour of English fans was outside our experience'.

While Croker's view contains some merit, it would have been more convincing if the policing problems to which he referred had not been the FA's only solution. But the authorities and the police had slowly come to believe that, as the problem was one of 'public order', then improved security methods were all that were necessary to stamp out the trouble. Issues such as the deteriorating conditions that genuine fans were subjected to in the stadia of the country, conditions which were tailor-made for anti-social activity, were left unaddressed. Moreover, little account was taken of the fact that increased or improved security affected law-abiding supporters just as much as it did the hooligans. Gradually, a policy was evolving which would punish the innocent along with the guilty as all supporters were treated as potential criminals, continually exhorted by the FA not to attend away games in Europe. At home the FA and League attempted to bring in restrictions on ticket allocations, making certain flashpoint games all-ticket, but this was never enforceable as large numbers of fans began to turn up at matches without tickets in the knowledge that they would eventually be let in. They knew full well that the police considered it safer to have them inside the ground rather than to allow them to rampage through city centres until it was time for their trains to leave for home. Supporters were welcome as turnstile fodder for the money they provided but more and more they were being treated like animals, caged to prevent them invading the pitch and policed with an increasing heavy-handedness. These measures would give the impression of containment for a time but they completely failed to deal with the problem and would lead only to an increased incidence of violence and to dangerous conditions on the terraces as security considerations became paramount.

After the Ibrox tragedy of 1971, British football was forced to comply with new regulations as safety at grounds was recognised by the Government to be totally inadequate. The Safety of Sports Grounds Act 1975 insisted that League clubs in the top divisions be required to possess a safety certificate from the local authority before their grounds could be used. Unlike, say, the Test and County Cricket Board, which ploughs back the profits from Test cricket to subsidise the County Championship and encourage the amateur game, the FA has never used the revenues from its major competitions in the same way. Neither has the Football League. To pay for the improvements ordered by the 1975 Act, football turned to the pools companies, which had been making large sums from betting on football matches for many years. The three major companies, Vernons, Littlewoods and Zetters, together with representatives of football in England and Scotland, formed the Football Grounds Improvement Trust in 1975, which used the profits from lucrative 'Spot the Ball' competitions to help clubs meet the cost of their obligations under the Act. The Trust was expanded in 1979, when the Football Trust was formed to provide money to tackle football-related social problems and to fund community initiatives. In 1984, the two Trusts acquired a higher public profile as they moved into the area of policing by setting money aside to help clubs pay for the cost of the police presence inside grounds. By 1988, the Trusts were also making significant contributions to a criminology research project in Oxford.

Few clubs took up the money on offer for community use. Between 1975 and 1987 clubs were paid a total of £20 million for 'safety' purposes whereas only £3 million was claimed for actual ground improvements or community plans. One of those that did use the community funds on offer was Millwall, whose success in London was helped by a donation of £80,000 from the Football Trust. Most clubs were quite happy to take large sums from both Trusts to help them meet the requirements of the Safety of Sports Grounds Act and to pay the costs of ever-more sophisticated policing and security, through such items as more fencing and closed circuit television. For all these measures, the English game was still careering towards Bradford, Heysel and Hillsborough.

While most clubs were spurning the opportunity to forge closer links with their communities; while the FA refused to enforce effective disciplinary measures, and while the Football League continued to devote its considerable resources to all manner of problems except hooliganism, the violence associated with the sport carried on unabated. The behaviour of supporters of the English national team in Spain at the 1982 World Cup became the subject of a study by the sociology department at Leicester University. The social scientists established the Sir Norman Chester Centre for Football Research at the University and produced two books on the problem, *Hooligans Abroad*, which covered the behaviour of the fans in Spain and *The Roots of Football Hooliganism*, which sought to place the problem in its historical and social context. Neither of the two main football authorities in England have contributed to the funding of the Centre or its projects, although a small number of individual clubs, such as Preston North End and Watford (which also maintains strong community links), commissioned the researchers for specific projects. In *Hooligans Abroad*, the authors put forward a package of measures which, they claimed, might go some way towards solving the problem of bad behaviour by English fans overseas, including colour-coded tickets and systems by which the FA could control the situation itself in the absence of practical support from the Government, UEFA or European clubs. However, the book's recommendations were ignored by the football authorities and were probably consigned to the Sir Nooorman Chester shelf at Lytham St Annes.

By 1985, the situation had become critical, although the fact went unrecognised by those whose job it was to deal with the problem. That all changed after the appalling events in Brussels on 29 May 1985. The Heysel stadium had more in common with its British counterparts than with most other large venues in continental Europe, being antiquated and, as it turned out, unsafe. It is also true that the organisation and policing of the event on the part of the Brussels authorities and UEFA left much to be desired. Nonetheless, the behaviour of the Liverpool fans was seen around the world for the national and human disgrace it had become. At Downing Street Margaret Thatcher watched the horrific scenes on television, just as she had when the Millwall fans rioted at Luton. This time of course, the result was far worse as 39 people, all supporters of Juventus, lost their lives. In Parliament the next day she announced a personal determination to act. If football's leaders could not put their own house in order, the Government would do it for them. The Prime Minister was forced to apologise to her Italian counterpart, Bettino Craxi, writing: 'No words can adequately express the horror and revulsion which I and millions of people felt at the scenes of violence . . . these terrible events have brought shame and disgrace on those responsible and on the country'. The world's press railed against the nation that invented the game. The feelings of many were summed up by *L'Equipe*: 'If this is what football has become, let it die'. *Bild Zeitung* in Germany declared: 'Why are these vandals allowed to leave their island? Never again allow these visitors into a stadium'.

The FA withdrew all English club sides from European competitions in the wake of the Heysel tragedy, although the same decision was not applied to the national team. Shortly afterwards, both FIFA and UEFA banned the country's clubs from playing anywhere in the world outside England. At the Football League's AGM in June, apart from a minute's silence, Heysel and its consequences were hardly discussed as the television negotiations and the superleague dominated proceedings. Some individual clubs had taken their own initiatives – there had been a novel idea from Ken Bates to instal electrified fences at Stamford Bridge, a plan scuppered by the local authority. While those in charge of the game continued to rely on the piecemeal responses of clubs which in turn devolved more responsibility to the police, the Government announced its own objectives after Margaret Thatcher had summoned the FA and the League to a meeting at Downing Street. These included more family enclosures, tougher action against offenders, more all-ticket matches, a clampdown on sales of alcohol, increased security at and around grounds and identity or membership cards if these measures proved insufficient.

The Prime Minister dismissed the arguments proffered by the game's officials that football clubs could not afford to implement the measures, citing the close season transfer of Gary Lineker from Leicester to Everton for £800,000 as evidence that the game was not as hard up as it claimed. To Margaret Thatcher, it seemed as if the administrators were incapable of appreciating the scale of the problem and the decisive action now required to tackle it. The prospect of a national membership scheme, in which every supporter would have to produce a membership card before being allowed into games, began to be seen by the Government as the only way in which the hooligan element could be controlled. Some clubs had already introduced partial membership schemes and the FA and League thought that by building on these existing arrangements, they could forestall legislation. The Minister for Sport, Neil MacFarlane, reminded them of the speed with which the Government expected them to come up with positive measures. 'We want safer grounds', he said. 'We want to stamp out hooliganism. We have to impress on the authorities the need for urgency, the new season is only ten weeks away.'

Events during the summer of 1985 propelled the Government to set up a judicial enquiry under Mr Justice Popplewell. Among the recommendations of his report were support for the Luton concept of banning away fans, more fencing, comprehensive closed circuit television at grounds, private security (used in the USA by the NFL) and a national membership scheme. The report spelled out the stakes when it said, 'Unless urgent steps are taken to produce some more efficient method of excluding hooligans, football may not be able to continue in its present form much longer'. Popplewell also hinted at the inadequacy of any proposed answers. 'I do not pretend that this [banning away supporters] is the perfect solution . . . and decent fans may be kept away. Nor can I guarantee that it will cure football hooliganism. It is not, however, possible for the present situation to continue any longer, with grounds resembling medieval fortresses.' Given this, it is curious that the Popplewell report did not exhort football clubs to follow the Millwall example or urge the game to listen to its consumers. It certainly didn't listen to Commander Fenton of the St John's Ambulance Brigade or James Tye, director general of the British Safety Council, both of whom made submissions to the Popplewell report and wrote offering safety instruction to the League clubs. They received only seven replies, prompting Tye to say: 'We felt we were wasting our time. Some people just don't learn'.

With increased security and a new mood of horror at the events in Brussels, the 1985–86 season saw a decrease in serious incidents for the first time in many years, although arrest figures increased in the first part of the season as the police presence was stepped up. Attending a football match was becoming an unpleasant experience, and not surprisingly gates dropped. The problem was to some extent contained, but the 'firms' and 'crews' still existed and trouble was still breaking out, often in the streets away from grounds. The atmosphere at many games remained intimidating and the Government reiterated its plans to introduce the membership scheme. Meanwhile the game paid £2.7 million in the 1985–86 season for policing,* a significant proportion of which was provided by the Football Trust.

When English clubs were allowed to compete in friendlies against foreign opposition in the summer of 1986, there was immediate trouble on a ferry carrying supporters to the continent for pre-season tournaments. Two hours out to sea the Dutch ship was turned into a battleground as fans of Manchester United and West Ham viciously set about each other using knives, bottles, fire extinguishers and furniture. The boat was turned around and taken back to Harwich where it was boarded by police who took off the injured and arrested 15 fans. The new Sports Minister, Dick Tracey, responded, 'This sort of behaviour could set us back years', while UEFA chief Hans Bangeter declared, 'We are very

*£4 million in 1988–89

disappointed. It is obvious that this illness has not been cured and this does not help bring English teams back to Europe. In fact, the whole situation has been aggravated'.

The 1986–87 season saw a widening gulf appear between football and the Government. Violent incidents once again appeared to be on the increase, while the clubs and the authorities seemed to be doing little beyond stating that everything was getting much better. Three days after 70 arrests were made at Darlington, FA chairman Bert Millichip said, 'We shall be back in Europe next year'. The season saw Leeds fans starting a fire, at Bradford of all places, and the club's FA Cup tie away to non-League Telford was transferred by police to West Bromwich Albion's ground in Birmingham, against West Brom's wishes as the Leeds fans had also started a fire at The Hawthorns some weeks before.

Thus hooliganism and the response to it had managed to destroy the very thing that makes the FA Cup such a glamorous competition, the romance of a small or non-League team's flirtation with the idea of winning the trophy, and the financial rewards that accrue when such a club is drawn against one of the big names of the game. Paul Leopold, assistant chief constable of West Midlands Police, commented: 'It's been a sad day for soccer. We've had those for ten years now. It's a sad day for civilisation really'. The Government again raised the spectre of the compulsory membership scheme when Dick Tracey said, 'We believe urgent action is now needed. I have asked the League to . . . let me have a report on the steps they have taken to introduce membership schemes'. The trouble was that football had not done very much to bring about its own voluntary schemes. Some clubs had up to 50 per cent of their grounds reserved for members but the actual schemes differed greatly from club to club and some, such as Arsenal, had no membership scheme at all. None of this was calculated to appease an angry Government.

Later Jack Dunnett, back at the League for a second spell as president, spoke of the situation at the time. 'Philip Carter [then League president] really believed he would never get the clubs to agree to some voluntary scheme. They would certainly never vote for it and in those circumstances he was persuaded that the Government better do what they wanted rather than try and do it through the League. The fact that the Government didn't do anything for a long time more and more convinced the clubs that the Government would not implement its threats but of course Governments never forget, they just take a long time to get going. The few voices such as myself – I think Ron Noades was another one – saying, "Look, it's better for us to do it rather than let the Government do it, it would be a lot easier for us," were disregarded.'

After the problems at the beginning of the centenary season, yet another new Sports Minister, Colin Moynihan, who had replaced Tracey after the 1987 election, went on the offensive. Both MacFarlane and Tracey had lost their jobs over the football issue, both had been 'too soft' for the Prime Minister's taste and Moynihan did not want the same fate to befall him. League president Philip Carter said in November, on the eve of the game between Everton and Bayern Munich, 'I would say our chances of getting back into Europe next season are very good as long as we don't have a major disaster'. What Carter had failed to take into account was the fact that he needed Moynihan's support in his efforts, as UEFA had made it perfectly clear that without Government backing, and unless there was good behaviour at the forthcoming European Championships in West Germany, there was no prospect of English teams being allowed back into European competitions. This was a reasonable stance for UEFA to take given the fact that the organisation had been charged after Heysel with criminal responsibility for the disaster. If the Government did not support English clubs playing in Europe, UEFA could face extremely serious consequences if it let the clubs back in and anything went wrong. For his part, Moynihan became determined to force the game to accept a national membership scheme, and this was the price of his support.

As the end of the centenary season approached there were further outbreaks of trouble, at the game between England and Scotland and at the play-off match between Chelsea and Middlesbrough. Colin Moynihan witnessed the violence at the England-Scotland match himself and afterwards slammed the administrators for the lack of effective segregation, adding, 'If UEFA wanted clear evidence on the depth of the problem in this country they witnessed it on Saturday'. Moynihan went on to declare what he saw as 'the ugliest scenes of violence for many years at a soccer international. I am going to take them [the FA] to town over this major setback'. The ineptitude of the arrangements for the game was certainly staggering. Contests between the two old enemies had produced crowd trouble for years. After widespread violence at Wembley the fixture had been moved to Glasgow in 1984 and 1985 and had been reintroduced at the England stadium only as midweek games. To take the risk of bringing the game back to its traditional Saturday, which enabled huge numbers of Scots to attend, and then to invite a hostile Sports Minister to watch what was always a volatile occasion displayed a remarkably complacent attitude in the face of potential trouble.

The centenary season had ended as it had begun, with scenes of violence and mayhem. Now the troublemakers turned their attention to the European Championships in West Germany. Although the problems that occurred in Germany in 1988 were exaggerated by the media in Britain – many newspapers had despatched news reporters to seek out trouble – the fact remains that English supporters once again demonstrated their propensity for violent and insulting behaviour. However, the official UEFA report emphasised that Dutch and Germans were also culprits. Moynihan, though, had lost patience. Reacting to the overblown media coverage, he severely criticised the authorities, demanding nothing less than a 100 per cent national membership scheme.

The trouble in Germany put paid to any hopes that English clubs might return to Europe but it also enraged the Government that football was still bringing shame on the country's image abroad. The authorities' record of abject failure was central to this thinking, and their objections to the membership scheme were viewed as further evidence of foot-dragging and avoidance of responsibilities. For years football had asked successive Governments to intervene. Now the intervention had arrived, it was in a form the game's leaders found unpalatable. Worse was to come as Moynihan confirmed that no Government cash would be made available to introduce the scheme. The new television deal with ITV was announced during the summer and thus any pleas of poverty were dismissed out of hand. Sir Norman Chester had prophetically stated in 1985: 'If the League was more compact and the regulations governing finance and facilities were tighter, the Government could then be properly approached for assistance. Safety has been improved, but once Bradford and Brussels have blown over in a year or so things will be the same . . . The Government won't want to help unless they are offered some assurances'.

When Colin Moynihan announced his plans, football, once again led by Jack Dunnett after the unseating of president Carter, launched into full scale opposition to the proposals. They were unworkable; they would not cure hooliganism; they would drive down crowds as casual supporters were dissuaded from attending; anyway the game could not afford the cost. Few in football saw any benefits in the idea. One who did was Luton chairman David Evans, who had become MP for Welwyn and Hatfield at the 1987 General Election and was a voluble supporter of Margaret Thatcher. Evans said: 'The 500,000 people who go to watch football have caused a lot of aggravation for the 50 million or so who don't. What I have tried to do is let the people of Luton and Dunstable have their freedom on a Saturday afternoon, which they haven't had for about 20 years. Asking supporters to carry a membership card seems a small price to pay'. It was quickly pointed out that the majority of the 500,000 to whom Evans referred did not cause anybody any aggravation, and tainting all supporters with allegations of troublemaking did little to solve the underlying problems that football faced. Luton, of course, was a special case. The thrust of the club's scheme was to ban away supporters, which the Government denied was its intention. One who put forward a more independent view in favour of the national scheme was Martin Lange, chairman of Brentford, who said: 'It will enable us to have closer contact with our supporters and market our clubs to them'.

The Millwall example showed that true membership could open up clubs to involve the fans, giving them privileges and incentives. If positively marketed such a scheme might be appealing to join and with sponsorship it could become self-financing. It could also give English supporters some of the influence enjoyed by fans on the continent, where members have a vote in the way clubs are run, or where local government involvement ensures more participation than is the case in Britain. It could, of course, be that this is precisely what the owners of professional clubs are trying to avoid, as the participation of fans could lead to a reduction in their power and interfere with their personal fiefdoms. It may be that Moynihan's plans were ill-conceived, but the complete absence of either an alternative strategy or the introduction of community schemes made the opposition case that much more difficult to argue convincingly. Writing in the *Guardian*, David Lacey summed up the situation: 'Irrelevant, authoritarian and an insult to football-lovers the compulsory membership scheme may be but by and large the clubs have got what they deserve'.

After Heysel a number of concerned fans had formed the Football Supporters' Association, an independent pressure group designed to increase the influence of fans in the running of the game. Despite some measure of success with specific campaigns, such as the fight against the proposed merger of west London clubs Fulham and Queens Park Rangers, and the proposal of Spurs to do away with the traditional standing area at White Hart Lane known as the Shelf, the organisation was generally shunned by both the clubs, who preferred the acquiescence of existing supporters' clubs, and the game's authorities, who saw the new association as another critic against whom to put up defences. It was only when the prospect of an enforced membership scheme seemed certain that the FSA was brought into the fold.

As the 1988–89 season got underway, the Government introduced the Football Spectators Bill, which dealt with the establishment of a compulsory national membership scheme and the introduction of measures for preventing convicted hooligans from travelling abroad, something Governments had always maintained could not be done as it contravened the basic human right of citizens to leave the country as and when they please. Football's authorities were asked to nominate members by 31 August 1989 to a new Football Membership Authority which would administer the scheme. If football refused to nominate members, the Government would appoint its own. The fact that Moynihan's proposals were likely to become law by the 1990–91 season did not prevent the football authorities from becoming even more vehement in their condemnations. A war of words ensued, with all manner of dubious statistics being cited to 'prove' either side's case. Irving Scholar took the fight directly to the House of Lords. 'The Government is abdicating its responsibility', he told the assembled peers. 'It is putting forward a Bill that is merely seeking to obtain from Parliament the power to enforce a 100 per cent national membership scheme and then inviting the football authorities to administer the scheme and carry the can. The Government knows it will not work, the football authorities know it will not work, the clubs and police know it will not work, and, most important of all, the public, whom this Bill is designed to protect, knows it will not work . . . The effect of this Bill, if it becomes law, would be that more damage would be caused to our national sport in one single act of legislation by politicians than any number of acts by hooligans.'

Football's leaders found a large measure of support for their opposition to the scheme from the police, the FSA and the all-party Parliamentary Football Committee. *Police Magazine* called the Bill 'a lamentable miscarriage of justice', which would put the police even further into the firing line. 'It would require more police on duty outside the ground than at present', the magazine continued. 'It is a threat to safety and public tranquility.' The Football League commissioned a report on the subject which pointed to the increased likelihood of trouble at the proposed computer-controlled turnstiles. Stayaway fans would cost the game £34 million, according to the report, which concluded, 'Clubs and police feel that few serious problems are now occurring within grounds'.

The Sir Norman Chester Centre for Football Research at Leicester University added its own independent view, concluding its critical report by saying: 'We remain unconvinced that a national scheme of this kind will "solve" the hooligan problem outside grounds or that it will be introduced with anything less than near chaos'. In a separate report on English fans who travelled to West Germany, the sociologists showed how the supporters were prone to provocation as at least 30 per cent spent one night or more without accommodation and many experienced up to two weeks on the streets. This point was taken up by the FSA in its plan, 'Europe 89', which contained ideas to control fans travelling abroad. Suggestions included no ticket sales for 48 hours before a match, a crackdown on touts who can ruin segregation arrangements and the establishment of travellers' clubs which would organise ticketing and realistically-priced hotels. The FSA also urged the FA and League to run low-cost packages with approved travel firms so that fans could be organised and controlled. But nothing now was about to move the Government, and the Football Spectators Bill made its way through the House of Lords stage with few meaningful amendments.

In April 1989, at a meeting in Lisbon, UEFA agreed to English clubs' readmission to the fold for the 1990–91 season, provided there was no more serious trouble and the Government supported the move. This was a little hopeful given the fact that the 1990 World Cup in Italy would give English hooligans perhaps their last opportunity to cause trouble in Europe before the introduction of banning orders preventing them from travelling abroad in future. Also, Colin Moynihan would only give the necessary support when the Football Spectators Bill became law. 'I'm concerned with one thing only,' he said, 'and that is to tackle hooliganism. That is my first consideration and my prime objective. The membership scheme, the ban on convicted hooligans travelling abroad, closed circuit television, effective segregation, good police intelligence and good police co-ordination are all absolutely essential.'

As the debate over the membership scheme raged on, few paid much attention to the potential dangers that still faced ordinary members of the public attending football games. In addition to the threat of violence, which though reduced still existed, policing took place in an environment in which all football fans were viewed as possible hooligans. In addition, poor facilities and fencing contributed to a feeling of alienation in people watching what should be an exciting sporting contest. 'What the FA and League appear to overlook', said David Miller in The Times, 'is that although the police – at an estimated annual gross cost of £40 million for the satisfactory surveillance of only 500,000 people – may often control crowd violence, the game is nonetheless played week by week under the permanent threat of intimidation, obscenity and property damage, not merely for law-abiding spectators but for citizens unconnected with football.' The idea that policing alone can solve the problem was further dented when a number of covert police actions took place in 1988 that marked a departure from pure crowd control operations to intelligence, surveillance and infiltration. When the cases came to trial many were dismissed amid widespread allegations of 'tainted' police evidence, much of which was not believed or shown to be false. Once again it had been seen that dependence on a security response alone was fraught with dangers.

On 15 April 1989 the football world, the nation and the people of Merseyside were shocked and devastated by the tragic accident at Hillsborough in which 95 Liverpool fans were killed in a crush behind one of the goals at the start of the FA Cup semi-final against Nottingham Forest. Since the Ibrox disaster in 1971, the country had seen the Safety of Sports Grounds Act which was supposed to ensure that such a thing could not happen again. Yet the Bradford fire had happened because the Act did not include Third Division grounds and now here was this latest tragedy. It was pointed out that in modern times Britain has lost more lives in accidents at football grounds than any other country except Peru, where more than 300 were killed in one incident in 1964. Such accidents have not occurred in Spain, in Italy or in Germany, yet they have become increasingly common on this side of the Channel. Unlike those in Britain, many continental football stadia have mainly been built or extensively rebuilt in the last 40 years, often in areas of parkland, and incorporate systems for funnelling large crowds safely into grounds. Facilities within grounds are often such that spectators are happy to turn up at the stadium in plenty of time to get in, thus avoiding a crush such as the one at Hillsborough. Every football fan in Britain has experienced a similar situation at some time, albeit with less disastrous results.

At Hillsborough, the limit of efficiency was breached, and almost 100 people lost their lives as a result. Police, used to dealing toughly with milling crowds, responded to the crush that built up outside the ground by opening the gates. As had become customary, fans arrived late or without tickets, confident that they would be allowed in, as they had always been in the past. When the gates were opened a more serious crush built up as supporters were squeezed against the fencing that had been installed to prevent pitch invasions, and the police, who for years had carried the brunt of hooliganism and who had become fixed in their methods of dealing with unruly fans, reacted slowly. The decision to award the more numerous Liverpool supporters the smaller end of the ground and the obstinate failure to postpone the kick-off time were two examples of administrative inefficiency that also contributed to the disaster.

In the shocked atmosphere that followed the tragedy all-seat stadia were called for. The membership scheme might have prevented the crush or made it worse, according to your point of view. A reluctant Government delayed the next stage of the Football Spectators Bill's parliamentary progress after the Hillsborough deaths, when it was pointed out that the enquiry that had been set up under Mr Justice Taylor might find it incompatible with any measures it might wish to recommend on safety. Given the precedent of the Popplewell Report, however, it is unlikely that Taylor will specifically condemn the membership scheme although he may call for modifications. The Government has in the meantime let it be known that the Football Spectators Bill is still an important plank in its legislative programme and it would be as well for football's authorities to recognise that determination.

Despite the fact that football's authorities have continually claimed that the hooligan problem is now under control, it is obvious to anybody who actually attends games that the threat is merely being contained. On the last day of the 1988–89 season, just weeks after Hillsborough, trouble erupted once again. Although the Birmingham fans who caused mayhem at Crystal Palace made the most news, the violence was country-wide. Police made 250 arrests in ten separate incidents. FA chairman Bert Millichip was aghast. 'Frankly, I don't know where we go from here', he said. 'This has left me frustrated. I don't know what course of action we can take but something has got to be done.' After 20 years, it seemed that the message had finally got through but it was much too late. Colin Moynihan commented: 'Sadly, this gives the lie to those who argue that present anti-hooligan methods have the problem under control'. The idea of a return to Europe in the forseeable future, always a remote prospect, receded further.

Days after the trouble at Crystal Palace and elsewhere, Millichip called for a total ban on away fans. Within 24 hours, Millichip's colleague at the FA, the new secretary Graham Kelly, sallied forth with his own proposals that were somewhat removed from his chairman's ideas. In fact Kelly's plan, that the FA should push for a partial home membership scheme and a 100 per cent away scheme, was not entirely original. It was first proposed in a report produced for the Football League by consultants Peat Marwick McLintock in 1987 which was ignored. Now installed at the FA, Kelly wheeled out the report's recommendations, which he had spurned two years previously, as the means to save the game. In the intervening period, the same idea had been advocated by Peter Mead in an article in *The Times*, but was, unsurprisingly, not acted upon by the League. The question of whether the ideas of Millichip or Kelly contained any merit was drowned in the publicity generated by the ludicrous situation in which two different sets of proposals came from the same organisation. It seemed as if the right hand did not know what the left hand was doing.

On the general subject of safety at grounds, when the comparison is made with the rest of Europe it becomes clear that nothing less than wholesale rebuilding of football grounds will provide safe, comfortable venues that will serve into the next century. Outside Britain, frameworks exist, as we have seen, for the provision of clean, safe stadia with excellent facilities. This is not to say that trouble does not occur. Hooliganism has become endemic in many countries as the violent elements in societies everywhere looked to the British example and copied it slavishly, even adopting the Union Jack as their emblem. However, the incidence of violence in other countries is far less than it is in England and, until Dutch and German fans clashed at a World Cup game in Rotterdam in April 1989, continental supporters had rarely ventured abroad to cause trouble. Once again, though, others have attempted far more radical solutions than the football authorities in England have countenanced. The Dutch federation, the KNVB, announced a 12-month experiment in January 1989 whereby supporters of five major clubs, which had all suffered from hooliganism, have to possess KNVB identity cards if they wish to watch away games. Spanish First Division team Real Oviedo have introduced electronic surveillance, based on the optical readers at supermarket checkouts, the first club in Europe to do so. Barcelona and Real Madrid are considering following suit, despite their huge crowds. In Italy, at the behest of Silvio Berlusconi, Saatchi and Saatchi produced an anti-hooligan commercial with the message 'he who loves football, hates violence!' This was transmitted extensively by Berlusconi's television network. When the same advertisement was offered free to the League and FA in England, no interest whatsoever was expressed in taking it up.

Antiquated stadia also exist on the continent, as Heysel shows, but this type of old facility is now in a minority. In addition, at a time when most English clubs were reducing ground capacities to comply with the Safety of Sports Grounds Act and by installing executive boxes, continental clubs were actually increasing their capacities. Wherever the gaze is cast, superb facilities can be seen: the Olympic Stadium in Munich, home of Bayern; the Nou Camp, with seating for 90,000 in Barcelona; the Calderon and Bernabeu in Madrid; the Stadium of Light in Lisbon; the Parc Lescure in Bordeaux; the San Siro in Milan. England has no ground that can be mentioned in the same breath as these, let alone the 11 enclosed domes that have been built in North America in recent years, three of which are in Canada. The newest of these, the Toronto SkyDome, has a retractable roof which can be opened or closed in 20 minutes. The $500 million needed to finance the stadium was raised through an imaginative mixture of public funding, private investment and the advance sale of boxes and seats. But it is not just in Europe and North America that facilities have improved. England has nothing to compare with the Aztec Stadium in Mexico or the Mohammed V in Morocco; both are third world countries with large debts, yet are still capable of providing their citizens with modern sporting facilities. England's national stadium at Wembley, despite the charisma of its name, cannot compete with any of these examples. Instead of isolated improvements perhaps it is time to tear down the old place with its 24 pillars that obstruct the view, and replace it with a modern, purpose-built facility.

In all the overseas cases, one common feature emerges that is lacking in Britain, except at a few clubs such as Millwall. It is the participation of the local community in the form of private members or local government. In Spain, the Bernabeu was built with contributions from the club's vast membership, which had a stake in the future of Real Madrid through the institution of meaningful membership enshrining voting rights. In Italy, the building and refurbishing of stadia is financed by the sale of bonds issued by the individual city, while in France direct municipal involvement ensures high-class grounds, the upkeep of which has been removed from the clubs and taken over by the local authority. In West Germany, stadia are also municipally owned and, as in many countries, are designed for multi-sports purposes. If the English game is ever to catch up, eradicate hooliganism and ensure that events like Bradford and Hillsborough do not happen in the future, some measure of official involvement is necessary. But, in return for this, clubs will have to be prepared to become more democratic, or at least recognise that they are a part of the communities they inhabit, and act accordingly. Excuses are no longer acceptable – that was before Hillsborough – and now football must find a way. After a large number of overseas clubs and federations made donations to the fund set up for bereaved families, an editorial in *The Times* said: 'The tragic chaos of Hillsborough has touched hearts around the world. In Britain it must also touch some minds'.

Perhaps one way in which major rebuilding work could be funded was first mooted in Sir Norman Chester's 1968 report. One recommendation was that a Football Levy be established, which would channel some of the money the Government receives in the betting tax imposed on the pools companies to improve facilities at grounds, along the lines of the existing levy for horse racing. In 1986 Labour MP Tom Pendry, chairman of the Parliamentary Football Committee, tried to introduce a Private Member's Bill to bring in such a levy but it fell through lack of time. Pendry repeated his call for the levy after the Hillsborough disaster. Considering that the betting tax on football is 42.5 per cent of turnover (compared to 8 per cent for horse racing), there certainly does appear to be room for a reduction. If the amount of tax was reduced to, say, 37.5 per cent, this would release £30 million for redevelopment. In return for such unaccustomed largesse, clubs and fans alike would have to accept the need for such things as edge-of-town stadia and shared grounds. For the treasury, such a move would be in line with the current crop of industry initiatives it sponsors and could be made contingent on local authority support or participation by supporters and private enterprise. Once again, the model for this approach is available in other countries, where pools income is used directly to fund improvements in many areas of the game.

Another possible source of cash could be the increased commercial income of clubs and the League which could be brought about by radical financial restructuring. Glasgow Rangers receives a mere 30 per cent of its revenue from gate receipts; the rest comes from lotteries and the club's other commercial activities, which have made it possible for the Ibrox stadium to be rebuilt. In 1989 plans were put forward to increase the stadium's capacity from 44,000 to 52,000, mainly financed by the sale of bonds and boxes. There is certainly no lack of atmosphere in the largely all-seater Ibrox – indeed it is a far more passionate place than any English ground and it offers standing accommodation for only 9,000. Small changes here and there and making room for executive boxes can in no way be compared with the full-scale rebuilding that Rangers undertook after the 1971 disaster.

In the absence of any serious action by the big English clubs we have to look to Scunthorpe (hardly a football hot-bed, although the town has provided two English internationals in recent years – three if you include their sometime first team player, Ian Botham – Kevin Keegan and Ray Clemence, both of whom were sold to Liverpool as young players) for the only example of a completely new stadium to be constructed in England for over 30 years. Scunthorpe's new, if small and homely, Glanford Park stadium with its capacity of 13,000 was paid for by selling the club's previous home, The Old Show Ground, to Safeway's supermarket chain for £3 million. The new stadium, opened in August 1988, cost £2.5 million and the profit wiped out Scunthorpe's overdraft. The land for the club's new home was provided by Glanford District Council, which has become Scunthorpe's sponsor. A similar arrangement has been effected by St Johnstone in Scotland. The Perth club sold its ground to the Asda supermarket group which built a new stadium on the edge of the town. Many football grounds in England occupy inner-city sites that are hopelessly inadequate for football but which suit other commercial purposes perfectly. With ground-sharing in the bigger cities, if such a thing can ever be considered in England, clubs could provide modern and, more importantly, safe stadia, where fans, to reiterate the words of Peter Mead at Millwall, can be proud of their environment and become its custodians.

Extra revenue could also be generated centrally by the Football League. At present there are many marketing opportunities open to the League that are not taken up because it is virtually impossible to get the co-operation of all 92 clubs, which jealously guard their individual marketing rights. The badges of clubs, for instance, would be worth far more if marketed as a complete set than individually. However, it only needs one club to refuse to join such a plan and the whole exercise is immediately devalued. Central marketing would involve the clubs giving up some of their individual power but the result would be the strengthening of the League as a whole and an increase in overall income, as is the case in America, where the NFL controls all marketing rights centrally.

The 'Insight' team of *The Sunday Times* put forward the idea of a Football Development Agency along the lines of the Welsh Development Agency and the London Docklands Development Corporation, with power over planning decisions and the authority to close down clubs that do not reach a given standard. The report said: 'England's football authorities are a contemptible mixture of incompetence and indifference; they must be by-passed, and only the Government can do that'. Any such development agency could perhaps be based on an expanded version of the Football Trust and could provide a number of marketing opportunities if embraced wholeheartedly. However, one thing is certain; there is no single answer to the twin problems of hooliganism and facilities. The former is a complex social problem, the resolution of which cannot lie in simple pleas to Government, police and courts to 'do something', while the latter requires huge amounts of investment. For years fans have been exploited by clubs, football authorities, Government and police. In the wake of Hillsborough, the English game must take steps to reach the position of the NFL and Major League Baseball in America, where fans are actively wooed to attend games and the interests of individual clubs are secondary to the interests of the whole entity. Only then will football in England cease to be what it has become, a slum sport.

It is now indisputable that English stadia are unsafe and unwelcoming edifices where hooliganism can thrive and that they are entirely unsuitable for the future. If further impetus were needed for the authorities and fans to get together and act, it exists in the attitude of FIFA. Improved standards and facilities such as all-seat stadia, which are becoming the norm in other countries, are to be formalised in new criteria for grounds that host World Cup matches. Pre-empting any opposition to this plan, Joseph Blatter, FIFA general secretary, stated: 'To those who say "Who is going to pay?" I would reply with another question, "What is a human life worth?" '. It may not be long before these regulations are extended to cover far more matches than at present. If that happens it will be simply too late for English clubs, the world will truly have passed them by. If this analysis seems far-fetched, an examination of the recent record of the world governing body will reveal how decisions affecting the future of the game that Britain invented are now taken, with very good reason, further and further from these shores.

13
YESTERDAY ENGLAND, TODAY THE WORLD

Only in a soccer stadium do I feel like a child again
ALBERT CAMUS

The 39th congress of the Fédération Internationale de Football Association (FIFA), held in Frankfurt on the eve of the 1974 World Cup, was marked by an extremely unusual event in the history of the organisation, a contested election for the office of president. As the delegates mounted the rostrum to place their voting papers in the glass bowl that served as a ballot box, it became increasingly clear that the outcome of the vote would change the face of world football forever. On the second ballot, after France and Portugal had switched sides, Joao Havelange finally acquired the majority he needed to become the leader of football's world governing body. Havelange, a Brazilian lawyer and businessman who had been in charge of his country's football association, the CBD, since 1958, was the first FIFA president to come from South America and had been elected on a programme of massive expansion. To fulfil the promises he had made to secure votes, Havelange now had to lead football into a new era dominated by commercialism, television and sponsorship.

The election also signalled the end of European, and particularly British, supremacy within world football. The defeated candidate, Sir Stanley Rous, had been president of FIFA since 1961 and had always been re-elected unopposed. Sir Stanley represented a generation out of step with the times, which had run FIFA like the British civil service and had failed to take into account the fact that Britain and Europe could no longer demand acquiescence from the rest of a world impatient for change. In the years after Rous was deposed the world game became more international while the

English consistently regressed as their administrators failed to heed the lessons of the 1974 vote.

In the run-up to the Frankfurt meeting, the issues surrounding the election were portrayed in England as an argument between the purity of the World Cup and its dilution to appease third world countries. Part of Havelange's programme contained a commitment to increase the number of teams participating in the final stages of World Cup tournaments from 16 to 24, and it was this proposal in a seven-point plan that was seized upon as the reason to oppose Havelange and support Rous, although Rous himself advocated limited expansion. The football correspondent of *The Sunday Times*, Brian Glanville, had put the case against expansion as far back as 1969: 'It is quite true that football in countries such as the USA and Ethiopia would be encouraged by World Cup participation, but only at the expense of cheapening the World Cup; a pretty heavy price to pay when this tournament is, or should be, the very zenith of the international game'. The extra teams in Havelange's plan would come in the main from South America and emerging football countries in Africa, Asia and Oceania, although there would also be an increase in European representation. Abroad, the move was seen as a necessary way of encouraging the growth of the game internationally, to ensure it remained the most popular sport in the world: an aim, it must be said, which was not really appreciated in Britain.

The English FA's relationship with FIFA has always been problematic. The organisation was first formed in 1904 without full British participation and England only joined a year later. Even when the English did become full members it was more to protect the status of the English game than to share in football's internationalisation, which was FIFA's objective. FIFA's second president, Englishman D.B. Woodfall, summed up the paternalistic attitude when he said: 'The FA should use its influence to regulate football on the continent as a pure sport and give all continental associations the full benefit of its many years experience'. Initially, the separate FAs of Scotland, Wales and Ireland (later Northern Ireland) were excluded as they were considered subsidiaries of the English FA, a situation that was resolved after years of lobbying in 1910, when the three independent associations were finally admitted. After the First World War the British FAs were reluctant to play against countries which had been enemies in the conflict and withdrew from FIFA. They rejoined in 1924, only to leave again four years later over a row about amateurism. They eventually rejoined in 1946, following a campaign by Stanley Rous.

During the Rous years as FIFA supremo a number of issues came to prominence that polarised opinion, not only in football, but in other sports bodies such as the International Olympic Committee. In 1961 Rous had seemed the ideal candidate, the third British president of the organisation out of six since FIFA's foundation, longstanding secretary of the English FA and a man of the old school. Exemplifying as he did a typical English establishment background in the days of the Empire – he was awarded the CBE in 1943 and knighted in 1949 – Rous was firm in the naïve belief, often expressed in Britain, that sport and politics do not mix. But the Rous presidency coincided with a decade of change; the British Empire was in retreat all over the globe and the independent nations that emerged in its wake demanded the fullest participation in international bodies, including those of sport. The time was rapidly approaching when the eurocentric view of FIFA would have to change – after all, it was a democratic organisation, one country, one vote, and the votes of third world countries would soon outnumber those of the traditional football nations. Rous seemed oblivious to this, the wind of change did not appear to blow in his direction, and thus the seeds of his downfall were sown virtually from the day he took office.

Rous's traditional way of doing things managed to alienate significant sections of world opinion. When this disaffection was allied to a natural desire on the part of the Latin American countries to have one of their own men as president, to right what they saw as an imbalance in an organisation that had always worked against them, the forces building up in opposition to Rous became overwhelming. The largest and most influential of these alienated blocs was Africa and the issue that set the continent's football administrators against Rous was South African Apartheid. Like many Europeans of his generation, Rous completely failed to appreciate the depth of feeling about South Africa as it built up in the 1960s and '70s. Although football managed to avoid the damaging splits that occurred in many other sports over the issue, the fact remains that Sir Stanley was identified from the very beginning of his term of office with the cause of white South Africa. The country was suspended from FIFA as far back as 1961, just as Rous was becoming president. Once installed in his new position he led a two-man delegation on a ten-day flying visit to the country to assess the position, which returned supporting a reinstatement of South Africa to world football. The suspension was duly lifted at a FIFA meeting in Cairo in 1963, after which the manager of the white-controlled South African League boasted, 'the decision is a defeat for communism'.

The new nations of black Africa, which had formed the Confederation of African Football (CAF), were outraged at the Cairo decision. It took a year of intensive lobbying to reverse the vote but at the 1964 Tokyo congress South Africa was once again suspended, a decision that would this time stick for 12 years before Joao Havelange finally expelled the country from FIFA in 1976. However, the damage was done and for the rest of his term Rous drew continual criticism for working towards South Africa's reintegration. The debate caused bitterness and friction and the African nations looked upon Rous as an appeaser of the Apartheid state.

There were also moves by the CAF to secure a place for Africa in the World Cup finals, led by the organisation's Ethiopian president, Ydnekatcheou Tassema. By 1966 the 16 places in the finals of the World Cup were split nine to Europe, four to the Americas and one to Asia, with the hosts and previous winners taking part as automatic qualifiers. No place was reserved for Africa and the continent's teams withdrew en masse from the World Cup. However, the performances of the Asian qualifiers, North Korea, in 1966 in England, where the team defeated Italy and made it to the quarter-finals of the competition, gave substance to the view that more participation from the non-traditional football world could only enhance the tournament. Rous was seen to oppose the moves that Tassema put forward on behalf of the CAF, although it was more the style than the substance of Rous's opposition to the progressive ideas coming out of Africa that really caused offence.

After all, Rous had actually been in the forefront of FIFA moves to aid the development of football in Africa, often in the face of fierce opposition from other European countries. The new-found power of the third world nations was felt for the first time at the Mexico congress in 1970, when a motion put forward by Tassema to end British exemption from the FIFA levy (paid from the receipts of all international matches) on games between the home countries was defeated by just one vote. The narrow defeat caused many delegates to begin questioning the status quo under which the single political entity of the United Kingdom had four representatives in the organisation and thus four votes.

Unpopular in black Africa, Rous also won few friends in Latin America. The beginnings of the disaffection were something the president could do nothing about. In all the years of FIFA not one president had come from the South American continent, and the Latin Americans felt that, despite their contribution to the game on the pitch, the system was loaded against them off it. Rous became closely involved in the organisation of the 1966 World Cup in England, a competition which many in South America saw as unfairly favouring the Europeans. According to the Latins, the referees were fixed so that European rule interpretations were enforced in crucial games. Two Uruguayans were sent off in the quarter-final against West Germany, refereed by an Englishman, and Antonio Rattin of Argentina was dismissed in the game against England by a West German referee. Perhaps worse, the great Pele was literally kicked out of the tournament in a bruising match between Brazil and Portugal. Rous's position on the referees' committee made him an obvious target for criticism over the appointment of officials and the fact that England became the first country to play all its games, including the final, in one stadium (Wembley) also rankled. Rous was actually against this, advocating that the England–Portugal semi-final be played in Liverpool, but the Latin Americans saw the hand of Rous behind every slight, real or imagined.

Perhaps what increased the ire of the Latin Americans was their collective impotence to change what they saw as an unjust situation. Europe still had more votes within FIFA – 33 to the Americas' 27 – and thus could always vote together to maintain European dominance, although by this time Africa actually held the balance of power. The famous quote of England manager Alf Ramsey after the game against Argentina, when he called the South Americans 'animals', was just about the last straw. It was an insult the whole of the continent would not forgive or forget. A movement began to find their own man who could look after their interests. By the 1970 congress in Mexico, however, the disparate nations of the continent had not been able to unite behind a popular candidate and Sir Stanley Rous was re-elected unopposed to a third term of office.

Almost as soon as the 1970 election was over, the campaign against Rous intensified, this time with support from an unexpected quarter. In Portugal, the newspaper *Mundo Desportivo* declared opposition to 'the dictatorial mandates of that big boss of soccer and his demands', and went on to say: 'It is time to settle accounts, time to send packing from the command of FIFA an individual who transformed the organisation into a puss-in-boots, with the amazing connivance and servility of many others. The shout of revolt has been launched in South America. It has reached Europe. It is the beginning of the end. Get out Sir Rous!'. With the momentum starting to turn in their direction, the South Americans finally agreed on a joint candidate for the presidency, and by October 1970 Joao Havelange had agreed to run for office.

When Havelange studied his chances for the next election, not due for another four years, he became convinced that he could win. Rous had never had to fight an election and might not have the stomach for a hard-fought contest; the increasing number of developing countries joining FIFA was altering the balance of votes within the organisation (in the 15 years from 1959 to Havelange's election in 1974 the number of countries affiliated to the organisation had grown from 95 to over 120); and Sir Stanley had anyway antagonised many groups, especially the Africans, who collectively could wield great power.

Joao Havelange, born in Rio de Janeiro in 1916, was no stranger to power and influence. He first came to prominence as a sportsman, representing his country as a swimmer in the 1936 Olympics and going on to feature in further Games in 1952 and 1956. After his active sporting career was over he turned to administration, becoming a member of the International Olympic

Committee as well as president of the Brazilian football federation, the CBD. He was also president or director of a number of leading Brazilian companies and had built a sizeable business empire. To Havelange, sport and politics in Brazil had always been indivisible and he understood the historic connection between the two. Sport has never, since the days of the first Olympic Games in ancient Greece, been apart from the political world. The myth that sport and politics are not connected is a peculiarly British invention of the middle years of the 20th century, and Havelange perceived this belief as one of Rous's major weaknesses. With the zeal of a man who still regularly swims a mile every day, Havelange took his campaign to all parts of the FIFA domain, visiting 86 countries between 1970 and 1974, building up contacts, listening to grievances, promising action, and above all, collecting votes.

Despite the numerous points in his favour, Havelange still faced considerable obstacles. The balance of power within FIFA could not be harnessed easily. Europe provided two-thirds of FIFA's budget and most of the world's top teams. A measure of European resistance to change can be seen in the events that took place halfway through Havelange's campaign at FIFA's Paris congress in 1972. As part of a plan to test the water, Uruguay, still seeking revenge for the refereeing decisions in England in 1966, threatened to bring to the vote the issue of Britain's four representatives, calling for a Great Britain team to be formed for FIFA tournaments. The four UK associations stated their intention to pull out of FIFA if the vote went against them. After intense behind-the-scenes manoeuvring, Uruguay was persuaded to withdraw the motion, although Britain did agree to pay the FIFA levy on home international matches.

Once news of Havelange's ambition had become public knowledge the opposition began its counter-attack. UEFA, the European Union of Association Football, could see its pre-eminent position in world football under threat and mobilised a campaign against the Brazilian. Stories began to appear in the European press alleging that certain 'inducements' were changing hands. Perhaps the only person who remained unconcerned over the threat posed by Havelange was Sir Stanley Rous, who stood aloof from it all until it was too late.

If proof were needed that sport and politics are indeed inter-twined it came in 1973 when global political issues drove a crucial wedge into the support for Rous in Europe. In Chile, Salvador Allende, the only elected Marxist head of state in the world, was overthrown in a bloody coup led by General Pinochet. The new regime used the national stadium in Santiago to hold large numbers of political prisoners, many of whom were tortured or killed, and the stadium became a symbol of international opposi-tion to the Pinochet Government. When the Soviet Union were drawn to play Chile in the qualifying competition for the 1974 World Cup they refused to play the game in the Santiago stadium. FIFA sent a delegation to Chile which reported that conditions were fit for the match to be played. The USSR offered to play the match on neutral territory but FIFA, supporting the Rous philosophy that sport and politics don't mix, ordered them to play at the stadium. They refused to do so, thus forfeiting a place in the World Cup finals. This inflexible attitude turned the Eastern Bloc against Rous and the resulting split within the ranks of UEFA hampered any concerted European campaign against Havelange as the important votes of Eastern Europe slipped from Rous's control. Once the East Europeans had been lost, the fate of Rous was sealed.

Never one to let an opportunity pass by, Havelange stepped up his campaign, using his extensive wealth to promote a dynamic, ambitious image. He issued his manifesto in a glossy brochure which laid out his plans should he win the election. The document was no mere list of promises to potential supporters. It was an extremely well worked-out platform which cleverly merged the disaffection in the developing countries of Africa and Asia, the traditional Latin American opposition to Europe and the new-found antagonism towards Rous from the USSR into a set of proposals acceptable to each group, but which also gave them collectively a significant stake in the future of the world game.

Havelange's whole plan rested on the premise that the time was right for a massive expansion in FIFA's activities. Football was to be encouraged in every country where it was played. A pyramid structure would be created with the World Cup, increased from 16 to 24 finalists, at its apex. In addition, new tournaments would be introduced at Under-20 and Under-16 levels to promote international football in countries whose dreams of becoming World Cup hosts were, for the moment, unrealistic. Wider participation in the Olympic Games would be pursued and international academies established to raise world standards. All this would be paid for by increased revenues generated through the expanded World Cup and sponsorship. Havelange was convinced that South Africa and Rhodesia should be expelled and promised to solve two other long-running political disputes, the seemingly intractable problem of China and Taiwan and the acceptance of Israel.

The weakened opposition to Havelange in Europe finally galvanised Rous into action, although his response was hardly inspired. The president sent a pamphlet to all FIFA delegates which stressed his record in office. It concluded: 'I can offer no special inducements to obtain support in my re-election, nor have I canvassed for votes except through this communication. I prefer to let the record speak for itself'. Rous's opposition to the Havelange challenge was too little, too late. The 79-year-old Rous had not recognised the way world football was changing. In England, where the idea of change has rarely found favour either within the game or among its supporters, the ramifications of the Havelange plan were largely ignored as the debate focused on the lowering of standards a 24-team World Cup would bring and vague allegations of corruption in the Havelange campaign.

After the Frankfurt election Rous was presented with a bouquet of flowers which he saw as 'more in the nature of a wreath'. Harry Cavan, the Northern Irish senior vice-president of FIFA said: 'It's the end of an era. The significant part of this congress has been the loud voice of Africa and the silence of Europe'. When the other business of the meeting was concluded the now ex-president declared of the congress: 'It was the most political I have ever attended'. One of the last votes of the congress saw a motion from Ydnekatcheou Tassema passed which underlined the new reality. From Frankfurt on, any FIFA member practising racial discrimination would be expelled.

The organisation that Havelange inherited in 1974 faced a number of urgent problems. On the political front, moves to expel South Africa and Rhodesia had to be put in train, China needed to be coaxed into membership of FIFA without the expulsion of Taiwan and a method had to be found to allow Israel to continue its participation in the World Cup without alienating the Arab countries. South Africa and Rhodesia were finally expelled in 1976 (the latter would be readmitted as Zimbabwe in 1980), while Taiwan and Israel, in the kind of pragmatic solution that was beyond the conception of other international bodies, were conveniently moved into the Oceania group for the purposes of World Cup qualification. Havelange's leadership and his method of 'Chinese diplomacy' shielded FIFA and the World Cup from the damaging political disputes and subsequent boycotts that blighted successive Olympic Games, the Commonwealth Games and other major events during the 1970s and '80s. In 1988, Havelange spoke about these early political difficulties. He said: 'The most difficult problem, one which had lasted for 50 years, was with the Republic of China. They had withdrawn in resentment since when they had strenuously resisted all attempts to readmit them. The Chinese put forward terms that were unacceptable as they didn't conform to our statutes. I was rebuffed at first but I persevered with an attitude that was "Chinese" in its patient approach to delicate situations. Today China is an integral part of FIFA alongside Formosa [Taiwan], whose expulsion China had previously insisted upon. Now China has organised with success the first Junior World Cup. On South Africa, FIFA had managed to run with the hare and the hounds with regard to the problem of Apartheid. Now, not only have we expelled South Africa but this type of racial issue is dealt with in our statutes. The third serious problem was that of Israel. There were a lot of problems relating to security but after laborious negotiations and a gentlemen's agreement we have arrived at an understanding which has given satisfaction to everybody'.

The other problems that faced Havelange were related to the finances of FIFA and the place that the World Cup occupied in the hierarchy of sporting events. FIFA had taken some tentative steps towards commercialism under Rous in the 1970 World Cup but now the involvement of business in football was positively encouraged. If Havelange wanted to fulfil his promises of more competitions and the vaunted academies, extra finance had to be generated. The man who provided Havelange with the means to achieve his aims was a German manufacturer of sports goods, Horst Dassler, president of Adidas.

Dassler had been involved in football for some time. His company sponsored a number of teams, including Bayern Munich, supplied the majority of World Cup teams with their kits and used players like Franz Beckenbauer for promotional purposes. Sport was fast becoming a global business and Dassler was among the first to realise the benefits a close liaison with FIFA could bring. He was the main impetus behind the drive for increased revenues that were to become a feature of Havelange's presidency. In return Adidas gained worldwide exposure for its products. In addition, Dassler became the supreme powerbroker of sport, bringing together multi-national corporations and sporting bodies in an innovative programme of sponsorship and advertising. Dassler also became one of the most powerful people in sport in his own right, having a significant input into a number of important decisions involving not just FIFA, but organisations such as the International Olympic Committee. Today, sponsorship and advertising in sport is taken for granted, so widespread has it become, but it was the union of Havelange and Dassler that began the industry's international expansion.

The man to whom Horst Dassler turned to realise his ideas was Patrick Nally, an English advertising and public relations executive. In *The Sports Business* by Neil Wilson, Nally said: 'Press and television did not accept the addition of a sponsor's name to a well-established competition. Events had to be created with a sponsor in mind'. Patrick Nally met Horst Dassler when he was carrying out public relations work for Adidas in the early 1970s. Dassler, although president of Adidas, could not use the company's funds himself, but a plan was devised allied to the marketing ideas of Nally to provide Havelange with the funds to implement his programme. Nally described the idea. 'Havelange needed money', he said. 'Dassler was dependent on soccer to sell Adidas equipment but couldn't afford to fund it from the company's budget. So I put forward all Havelange had promised, and a bit more, as a marketing package and presented it to international companies. There was no way the international sports federations

like FIFA could do it for themselves. They were small outfits then.
FIFA was a general secretary . . . and a couple of assistants.'

The results of the new association took over a year to finalise
but when they finally emerged, they were far-reaching. Coca-
Cola was to sponsor the Under-20 tournament, to be called the
Coca-Cola Cup, for £3 million over four years. In addition,
Coca-Cola would sponsor a world-wide expansion and development package, an updated and modified version of the academies, incorporating medical facilities, coaching exchanges and
teaching courses. Havelange took the competition to new football venues; Tunisia in 1977, Japan in 1979, Australia in 1981:
all places where the tournament could help stimulate interest in
the game, particularly at grass-roots level. It is often forgotten
that an important part of the Havelange regime has been taken
up with encouraging football at this level in a large number of
countries. At the same time the Brazilian liberalised the rules for
Olympic eligibility, helping to widen football's participation.
However, he was careful not to allow Olympic qualification to
overshadow the World Cup. Although the rules were relaxed,
European and South American professionals were allowed to
play only if they had not appeared in the World Cup, so that
the new rules retained the World Cup's unique place at the head
of the world game. Nonetheless, many football-playing countries
have used these other tournaments to give young players a taste
of international competition. Players such as Marco van Basten
and Diego Maradona (Coca-Cola Cup) and Michel Platini and
Hugo Sanchez (Olympic Games) were introduced to international
football through these competitions. Needless to say, the competitions have largely been ignored in England, where the League
programme is too important to allow for the release of young
players! Since the European ban, an ideal way to bring on the
best youngsters would surely be to utilise these youth tournaments to the full. Sadly, though unsurprisingly, it has not happened.

Meanwhile, Dassler had secured the rights to the advertising
of the 1978 World Cup in Argentina, and with financial backing
from Coca-Cola acquired most of the other commercial rights too.
Nally brought in five more multi-national companies, including

Seiko, Gillette and Kodak to join Coca-Cola in becoming long-term sponsors of FIFA competitions. Adidas, of course, gained world-wide exposure for all of its products.

For the 1982 World Cup in Spain, Dassler again secured marketing rights, this time under the umbrella of a new marketing company, ISL, but only after he guaranteed FIFA an income of £30 million to underwrite the expansion of the competition to 24 teams. The money was generated by a series of closely defined sponsorship packages which now offered exclusivity within a product range for a period of four years. It was the formula which was later applied to the Los Angeles Olympic Games of 1984, and it saved the Olympic movement from financial disaster after host cities, particularly Montreal in 1976, suffered massive losses.

In 1985 Havelange instituted a new Under-16 competition, now sponsored by Japanese electronics company JVC, which has so far been played in China and Canada and was contested in Scotland in 1989. All over the world there has been strong interest in the new tournaments and television coverage has been widespread. Once again, in England they are almost unknown, and not one of the events has ever been televised. The Scottish experience showed that the British public is far more interested in these tournaments than the authorities or the media realise. Crowds for the 1989 competition were the largest since its inception – 28,000 packed into Tynecastle for the semi-final between Scotland and Portugal and 5,000 more were locked out. The final at Hampden drew a massive 51,000 spectators. The Scottish media eventually caught up with their consumers and began extensive coverage of the tournament. In England, it was difficult to find even the results of the early games. The English FA did not see fit to enter a team and showed its lack of understanding of the event's importance by scheduling a schoolboy international against West Germany on the day the competition in Scotland started. And how many in the UK are aware of the coaching seminars which have been carried out in Africa, Asia and Oceania with the intention of raising standards?

When the World Cup was expanded to 24 teams in 1982, England was able to qualify for the tournament only because of the extra number of teams Havelange and Dassler had masterminded.

Europe's representation had been increased from nine to 14, along with guaranteed places for Africa, Asia and Oceania and more places for the Americas. Thus England, which finished second in its qualifying group, made it to Spain on the back of a policy that most English pundits had attacked for its lowering of standards. By contrast, the FA Cup has never been regarded as a devalued tournament because of participation by non-League teams. Indeed, it could be argued that the potential for giant-killing is the true spirit of the competition. The opposition to the expansion of the World Cup in England is all the more difficult to understand given the performances of the North Koreans in 1966. In the years since the increase to 24 teams unfancied countries have often surprised their so-called superiors and most would now surely admit that the World Cup itself, and global standards of football, have improved as a result. Algeria beat West Germany 2–1 in 1982 and was eliminated only after an extremely dubious 1–0 win by the Germans over their Austrian neighbours. Cameroon was eliminated on goal difference after drawing with Peru, Poland and the eventual winners, Italy. And in 1986 Morocco topped its group over England, Portugal and Poland. All in the game now agree that there are no longer any easy matches at international level. This has not happened by accident, and the proactive administration of Havelange is a major reason why it has taken place.

Havelange has also increased World Cup income from television. From total revenues for the 1970 World Cup in Mexico of £4 million, television alone provided £12.5 million in 1982, £20 million in 1986 and is expected to bring in £35 million from Italy in 1990. Although there has been justified criticism of television's influence on the scheduling of World Cup games, particularly in the heat and altitude of Mexico, the reliance on the medium has, if anything, lessened in the Havelange years, at least as far as income is concerned. While global television coverage is necessary to maintain the status of the event and to keep sponsors interested the money that television pays is now equalled, if not surpassed, by other commercial partners. Total income for the Mexico World Cup of 1986 was £55 million and the tournament turned in a profit of £25 million. The World Cup is now the undisputed number one sporting event in the world, eclipsing even the Olympic Games. It is also a television spectacular and an industry in itself – there are ten major sponsors already lined up for 1990, paying over £40 million between them. Yet the World Cup, unlike the English League, has not had to take on a 'title' sponsor, and there has never been any complaint that sponsors' interests have outweighed those of spectators or television viewers. For instance, the referee is not instructed to stop and start games according to the duration of the commercial breaks on television, as he is in American Football. Nor has FIFA been compelled to alter the length of half-time intervals to accommodate television's priorities as the English League has been forced to do.

Another major innovation during Havelange's term of office was the decision to make the USA hosts for the 1994 World Cup after their previous bid to host the competition in 1986, on the withdrawal of the original choice, Colombia, was rejected. The 1994 tournament will be the first World Cup to be held outside Europe or South America and this bold move is designed to further football in the USA and to maximise income in the home of commercialism. Havelange said of the decision: 'I'm convinced after 14 years in office and of developing soccer around the world that the organisation of the World Cup in the USA will be my highest achievement because soccer will be recognised in that country, where it hasn't been in the past'. Havelange's own country, Brazil, put in a bid, as did Morocco, but the president was a tacit supporter of the USA and after the decision was taken announced his intention to take the World Cup to a succession of new venues in the future, possibly including China. In fact, Morocco did not have all its planned facilities in place despite having successfully hosted the 1988 African Nations Cup and economic problems made it almost impossible for Brazil to hold a World Cup, and thus the USA became the inevitable choice.

The long-term strategic thinking behind these moves was summed up by Havelange: 'We have come to terms with the modern world of marketing, particularly in the areas of advertising and sponsorship. In 1982 we went from 16 to 24 countries for the final stages of the World Cup. The interest of spectators has grown. At the last World Cup in Mexico the combined audiences for all the matches added up to 12 billion people – two and a half times the population of the world. The additional receipts have allowed us to take our proselytising to the underprivileged regions and to innovate with new competitions for the youth of the entire world'.

The evolution of the World Cup and the way FIFA operates have not passed by entirely without criticism. Much of the early opposition arose in Europe simply because Havelange came from South America. At the UEFA congress in Edinburgh in 1974 there were mutterings of a possible FIFA–UEFA split, with Sir Stanley Rous making a plea to 'keep FIFA European', while Belgian representative Louis Wouters condemned the 'inordinate ambition' of the Afro–Asian axis. However, UEFA opposition ran out of steam when Artemio Franchi took over as president of the European organisation and became embroiled in controversies in his own backyard. Individual criticism of Havelange has still surfaced from time to time, however. In 1978 Hermann Neuberger, a vice-president of FIFA and chairman of the German FA, questioned Havelange's propriety after it was revealed that the Brazilian was connected to an insurance company that had bid for the £2 million contract to insure the new World Cup, the so-called 'Boavista Affair'. It is Havelange's longstanding relationship with Horst Dassler, though, that has drawn the majority of criticism to his presidency.

In 1979 Neuberger renewed his attack in a letter to Havelange in which he called on the president to ensure that Dassler 'steps down . . . and refrains from all sports politics'. The issue, which Neuberger described as a 'Watergate', concerned allegations made by Rolf Deyhle, boss of a German sports marketing company called Sport Billy which had contracts with FIFA but had been in dispute with Dassler for some time. The allegations centred on the charge that Dassler controlled a secret Swiss bank account which was used to make illegal payments to FIFA personnel. FIFA's executive committee met to consider the matter, but not surprisingly rejected Deyhle's allegations. In 1983, however, the (British) Howell report on sponsorship said: 'We are concerned at the close relationship between Mr Dassler and Adidas with FIFA and we consider that there should be a proper examination of the situation'. It was certainly true that Dassler was now in an important position within FIFA, wielding much influence until his death in 1987. He managed to secure rights for ISL to the 1990, 1994 and 1998 World Cups, although this can also be seen as recognition of Dassler's efforts in the early days. Whatever the case it is in line with Havelange's policies in other areas. The television rights to the same World Cups, for instance, have been sold for over £100 million to a consortium of broadcasting unions, including the European Broadcasting Union, and no one has ever suggested that that contract is in any way tainted by corruption.

Havelange, far from being reluctant to discuss the sale of rights so far into the future, actually seems proud of the deal. He said: 'One of our contracts has had a great impact in the world of finance as well as in the world of advertising and publicity. FIFA has negotiated, at one sitting, the World Cups for 1990, 1994 and 1998. This is a gesture of courage which has been worthy of the approval it has drawn from marketing people. It has enabled them to look at long-term plans for their own strategy until practically the year 2000. This . . . provides a good model for the world of business, for federations, if not even for certain governments . . . Our initiative has firmed up a north-south action which is like a canal which runs to the third world'. On the subject of the money participating countries can earn out of the World Cup, the president declared: 'When the draw is made each qualified team rapidly receives $200,000. If there is a need we are ready to pay in advance a similar amount for their preparation. This sum will be reimbursed when we have final accounts. FIFA pays for all the travel, lodgings and local transport and in addition gives $150 per day to every delegate from every delegation. The teams receive $400,000 per match. Let us say each match costs FIFA $1,200,000. The competition has 52 matches, so to balance such a budget requires a certain sense of business affairs and administration'.

Although no outright corruption has been proved in the case of Joao Havelange and Horst Dassler the connections between the two certainly raise questions. The basic argument centres around the conflict of interest between Dassler's dual roles. On the one hand he was chairman of a multi-national company selling sports-based products in 150 countries while at the same time he was the man in charge of negotiating marketing rights to the World Cup. Patrick Nally at least saw the dangers in the potential conflict of interests, although he is quick to point out that in the early days Dassler had to carry out both tasks as there was no one else who could do it. It is also the case that before Dassler, there was hardly any marketing of football or any other sport outside the USA. Dassler and Nally more or less made it up as they went along, using the US experience for guidance, and undoubtedly large sums of money have accrued to FIFA as a result of their efforts. And is it conceivable that the FA in England would use such influxes of cash in the constructive way FIFA has managed? FIFA has moved to a new purpose-built headquarters in Zurich and the efficiency of its administration has been improved beyond all recognition. Continuous programmes have been inaugurated to raise playing standards around the world, and in addition to the promotion of the game at youth levels, indoor and women's football have been embraced for the first time. Those corporate sponsors that have involved themselves with FIFA have generally renewed their contracts while many more wait in line.

Allegations of corruption surfaced again during the World Cup in Mexico in 1986. The television lines to the rest of the world went dead at the beginning of the tournament. A spokesman for the European Broadcasting Union called it 'the biggest telecommunications disaster in sporting history'. Although the problem was quickly solved the incident focused attention on the television arrangements. It was alleged that Havelange had a financial association with Emilio Ascarraga, a leading Mexican businessman who owns television stations, hotels and the Aztec Stadium in Mexico City. Defending the links when questioned by the ITV current affairs programme 'World In Action' in June 1986, Havelange said: 'FIFA has taken on an importance which it never had under former presidents. Because of football's image everyone wants television rights, everyone wants to use it. Football sells products all over the world, all this is due to my work'. Large profits from the televising of the 1986 World Cup were also alleged to have gone to a FIFA vice-president, Guillermo Canedo, who controlled local television rights with Ascarraga. When the decision was announced to take the 1994 World Cup to the USA, Canedo was appointed to oversee the organisation and Ascarraga gained partial television rights through his links with Univision, North America's Spanish language network.

Despite the criticisms, on balance it should be recognised that Havelange's achievements are significant. Opposition to the expanded World Cup cannot detract from the fact that it is a popular and commercial success, and gives more nations an incentive to improve their football at all levels. That this had to be achieved by closer commercial links with companies and entrepreneurs than the purists would like is one of the features of the modern world with which all sports are having to come to terms. Even the USSR is examining ways of introducing more commercialism into its football. And there is an element of corruption wherever there is money and power, which has not been noticeably better handled when it has surfaced in Britain or Europe than anywhere else. The allegations of corruption within UEFA in the 1970s, for instance charges of match-fixing and bribery of referees, have never been satisfactorily explained.

Joao Havelange has also shown himself to be a friend of Britain. He has consistently defended the right of the United Kingdom to its four FIFA representatives and there is little prospect of the position changing while he is in charge. However, the growing influence of developing countries will surely one day bring about a vote to end this historic privilege, unless the British FAs recognise the threat and head it off at the pass. Perhaps it is time to repay Havelange's support for Britain by embracing his development programme wholeheartedly and to take the lead in encouraging football in every country where it is played. This would be nothing less than the revival of Britain's original contribution to the world game, a role which was neglected for so long that it was taken up by others. A good start would be to invite an African team to play at Wembley. Bringing young players from developing countries to the Lilleshall Centre might also help to convince other nations that the status quo is worth preserving. One positive step was the announcement by the FA of a limited programme of overseas coaching in May 1989, to be sponsored by British Aerospace.

Havelange's swansong, and what could turn out to be his major achievement, will be the 1994 World Cup in the USA. What better way is there to secure the future of the game than to take on

American Football in its own backyard? After all, the NFL is currently finalising plans to expand into Europe and Japan with a view to forming a world league to complement business at home. If the 1994 World Cup is successful, the implications for world soccer will be enormous. In the meantime, the amount of cash the tournament will bring to FIFA will secure the funding of its activities into the next century. Havelange has made FIFA more important than the sum of its parts; no single country or handful of nations can dictate its policy. There are now 166 member countries, more than are affiliated to the United Nations. In presiding over this evolution of football to the status of the greatest game in history, the Brazilian has proved himself a man of vision. The same can be said about the other entrepreneurs from Europe who have featured in this book. Whichever country is examined, innovative systems of administering football can be seen. While checks and balances within their structures have been devised to give people what they want, it has not prevented the emergence of visionaries. In England, on the other hand, the dead hand of administrators and owners alike has brought the country's game to the brink of disaster, from which any recovery will be painful and slow.

The lessons of Berlusconi, Bez and Gil show that businessmen are not necessarily bad for football provided they work in a system which encourages them to be progressive and to take into account the wishes of supporters. In Spain presidents will be ousted if they lose the support of members; in France and Italy owners are constrained by the involvement of local government from the kind of excesses that have been seen in England. And in all these countries football has retained its unique place in society, which enables the game to grow from generation to generation rather than diminish as it has in England. The English system achieves none of the possible benefits outlined in this book. It neither constrains owners nor does it encourage the best of them to be progressive. At the same time little notice is taken of the needs of spectators. Whereas everywhere else the national team comes first, in England the clubs come first and any success they have enjoyed has been at the expense of the England team's prospects.

Riven by damaging splits and faction fighting, incapable of utilising the experience of its best players and unable to agree on the simplest of decisions, such as how many teams should ideally be in the First Division, the English game stands at the crossroads. The global designs of Berlusconi and his like will not include the English as long as English clubs fail to solve the game's endemic problems. Referring to his proposal for a European superleague, Berlusconi said: 'English clubs would have to improve their stadia greatly and reduce violence considerably before we would even consider them for our League'. The result of the authorities' inability in so many areas has been isolation and the worst image football has ever had. If an unsympathetic membership scheme is forced on a reluctant football establishment that offers little co-operation then the future is certainly bleak. Post-Hillsborough, it is time for the Sir Norman Chester Shelf to be dusted off at Lytham St Annes and for the lessons the world can teach us to be absorbed.

Britain invented football. It is perhaps one of the country's great contributions to the world. Ordinary British people took the game to all parts of the globe. Today, the game in England has two ways to go. If fundamental change does not take place in the way football is run, then the European superleague will happen without us and English football will be reduced to the European equivalent of the Beazer Homes League as teams from Scotland are left to carry the British torch and the best English players are plundered in ever-increasing numbers. The other path could lead to prosperity and a new deal for the greatest sponsors of the English game, the ordinary supporters. Like the rest of the world, England must build safe stadia and rid the game of its intimidating and anti-social atmosphere. If this means embracing a less than perfect member-ship scheme then so be it, football will have to be rebuilt anew from there. To achieve this the League must be reorganised to maximise its impact and get itself ready for the 21st century. As FIFA did, it must find a leader of vision with the power to take tough decisions. Any leader should ideally come from outside the game, someone not associated with the failures of the past, and most important, it should be someone totally independent of any specific club who can view the whole game in its true perspective.

But the simple appointment of a supremo is not a panacea. The FA must become more professional and the relationship between the governing body and the League must be reappraised so that a supreme body can be created. In this way the dividing line between the interest of the League and the interest of the national team will no longer be blurred and all competitions can be organised to maximum effect.

Finally, the clubs themselves must be forced to realise that narrow self-interest will do none of them any good in the long term and they must be reformed. The time has passed when tinkering was enough. Moves are already taking place which will see large scale changes after 1992. Scotland will be there; Spain will be there; Italy will be there; France will be there; West Germany will be there; Holland and Portugal will be there. Evolution will no longer suffice, there must be revolution now, otherwise we shall have lost the right to compete on the international stage. The game in this country will then wither and die, its glorious past consigned to a fading image on an old videotape, its achievements just a dim and distant memory.

Aitken, Mike and Mercer, Wallace: *Heart to Heart: The Anatomy of a Football Club* (Mainstream, Edinburgh, 1988)

Archer, R. and Boulillon, Antoine: *The South African Game: Sport and Racism* (Zed Press, London, 1982)

Ball, Peter and Shaw, Phil: *The Book of Football Quotations* (Stanley Paul, London, 1984)

Beltrami, A. (ed): *Almanacco del Calcio* (Edizioni Panini, Modena, various editions)

Business Ratio Report: *Association Football Clubs* (ICC)

Butler, Bryon: *The Football League 1888–1988* (Macdonald Queen Anne Press, London, 1987)

Crick, Michael and Smith, David: *Manchester United: The Betrayal of a Legend* (Pelham, London, 1989)

Davies, Hunter: *The Glory Game* (Mainstream, Edinburgh, 1985)

Docherty, D.: *The Rangers Football Companion* (John Donald and Rangers FC, Edinburgh, 1986)

Dunning, Eric; Murphy, Patrick and Williams, John: *Hooligans Abroad* (Routledge & Kegan Paul, London, 1984)

Dunning, Eric; Murphy, Patrick and Williams, John: *The Roots of Football Hooliganism* (Routledge & Kegan Paul, London, 1988)

FIFA Technical Report on 1986 World Cup

The Football Trust: *Digest of Football Statistics* (1985 and 1987)

Gibbs, Nick: *England, the Football Facts* (Facer, London, 1988)

Glanville, Brian: *The History of the World Cup* (Faber and Faber, London, 1980)

Golesworthy, Maurice: *The Encyclopaedia of Association Football* (Robert Hale, London, various editions)

Green, Geoffrey: *Soccer: The World Game* (Sportsman's Book Club, London, 1954)

Greenwood, Ron: *Yours Sincerely* (Collins, London, 1984)

Hammond, Mike (ed): *European Football Yearbook* (Facer, London, 1988)

Inglis, Simon: *League Football and the Men Who Made It* (Collins Willow, London, 1988)

Inglis, Simon: *The Football Grounds of Great Britain* (Collins, London, 1987)

Jordans – 1987: *A Survey of Football League Clubs*

Miller, David: *World Cup: The Argentina Story* (Frederick Warne, London, 1978)

Murray, Bill: *The Old Firm: Sectarianism, Sport and Society in Scotland* (John Donald, Edinburgh, 1984)

Murray, Bill: *Glasgow's Giants: 100 Years of the Old Firm* (Mainstream, Edinburgh, 1988)

Murray, James: *Millwall, Lions of the South* (Indispensable and Millwall FC, London, 1988)

Nickolds, Andrew and Hey, Stan (eds): *The Foul Book of Football No. 1* (London, 1976)

Platini, Michel and Mahe, Patrick: *Ma Vie comme un Match*, (Robert Laffont, Paris, 1987)

Rethacker, Jean-Philippe (ed): *Football '89:* (*L'Equipe*, various editions)

Rippon, Anton: *Soccer: The Road to Crisis* (Moorland, Ashbourne, 1983)

Robinson, John: *The European Championship 1958–88* (Marksman, Cleethorpes, 1988)

Rothmans Football Yearbook (Macdonald Queen Anne Press, various editions)

Rous, Stanley: *Football Worlds: A Life in Sport* (Faber and Faber, London, 1978)

Ticher, Mike (ed): *Foul 1972–76* (Simon & Schuster, London, 1987)

Tomlinson, Alan and Whannel, Gary (eds): *Off The Ball* (Pluto, London, 1986)

UEFA Technical Report on European Championships (1988)

Wagg, Stephen: *The Football World* (Harvester, London, 1984)

Wilson, Neil: *The Sports Business, the Men and the Money* (Judy Piatkus, London, 1988)

Woodcock, Tony and Ball, Peter: *Inside Soccer* (Macdonald Queen Anne Press, London, 1985)

Young, Chick: *Rebirth of the Blues* (Mainstream, Edinburgh, 1987)

INDEX